Communications
in Computer and Information Science   1366

More information about this series at http://www.springer.com/series/7899

Sabu M. Thampi · Selwyn Piramuthu ·
Kuan-Ching Li · Stefano Berretti ·
Michal Wozniak · Dhananjay Singh (Eds.)

Machine Learning and Metaheuristics Algorithms, and Applications

Second Symposium, SoMMA 2020
Chennai, India, October 14–17, 2020
Revised Selected Papers

 Springer

Editors
Sabu M. Thampi
Indian Institute of Information Technology
and Management - Kerala
Trivandrum, India

Kuan-Ching Li
Providence University
Taichung, Taiwan

Michal Wozniak
Wrocław University of Technology
Wrocław, Poland

Selwyn Piramuthu
University of Florida
Gainesville, FL, USA

Stefano Berretti ⓘD
Università degli Studi di Firenze
Florence, Italy

Dhananjay Singh ⓘD
Hankuk University of Foreign Studies
Yongin, Korea (Republic of)

ISSN 1865-0929   ISSN 1865-0937 (electronic)
Communications in Computer and Information Science
ISBN 978-981-16-0418-8   ISBN 978-981-16-0419-5 (eBook)
https://doi.org/10.1007/978-981-16-0419-5

This Springer imprint is published by the registered company Springer Nature Singapore Pte Ltd.
The registered company address is: 152 Beach Road, #21-01/04 Gateway East, Singapore 189721, Singapore

Preface

The Second Symposium on Machine Learning and Metaheuristics Algorithms, and Applications (SoMMA'20) provided a forum for scientists and researchers to present their latest results and a means to discuss the recent developments in machine learning, metaheuristics, and their applications. The Symposium was organised by Vellore Institute of Technology (VIT), Chennai, India during October 14–17, 2020. Due to the recent pandemic situation, it was conducted as a virtual event. SoMMA'20 was co-located with the International Conference on Applied Soft Computing and Communication Networks (ACN'20).

This year, we received 40 submissions, of which 19 papers (12 regular and 7 short papers) were accepted. The papers were subject to a double-blind peer review where significance, novelty, and technical quality of submissions were considered by the Technical Program Committee. The papers cover different areas such as image processing, computer vision, pattern recognition, big data, machine learning, and cybersecurity.

We thank the program chairs for their wise guidance and brilliant suggestions in organizing the technical program. Thanks to all members of the Technical Program Committee, and the external reviewers, for their hard work in reviewing the papers. We sincerely thank all the keynote speakers who shared their experience and expertise with us. Moreover, our warm gratitude should be given to all the authors who submitted their work to SoMMA'20. During the submission, review, and editing stages, the EDAS conference system proved very helpful.

We are grateful to Vellore Institute of Technology (VIT), Chennai for organizing the Symposium. It could not have taken place without the commitment of the Local Organizing Committee, which in many ways helped to effectively coordinate the event. Finally, we would like to thank our publisher Springer for their cooperation.

October 2020

Sabu M. Thampi
Selwyn Piramuthu
Kuan-Ching Li
Stefano Berretti
Michał Woźniak
Dhananjay Singh

Conference Organization

Chief Patron

G. Viswanathan   Vellore Institute of Technology, India
(Chancellor)

Patrons

Sankar Viswanathan   Vellore Institute of Technology, India
(Vice-president)
Sekar Viswanathan   Vellore Institute of Technology, India
(Vice-president)
G. V. Selvam   Vellore Institute of Technology, India
(Vice-president)
Sandhya Pentareddy   Vellore Institute of Technology, India
(Executive Director)
Kadhambari S. Viswanathan Vellore Institute of Technology, India
(Assistant Vice-president)
Rambabu Kodali   Vellore Institute of Technology, India
(Vice Chancellor)
S. Narayanan   Vellore Institute of Technology, Vellore, India
(Pro-vice Chancellor)
V. S. Kanchana Bhaaskaran Vellore Institute of Technology, India
(Pro-vice Chancellor)
P. K. Manoharan   Vellore Institute of Technology, India
(Additional Registrar)

General Chairs

Selwyn Piramuthu   University of Florida, USA
Kuan-Ching Li   Providence University, Taiwan
Sabu M. Thampi   IIITM-Kerala, India

Program Chairs

Stefano Berretti   University of Florence, Italy
Michał Woźniak   Wrocław University, Warsaw, Poland
Dhananjay Singh   Hankuk University of Foreign Studies, South Korea

Organizing Chairs

Geetha S.	VIT, Chennai, India
Jagadeesh Kannan R.	VIT, Chennai, India

Organizing Co-chairs

Asha S.	VIT, Chennai, India
Pattabiraman V.	VIT, Chennai, India
Viswanathan V.	VIT, Chennai, India

Organizing Secretaries

Sweetlin Hemalatha C.	VIT, Chennai, India
Suganya G.	VIT, Chennai, India
Kumar R.	VIT, Chennai, India

TPC Members

http://www.acn-conference.org/2020/somma2020/committee.html

Organized by

Vellore Institute of Technology (VIT), Chennai, India

VIT®

Vellore Institute of Technology

(Deemed to be University under section 3 of UGC Act, 1956)

Contents

Learning 3DMM Deformation Coefficients for Action Unit Detection

Luigi Ariano, Claudio Ferrari, and Stefano Berretti[✉]🆔

Media Integration and Communication Center, University of Florence, Florence, Italy
stefano.berretti@unifi.it

Abstract. Facial Action Units (AUs) correspond to the deformation/contraction of individual or combinations of facial muscles. As such, each AU affects just a small portion of the face, with deformations that are asymmetric in many cases. Analysing AUs in 3D is particularly relevant for the potential applications it can enable. In this paper, we propose a solution for AUs detection by developing on a newly defined 3D Morphable Model (3DMM) of the face. Differently from most of the 3DMMs existing in the literature, that mainly model global variations of the face and show limitations in adapting to local and asymmetric deformations, the proposed solution is specifically devised to cope with such difficult morphings. During a learning phase, the deformation coefficients are learned that enable the 3DMM to deform to 3D target scans showing neutral and facial expression of a same individual, thus decoupling expression from identity deformations. Then, such deformation coefficients are used to train an AU classifier. We experimented the proposed approach in a difficult cross-dataset experiment, where the 3DMM is constructed on one dataset (BU-3DFE) and tested on a different one (Bosphorus). Results evidence that effective AU detection is obtained by SVM learning of deformation coefficients from a small training set.

Keywords: AU detection · 3D morphable model · Deformation coefficient learning

1 Introduction

Developing methods for automatic generation and recognition of facial expressions has a vast interest, which is both theoretical and practical. In fact, facial expressions are largely studied from a theoretical point of view in disciplines like Cognitive Sciences, Psychology, and Medicine; Important practical applications have been designed in surveillance, where the human emotional state can be analyzed for discovering suspect actions, in monitoring, for fatigue detection especially for drives, in gaming or Human Computer Interaction, where it can help in developing innovative and more friendly interaction paradigms.

From a physiological point of view, facial expressions can be seen as resulting from the contraction of facial muscles that deform the visible skin tissue. Usually, the type and intensity of facial expressions depend in a complex way on

© Springer Nature Singapore Pte Ltd. 2021
S. M. Thampi et al. (Eds.): SoMMA 2020, CCIS 1366, pp. 1–14, 2021.
https://doi.org/10.1007/978-981-16-0419-5_1

the level of activation of several muscles and their combined effect. Looking to the deformation of individual muscles or their combination, Ekman and Friesen defined the Facial Action Coding System (FACS) [14] that relates facial expressions with the activation of Action Units (AUs), *i.e.*, deformations of individual muscles. Though facial expressions and AUs can be detected from 2D images, analyzing AUs in 3D allows a direct evaluation of geometric deformations of the face in the 3D space where they take place, rather than from their 2D projection in RGB images [4].

In this paper, we propose a method for AU detection in 3D using a 3DMM of the face. This has been obtained by using a particular 3DMM, called *Sparse and Locally Coherent* (SLC) 3DMM [16], which has the capability of modeling local deformation of the face. This capacity of the SLC-3DMM derives from three specific properties: *(i)* It is trained with 3D facial scans showing expressions at different levels of intensity. This feature is not exposed by most of the existing 3DMMs that typically use neutral scans for training; *(ii)* The components that deform the SLC-average model are learned by solving a *dictionary learning* problem, so that the resulting atoms are sparse; *(iii)* In the standard 3DMM formulation, Principal Component Analysis (PCA) is used as mathematical tool to learn the deformation components. As a result of this approach, each component deform the average model of the face at a global level; Instead, using the dictionary learning approach, atoms capture the deformations of the face at a local level. An additional reason for this resides in the fact the learned atoms identity vertices and local regions around them that are deformed in a consistent way, rather than face instances as in the traditional 3DMM construction. This 3DMM can be efficiently fit to a target 3D scan using an iterative process that results into a 3D reconstructed model of the target subject, which is semantically consistent, *i.e.*, in dense correspondence, with the 3DMM. In doing so, a set of deformation coefficients (weights) balancing the contribution of each atom are identified. There are two main steps in the fitting procedure: *(i)* In an initial step, the 3DMM is deformed to a 3D scan showing a neutral expression; In this way, a person-specific reconstruction of the face is produced, which is then used in the subsequent step. In practice, it is like a person-specific neutral 3DMM is obtained; *(ii)* This reconstructed model is then used to fit a 3D face scan with expressions of the same subject. The deformation coefficients that regulates this second step of deformation are collected representing the way it is possible to pass from neutral to a specific expression in a subject dependent way. Ultimately, this separates the deformations that model identity traits from the ones modeling AUs. The task of AU classification can then be performed on such coefficients collected for all the subjects and AU: What we want to discover are recurrent patterns in the coefficients that can be related to individual AUs so as to perform AU detection. We experiments this strategy in a set of experiments showing that it is possible to recover such coefficients in a quite simple way even in a cross-dataset scenario, where the 3DMM is learned on one dataset (*i.e.*, Binghamton University 3D facial expression–BU-3DFE), while AU detection is performed on a different one (*i.e.*, Bosphorus).

In summary, this work includes two main contributions:

- We identify a specific 3DMM, which is able to capture localized deformations of the face, and show how it has sufficient representation power and versatility to enable action unit detection in 3D;
- We propose a fully framework for learning the 3DMM deformation coefficients that control AU-specific deformations through an original two-steps approach, and successfully apply the learned classifier to AU detection from 3D scans in a difficult cross-dataset scenario.

The paper is organized as reported in the following: The work in the literature on 3DMM construction and 3D AU detection that are most closely related to our proposal are summarized in Sect. 2; To make the presentation of our proposal self-contained as much as possible, we summarize the SLC-3DMM and its characteristics that are relevant for our application in Sect. 3; In Sect. 4, the proposed method for deformation coefficients learning is illustrated, together with details about the way such coefficients are used for AU detection; In Sect. 5, we report quantitative results for AU detection; A discussion with conclusive remarks are finally given in Sect. 6.

2   Related Work

In the following, we first summarize different solutions from 3DMM construction, then we shortly report on 3DMM applications aiming at modeling local variations of the face as induced by facial expressions and AUs.

The first complete solution for a 3DMM of the face was presented by Blanz and Vetter in their seminal work [5]. They were the first to derive a 3DMM by taking a training set of 3D face scans and transforming the shape and texture information included in the training into a vector space representation using Principal Component Analysis (PCA). One limitation of this approach was represented by the limited number of tarining scans (i.e., they used 200 scans of young Caucasians showing neutral facial expressions). This limited variability in the training faces resulted in a reduced capability of the model to generalize to the modeling of subjects with different ethnicity and non-neutral expressions. Though constrained by the above limitations, the 3DMM proved to be effective in different tasks, such as face analysis from 2D images, also resulting the main inspiring approach for most of the subsequent work. The Blanz and Vetter' 3DMM represented a seminal contribution that inspired many of the subsequent works on this topic. Paysan et al. [25] refined the original 3DMM proposal into the Basel Face Model. This model also used a better scanning device allowing a higher accuracy in capturing shape and texture information and also reducing the number of artifacts in the correspondences established by the dense registration. This latter results was obtained by exploiting the improved performance of the Non-rigid Iterative Closest Point (NICP) [2] algorithm in registering the 3D scans. However, this solution was still limited by the fact that NICP cannot handle topological variations and large missing regions of the face, so that also in this case expressive scans were not included in the training data. An additional limitation shown by these solutions is that both the optical-flow method used in [5] and the NICP method used in [1, 25] were both based on the idea of using a reference model to transfer the vertex index to all the scans in the training. A clear disadvantage of this solution is that the quality of the detected correspondences, and so of the resulting 3DMM, depends from the face model which is used as reference. A complete pipeline for constructing a 3DMM was introduce by Booth *et al.* [7]. They started by estimating a dense correspondence among all the training scans by using NICP to deform a template model. PCA was then applied to derive the deformation components on a dataset of 9,663 scans with a large variability in terms of age, gender, and ethnicity. Though being the largest dataset compared to the current state-of-the-art, the face scans used for training were still in neutral expression. The resulting model was called LSFM-3DMM.

Other works proposed alternative solutions to the use of PCA in the learning of 3DMM deformation components. For example, Patel and Smith [24] used Thin-Plate Splines (TPS) and Procrustes analysis. Cosker *et al.* [11] constructed a 3DMM incorporating dynamic data. This was obtained by developing on Active Appearance Model and TPS for 3D mesh non-rigid registration and correspondence. Results showed this method is capable of overcoming optical-flow based solutions that are impaired by temporal drift. Lüthi *et al.* [22] developed a *Gaussian Process* Morphable Model (GPMM), which generalizes PCA-based statistical shape models. In [8], Brunton *et al.* proposed a statistical model for 3D expressive faces. A wavelet transform was used to decompose the face and learn localized, decorrelated multilinear models on the resulting coefficients.

At coarse level, 3DMM has been mainly used for face recognition and synthesis. For example, Blanz and Vetter [6] applied their 3DMM for face recognition in 2D. This was obtained by deforming the 3D model on target images in such a way that rendering an image from the shape and texture of the deformed resulted as similar as possible to the target image. In the work by Romdhani and Vetter [27], the 3DMM was used again for the task of face recognition, with am improved deformation algorithm that also includes various image features. In [31], Yi *et al.* used a 3DMM to estimate the 3D pose of a face in a 2D image; this was based on a fast fitting algorithm of the 3DMM. Zhu *et al.* [33] extended this idea by fitting a dense 3DMM to an image via a Convolutional Neural Network (CNN). Grupp *et al.* [19] fitted a 3DMM based exclusively on facial landmarks, corrected the pose of the face and transformed it back to a frontal 2D representation for face recognition. Hu *et al.* [20] proposed a Unified-3DMM capturing intra-personal variations due to illumination and occlusions, showing its performance in 3D-assisted 2D face recognition in scenarios where the input image is of low-quality or exhibits intra-personal variations. Recent solutions also used deep neural networks to learn complex non-linear regressor functions mapping a 2D facial image to optimal 3DMM parameters [13, 29].

In the methods summarized above, the 3DMM was mainly used to compensate for pose variations of the face, while some other examples also performed illumination normalization. In the literature, there are very few examples that considered 3DMMs in applications that involve expression variations of the face, with some example existing for expression recognition [3,9]. For example, Ramanathan *et al.* [26] constructed a 3DMM incorporating face variations that are emotion-dependent. This was obtained by using morphing parameters for recognizing four emotions. Ujir and Spann [30] addressed the problem of facial expression recognition by combining a 3DMM with Modular PCA and Facial Animation Parameters (FAP). The resulting deformation, however, is mainly due to the action of FAP rather than to the learned components. Cosker *et al.* [12] explored the effect of linear and non-linear facial movement on expression recognition using a dynamic 3DMM [10]. They also developed a user based test to evaluate animated frames. A cascaded-regressor based face tracking and a 3DMM shape fitting for 3D face reconstruction from monocular in-the-wild videos was proposed by Huber *et al.* [21]. Ferrari *et al.* [18] proposed the Dictionary Learning based 3DMM (DL-3DMM). This 3DMM is particularly promising since it is capable of producing realistic facial expressions by deforming the average model. One specific aspect of this model that motivate such results, is the use of a dense alignment procedure which is guided by facial landmarks. This allows face partitioning into regions and subsequent resampling, of the regions with a same number of points. Ultimately, this enables the enrollment in the training set of facial scans with topological variations and facial expressions. This 3DMM has been experimented in the tasks of facial expression and action unit recognition from 2D still images and videos. Looking to the 3DMM construction problem from a different perspective, Ferrari *et al.* [16] proposed the *Sparse and Locally-Coherent* (SLC) 3DMM, where the learned components of deformation are no more in correspondence with face instances, rather with vertices and local patches of the face that are subject to consistent movements when facial muscles are activated. This revealed to be decisive to model very localized face deformations at a fine level.

3 3D Morphable Model with Local Deformation Capabilities

When the different solutions for constructing a 3DMM are considered, it is evident there are some aspects that have a major importance in determining the properties of the resulting model: *(i)* The number and heterogeneity of training scans. Including as much variability of the human face as possible in the training scans is decisive in making the resulting model capable to generalize to a broader set of target scans; *(ii)* The presence of expressive scans and scans showing AUs in the training data. This makes visible during the training local deformations of the face, thus enabling the model to account for local deformations.

We identified the *Sparse and Locally-Coherent* (SLC)-3DMM proposed by Ferrari *et al.* [16] as one of the few models in the literature that exhibit both these characteristics. Since in our proposal we exploit the SLC-3DMM potential, below we summarize the construction and fitting operations of the SLC-3DMM and the properties that make it suitable for our purposes. This also helps to make the paper self-contained.

3.1 3DMM Construction

Selecting a suitable set of training data is the first problem to be solved is the construction of a 3DMM. This set should include sufficient variability in terms of ethnicity, gender, age, expressions, *etc.*, thus allowing the model to account for a large variability in the data. One a training set is identified, the facial scans must be posed in dense point-to-point correspondence. This is a difficult task since the correspondence should be guided by the semantic meaning of each point of the face (*e.g.*, the left mouth corner across all the scans must the identified by the same vertex number in the model, and this must be assured for any other vertex). The optical-flow method was used to solve this problem in the original work by Blanz and Vetter [5]. Though optical-flow resulted effective in providing reasonable results in the case of neutral scans it resulted not capable of addressing the difficulties posed by expressive scans; as a consequence, several subsequent works replaced the optical-flow solution with the non-rigid variants of the ICP algorithm. However, also these latter solutions did not show the capability of addressing topological variations, like those induced by opening the mouth, and large facial expressions.

For the SLC-3DMM, dense alignment of the training data was obtained in [16] with a solution based on 3D face landmarks. Landmarks were used to partition the face into a set of non-overlapping regions, each one identifying the same part of the face across all the scans. Using the contour of the regions to re-sample the surface of the interior of the region, a dense correspondence was derived region-by-region and so for the entire face. Such method was first proposed in [17, 18], and showed to be robust also to large expression variations, also including topological variations, as those occurring in the BU-3DFE database [32]. This latter dataset was used in the construction of the SLC-3DMM.

In the SLC-3DMM [16], the geometry of a training 3D face with m vertices is represented by a vector $\mathbf{f}_i = [x_1, y_1, z_1, \cdots, x_m, y_m, z_m]^T \in \mathbb{R}^{3m}$ that contains the linearized (x, y, z) coordinates of the vertices. Let $\mathbf{F} = [\mathbf{f}_1|, \ldots, |\mathbf{f}_N] \in \mathbb{R}^{3m \times N}$ be the matrix of the N training scans, each with m vertices arranged column-wise. Then, the average of the densely aligned training scans is computed as:

$$\mathbf{m} = \frac{1}{N} \sum_{i=1}^{N} \mathbf{f}_i, \tag{1}$$

and the difference between each training scan and the average 3D face is also derived $\mathbf{v}_i = \mathbf{f}_i - \mathbf{m}, \ \forall \mathbf{f}_i \in \mathbf{F}$. In doing so, each $\mathbf{v}_i$ represents the set of directions that transform the average model $\mathbf{m}$ into a training scan $\mathbf{f}_i$. Such $\mathbf{v}_i$ are collected into the training matrix $\mathbf{V} = [\mathbf{v}_1|, \ldots, |\mathbf{v}_N] \in \mathbb{R}^{3m \times N}$.

With respect to the usual approach for 3DMM construction, the used SLC-3DMM changes the way training data are considered: Instead of using each $\mathbf{v}_i$ as a separate training sample, each vertex coordinate is managed independently, *i.e.*, the displacements of each coordinate across the N scans are used as training samples. In this way, each sample is regarded as an N-dimensional data point $\mathbf{v}'_i \in \mathbb{R}^N$, which represents the statistics of variation each vertex coordinate is subject to ($3m$ training samples in total). Practically, this is obtained by transposing the training matrix $\mathbf{V}$. The estimation of the primary directions and expansion coefficients is formulated as a *sparse-coding problem*, in which the goal is to find a set of directions that can be sparsely combined to reconstruct the training data. This procedure is summarized in the following.

Let $\mathbf{V}' = \mathbf{V}^T \in \mathbb{R}^{N \times 3m}$ be the transposed training matrix. The objective is to find a set of $k \ll 3m$ primary directions $\mathbf{D} \in \mathbb{R}^{N \times k}$ and sparse expansion coefficients $\mathbf{C} = [\mathbf{c}_1|, \ldots, |\mathbf{c}_{3m}] \in \mathbb{R}^{k \times 3m}$ that allow optimally reconstructing the input data, *i.e.*, such that $\|\mathbf{V}' - \mathbf{DC}\|_2^2$ is minimized and $\mathbf{C}$ is sparse. To obtain realistic deformations, the coefficients should also be smooth enough to prevent discontinuities. In [16], the problem is formulated as:

$$\min_{\mathbf{c}_i, \mathbf{D}} \frac{1}{3m} \sum_{i=1}^{3m} \|\mathbf{v}'_i - \mathbf{Dc}_i\|_2^2 + l_{1,2}, \quad s.t. \ \mathbf{D} \geq 0, \ \mathbf{C} \geq 0, \tag{2}$$

being $l_{1,2} = \lambda_1 \|\mathbf{c}_i\|_1 + \lambda_2 \|\mathbf{c}_i\|_2^2$. In particular, the ℓ_1 penalty forces *sparsity* of the solution, while the ℓ_2 regularization encourages *grouping* [34]. Overall, it results the learned $\mathbf{c}_i$ contain similar values that are in turn spatially grouped. Each of the k row vectors of $\mathbf{C}$ has the effect of expanding the primary directions $\mathbf{d}_i$ to a sparse, spatially bounded subset of the $3m$ vertex coordinates, which allows reproducing local face deformations. A positivity constraint is also forced in (2), which induces additional sparsity to the solution by promoting the complementarity of each learned atom [23].

The sparse components $\mathbf{C}$, the average model $\mathbf{m}$, plus the weight vector $\boldsymbol{\mu} = \frac{1}{N} \sum_{i=1}^{N} D_{i,j} \ \forall j$ balancing the contribution of different components, constitute the SLC-3DMM as first proposed in [16] (see the original paper for more details).

3.2 Fitting the 3DMM to Target Scans

Fitting the SLC-3DMM to a 3D target face scan $\hat{\mathbf{t}}$ allows a coarse 3D reconstruction of the face, which is obtained by the new parameterizations established by the vertex association between the 3DMM and the target. The process is started by an ICP step that is performed once with the aim to pose the two scans in a reasonably good initial alignment. Then, the following steps are iterated till a stopping condition is reached (more details can be found in [16]):

1. A vertex correspondence is established between vertices in the 3DMM and the target. The target model, re-indexed according to the 3DMM vertices is indicated as $\hat{\mathbf{t}}^c$;
2. A transformation accounting for rotation, scale and translation is estimated between the average 3DMM $\mathbf{S}$ and the target $\hat{\mathbf{t}}^c$: $\mathbf{S} = \hat{\mathbf{t}}^c \cdot \mathbf{P} + \mathbf{T}$. In the latter equation, $\mathbf{T} \in \mathbb{R}^3$ is the 3D translation, and $\mathbf{P} \in \mathbb{R}^{3 \times 3}$ contains the 3D rotation and scale parameters. $\mathbf{P}$ is found in closed-form solving the problem:

$$\underset{\mathbf{P}}{\arg\min} \left\| \mathbf{S} - \hat{\mathbf{t}}^c \cdot \mathbf{P} \right\|_2^2. \tag{3}$$

A solution to (3) is given by $\mathbf{P} = \mathbf{S} \cdot \hat{\mathbf{t}}^{c\dagger}$, where $\hat{\mathbf{t}}^{c\dagger}$ is the pseudo-inverse of $\hat{\mathbf{t}}^c$. The translation is then recovered as $\mathbf{T} = \mathbf{S} - \mathbf{P} \cdot \hat{\mathbf{t}}^c$. Rotation and scale matrices $[\mathbf{R}, \mathbf{S}_c] \in \mathbb{R}^{3 \times 3}$ can be retrieved applying QR decomposition to $\mathbf{P}$. Using $[\mathbf{R}, \mathbf{S}_c]$ and $\mathbf{T}$, both $\hat{\mathbf{t}}^c$ and $\hat{\mathbf{t}}$ are re-aligned to $\mathbf{S}$ before performing the deformation $\hat{\mathbf{t}}^c = (\hat{\mathbf{t}}^c \cdot \mathbf{R}) \cdot \mathbf{S}_c + \mathbf{T}$;

3. To deform $\mathbf{S}$, the optimal set of deformation coefficients $\boldsymbol{\alpha} \in \mathbb{R}^k$ should be found so that the per-vertex distance between the two point sets is minimized. Similar to other works using a morphable model [15,18], the problem is formulated as a regularized least-squares:

$$\min_{\boldsymbol{\alpha}} \left\| \hat{\mathbf{t}}^c - \mathbf{S} - \mathbf{C}\boldsymbol{\alpha} \right\|_2^2 + \lambda \left\| \boldsymbol{\alpha} \circ \boldsymbol{\mu}^{-1} \right\|_2, \tag{4}$$

where λ balances between the fitting accuracy and smoothness of the deformation. The deformation regularization is obtained by using $\boldsymbol{\mu}^{-1}$ so that the contribution of each component is weighed with respect to its average intensity. By pre-computing $\mathbf{X} = \hat{\mathbf{t}}^c - \mathbf{S}$, the solution is found in closed form: $\boldsymbol{\alpha} = \left(\mathbf{C}^T \mathbf{C} + \lambda \cdot \mathrm{diag}(\hat{\boldsymbol{\mu}}^{-1}) \right)^{-1} \mathbf{C}^T \mathbf{X}$, where $\mathrm{diag}(\hat{\boldsymbol{\mu}}^{-1})$ is the diagonal matrix with vector $\hat{\boldsymbol{\mu}}^{-1}$ on its diagonal. $\mathbf{S}$ is then deformed using: $\mathbf{m} + \sum_{i=1}^k \mathbf{C}_i \alpha_i$. Finally, the per-vertex error of the deformed model is computed as the average Euclidean distance between each vertex of $\mathbf{S}$ and its nearest-neighbor in $\hat{\mathbf{t}}$.

The above procedure is repeated until the error between subsequent iterations is above some threshold τ_e, or a maximum number of iterations is reached. At this point, the 3DMM has been optimally fit to the target shape. For a more detailed description of the procedure the reader can refer to [16].

4   Learning Deformation Coefficients

As introduced in the previous section, fitting the SLC-3DMM to a target scan results into a set of coefficients $\boldsymbol{\alpha}$ that deform the average model using the linear combination $\mathbf{m} + \sum_{i=1}^k \mathbf{C}_i \alpha_i$. Coefficients α codify the deformation the model should undergo to be transformed as similar as possible to the target scan. This includes both deformation due to the identity and to the contraction of facial muscles due to expressions and action units.

Our main goal here is to obtain the set of coefficients that deform the average face to the specific action unit. To do so, we proceed with a two step approach. First, we isolate the identity component from the deformation one. This is obtained by fitting the SLC-3DMM to a face scan in neutral expression so that the deformation coefficients related to the identity are discovered $\boldsymbol{\alpha}_{id}$. Then, the neutral model resulting from the previous step is used in place of the average model to fit an expressive face scan of the same subject showing a specific action unit. In this way, we obtain a set of coefficients $\boldsymbol{\alpha}_{expr}$ that codify the sole action unit. The final step is to find recurrent patterns in the α_{expr} coefficients, separately for each AU. We addressed this task by training a Support Vector Machine (SVM) with a Radial Basis Function (RBF) kernel.

5 Experimental Results

Experiments have been performed on the Bosphorus [28] dataset, which is one of the few datasets including 3D face scans with coded AUs. The Bosphorus dataset comprises 4,666 high-resolution scans of 105 individuals. There are up to 54 scans per subject, which include prototypical expressions, facial action units activation, rotations and occlusions. Scans of Bosphorus have an average of $30K$ vertices on the face region. Bosphorus also contains scans with posed Action Units coded according to the Facial Action Coding System (FACS) [14]. The list of posed AUs, which also involve a few combinations, and intensity and asymmetry variations are given in Table 1.

Table 1. List of the AUs that are included in the Bosphorus dataset

Lower Face Action Units
Lower Lip Depressor - AU16
Lips Part - AU25
Jaw Drop - AU26
Mouth Stretch - AU27
Lip Corner Puller - AU12
Left Lip Corner Puller - AU12L
Right Lip Corner Puller - AU12R
Low Intensity Lip Corner Puller - AU12LW
Dimpler - AU14
Lip Stretcher - AU20
Lip Corner Depressor - AU15
Chin Raiser - AU17
Lip Funneler - AU22
Lip Puckerer - AU18
Lip Tightener - AU23
Lip Presser - AU24
Lip Suck - AU28
Upper Lip Raiser - AU10
Nose Wrinkler - AU9
Cheek Puff - AU34

Upper Face Action Units
Outer Brow Raiser - AU2
Brow Lowerer - AU4
Inner Brow Raiser - AU1
Squint - AU44
Eyes Closed - AU43

Some Action Unit Combinations
AU26 + AU12LW
AU22 + AU25
AU12 + AU15

Examples of some of the AUs included in the Bosphorus dataset are illustrated in Fig. 1.

In the evaluation, we compared three different approaches to derive the 3DMM deformation components:

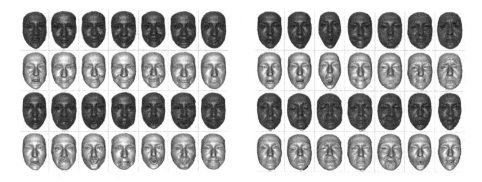

Fig. 1. AU examples from the Bosphorus dataset

- 3DMM with 50 components learned using PCA according to the standard 3DMM construction approach. Results for the deformation coefficients obtained using this solution are indicated as alpha-PCA50;
- 3DMM with 50 components learned using the SLC approach. The acronym used for this solution is alpha-SLC50;
- 3DMM with 300 components learned using the SLC approach (alpha-SLC300).

The 3DMM for each of the three solutions above has been deformed to each of the 3D scans of the Bosphorus dataset representing an AU using the fitting procedure illustrated in Sect. 3.2. We recall here that for scans with AUs we first deformed the 3DMM on the neutral scans of a subject, then from this to the expressive scans of the same subject. In this way, the α coefficients capture the shape deformation to pass from a neutral to an expressive scan for a specific identity.

We followed a *leave-one-subject-out* protocol computing the F1-score and the Area Under the Receiving Operating Characteristic (ROC) curve, *i.e.*, AUC. The F1-score is computed as:

$$F1 = 2 \cdot \frac{Precision \times Recall}{Precision + Recall}. \tag{5}$$

To illustrate the effectiveness of the classifier in a more detailed way, three F1-score measures are computed:

- The *macro-averaged* F1-score, or the macro-F1 for short, as the arithmetic mean of per-class F1-scores;
- When averaging the macro-F1, an equal weights is given to each class. In the *weighted-average F1-score*, or weighted-F1, instead, we weight the F1-score of each class by the number of samples from that class itself;
- The *micro-averaged F1-score*, or micro-F1, which is computed from micro-averaged precision and micro-averaged recall over all the samples, and then combining the two. It results *micro-F1 = micro-precision = micro-recall = accuracy*.

Results using the above indicators are reported in Table 2. Overall, the three 3DMMs under comparison score similar values with a slight increment observed for the SLC-3DMM.

Table 2. AUs detection results using F1-score and AUC

	$\alpha-$PCA50	$\alpha-$SLC50	$\alpha-$SLC300
F1-micro	0.710	0.703	0.7
F1-macro	0.711	0.702	0.713
F1-weighted	0.711	0.705	0.711
AUC-macro	0.953	0.958	0.956
AUC-weighted	0.953	0.958	0.956

Table 3. Values of the F1-score and AUC for each AU for the SLC50-3DMM

AU code	F1-micro	F1-macro	F1-weighted	AUC-macro	AUC-weighted
LFAU - AU10	0.78	0.13	0.87	0.99	0.99
LFAU - AU12	0.78	0.09	0.88	0.0	0.0
LFAU - AU12L	0.55	0.07	0.70	0.79	0.79
LFAU - AU12LW	0.74	0.07	0.85	0.0	0.0
LFAU - AU12R	0.84	0.15	0.92	0.13	0.13
LFAU - AU14	0.72	0.08	0.84	0.93	0.93
LFAU - AU15	0.77	0.12	0.87	0.95	0.95
LFAU - AU16	0.55	0.04	0.72	0.71	0.71
LFAU - AU17	0.69	0.05	0.82	0.86	0.86
LFAU - AU18	0.62	0.06	0.77	0.86	0.86
LFAU - AU20	0.75	0.09	0.85	0.95	0.95
LFAU - AU22	0.6	0.06	0.75	0.96	0.96
LFAU - AU23	0.63	0.06	0.77	0.87	0.87
LFAU - AU24	0.58	0.06	0.73	0.87	0.87
LFAU - AU25	0.59	0.04	0.75	0.84	0.84
LFAU - AU26	0.70	0.07	0.82	0.88	0.88
LFAU - AU27	0.76	0.08	0.86	0.88	0.88
LFAU - AU28	0.85	0.09	0.92	0.97	0.97
LFAU - AU34	0.82	0.07	0.90	0.97	0.97
LFAU - AU9	0.85	0.07	0.92	0.96	0.96
UFAU - AU1	0.54	0.09	0.70	0.91	0.91
UFAU - AU2	0.68	0.06	0.81	0.86	0.86
UFAU - AU4	0.67	0.06	0.8	0.0	0.0
UFAU - AU43	0.72	0.06	0.84	0.38	0.38
UFAU - AU44	0.52	0.05	0.69	0.44	0.44

Results of the SLC50-3DMM for each AU of the Bosphorus dataset are reported in Table 3. Overall, it emerges there are some critical AUs, like LFAU-AU12, LFAU-AU12LW, and UFAU-AU4, UFAU-AU43. The first two are related to lip corner movements: those points can be modeled by the 3DMM with lower precision that reflects in deformation coefficients α that are not so well characterized. The third and forth ones are related to brow lowerer and eyes closed that represent, respectively, a quite slight variation of the 3D shape that can be modeled with difficulty by the fitting process, and a 3D feature that is difficulty captured by a 3D scan.

6   Conclusions

In this paper, we have proposed a method to isolate the action unit-specific deformation coefficients of a 3DMM and applied them to perform action unit detection. We exploited a particular 3DMM implementation based on learning a sparse set of localized deformation components, which is able to reproduce action units thanks to the inclusion of expressive scans in the training set. The model also exploits a different interpretation of the learning, where points and their local movements are considered as training instances rather than full face scans. We also showed that the 3DMM fitting operated in two subsequent steps is effective in removing the identity component from the deformed 3DMM; it results that recurrent patterns can be found in the deformation coefficients of the subject-specific 3DMM that well relates to specific action units. Results are encouraging also considering the proposed approach is, to the best of our knowledge, the first solution that uses the deformation coefficients of a 3DMM to perform action unit detection from 3D scans.

Finally, we point out our solution is not exempt from limitations, that are mostly evidenced by the difficulty in detecting a subset of action units. Though these are in part due to the quality of the given 3D scans, an additional investigation is required to make the fitting process more accurate, while also increasing the number of vertices comprised by the 3DMM.

References

1. Amberg, B., Knothe, R., Vetter, T.: Expression invariant 3D face recognition with a morphable model. In: IEEE International Conference on Automatic Face and Gesture Recognition (2008)
2. Amberg, B., Romdhani, S., Vetter, T.: Optimal step nonrigid ICP algorithms for surface registration. In: IEEE International Conference on Computer Vision and Pattern Recognition, pp. 1–8 (2007)
3. Bejaoui, H., Ghazouani, H., Barhoumi, W.: Fully automated facial expression recognition using 3D morphable model and mesh-local binary pattern. In: Blanc-Talon, J., Penne, R., Philips, W., Popescu, D., Scheunders, P. (eds.) ACIVS 2017. LNCS, vol. 10617, pp. 39–50. Springer, Cham (2017). https://doi.org/10.1007/978-3-319-70353-4_4
4. Berretti, S., Daoudi, M., Turaga, P., Basu, A.: Representation, analysis and recognition of 3D humans: a survey. ACM Trans. Multimedia Comput. Commun. Appl. **14**(1s), 1–35 (2018)

5. Blanz, V., Vetter, T.: A morphable model for the synthesis of 3D faces. In: ACM Conference on Computer Graphics and Interactive Techniques, pp. 187–194 (1999)
6. Blanz, V., Vetter, T.: Face recognition based on fitting a 3D morphable model. IEEE Trans. Pattern Anal. Mach. Intell. **25**(9), 1063–1074 (2003)
7. Booth, J., Roussos, A., Zafeiriou, S., Ponniahand, A., Dunaway, D.: A 3D morphable model learnt from 10,000 faces. In: IEEE Conference on Computer Vision and Pattern Recognition, pp. 5543–5552 (2016)
8. Brunton, A., Bolkart, T., Wuhrer, S.: Multilinear wavelets: a statistical shape space for human faces. In: Fleet, D., Pajdla, T., Schiele, B., Tuytelaars, T. (eds.) ECCV 2014. LNCS, vol. 8689, pp. 297–312. Springer, Cham (2014). https://doi.org/10.1007/978-3-319-10590-1_20
9. Chang, F.J., Tran, A., Hassner, T., Masi, I., Nevatia, R., Medioni, G.: Expnet: landmark-free, deep, 3D facial expressions. In: IEEE Conference on Automatic Face and Gesture Recognition (2018)
10. Cosker, D., Krumhuber, E., Hilton, A.: Perception of linear and nonlinear motion properties using a FACS validated 3D facial model. In: ACM Applied Perception in Graphics and Vision (2010)
11. Cosker, D., Krumhuber, E., Hilton, A.: A FACS valid 3D dynamic action unit database with applications to 3D dynamic morphable facial modeling. In: International Conference on Computer Vision (ICCV) (2011)
12. Cosker, D., Krumhuber, E., Hilton, A.: Perceived emotionality of linear and non-linear AUs synthesised using a 3D dynamic morphable facial model. In: Proceedings of the Facial Analysis and Animation, pp. 7:1–7:1. FAA 2015. ACM (2015)
13. Dou, P., Shah, S.K., Kakadiaris, I.A.: End-to-end 3D face reconstruction with deep neural networks. In: IEEE Conference on Computer Vision and Pattern Recognition (CVPR), pp. 1503–1512, July 2017. https://doi.org/10.1109/CVPR.2017.164
14. Ekman, P., Friesen, W.: Facial Action Coding System: A Technique for the Measurement of Facial Movement. Consulting Psychologists Press, Palo Alto (1978)
15. Fan, Z., Hu, X., Chen, C., Peng, S.: Dense semantic and topological correspondence of 3D faces without landmarks. In: Ferrari, V., Hebert, M., Sminchisescu, C., Weiss, Y. (eds.) ECCV 2018. LNCS, vol. 11220, pp. 541–558. Springer, Cham (2018). https://doi.org/10.1007/978-3-030-01270-0_32
16. Ferrari, C., Berretti, S., Pala, P., Del Bimbo, A.: A sparse and locally coherent morphable face model for dense semantic correspondence across heterogeneous 3D faces. CoRR abs/2006.03840 (2020). https://arxiv.org/abs/2006.03840
17. Ferrari, C., Lisanti, G., Berretti, S., Del Bimbo, A.: Dictionary learning based 3D morphable model construction for face recognition with varying expression and pose. In: International Conference on 3D Vision (2015)
18. Ferrari, C., Lisanti, G., Berretti, S., Del Bimbo, A.: A dictionary learning-based 3D morphable shape model. IEEE Trans. Multimedia **19**(12), 2666–2679 (2017)
19. Grupp, M., Kopp, P., Huber, P., Rätsch, M.: A 3D face modelling approach for pose-invariant face recognition in a human-robot environment. CoRR abs/1606.00474 (2016)
20. Hu, G., et al.: Face recognition using a unified 3D morphable model. In: Leibe, B., Matas, J., Sebe, N., Welling, M. (eds.) ECCV 2016. LNCS, vol. 9912, pp. 73–89. Springer, Cham (2016). https://doi.org/10.1007/978-3-319-46484-8_5
21. Huber, P., Kopp, P., Rätsch, M., Christmas, W.J., Kittler, J.: 3D face tracking and texture fusion in the wild. CoRR abs/1605.06764 (2016). http://arxiv.org/abs/1605.06764
22. Lüthi, M., Jud, C., Gerig, T., Vetter, T.: Gaussian process morphable models. CoRR abs/1603.07254 (2016). http://arxiv.org/abs/1603.07254

23. Mairal, J., Bach, F., Ponce, J., Sapiro, G.: Online learning for matrix factorization and sparse coding. J. Mach. Learn. Res. **11**, 19–60 (2010)
24. Patel, A., Smith, W.A.P.: 3D morphable face models revisited. In: IEEE Conference on Computer Vision and Pattern Recognition, pp. 1327–1334 (2009)
25. Paysan, P., Knothe, R., Amberg, B., Romdhani, S., Vetter, T.: A 3D face model for pose and illumination invariant face recognition. In: IEEE International Conference on Advanced Video and Signal Based Surveillance (AVSS), pp. 296–301 (2009)
26. Ramanathan, S., Kassim, A., Venkatesh, Y.V., Wah, W.S.: Human facial expression recognition using a 3D morphable model. In: International Conference on Image Processing (2006)
27. Romdhani, S., Vetter, T.: Estimating 3D shape and texture using pixel intensity, edges, specular highlights, texture constraints and a prior. In: IEEE Conference on Computer Vision and Pattern Recognition (2005)
28. Savran, A., et al.: Bosphorus database for 3D face analysis. In: Schouten, B., Juul, N.C., Drygajlo, A., Tistarelli, M. (eds.) BioID 2008. LNCS, vol. 5372, pp. 47–56. Springer, Heidelberg (2008). https://doi.org/10.1007/978-3-540-89991-4_6
29. Tran, A.T., Hassner, T., Masi, I., Medioni, G.: Regressing robust and discriminative 3D morphable models with a very deep neural network. In: IEEE Conference on Computer Vision and Pattern Recognition (CVPR), pp. 5163–5172, July 2017
30. Ujir, H., Spann, M.: Facial expression recognition using FAPs-based 3DMM. In: Tavares, J., Natal Jorge, R. (eds.) Topics in Medical Image Processing and Computational Vision, pp. 33–47. Lecture Notes in Computer Science. Springer, Heidelberg (2013). https://doi.org/10.1007/978-94-007-0726-9_2
31. Yi, D., Lei, Z., Li, S.Z.: Towards pose robust face recognition. In: IEEE Conference on Computer Vision and Pattern Recognition (2013)
32. Yin, L., Wei, X., Sun, Y., Wang, J., Rosato, M.: A 3D facial expression database for facial behavior research. In: IEEE International Conference on Automatic Face and Gesture Recognition (2006)
33. Zhu, X., Lei, Z., Liu, X., Shi, H., Li, S.Z.: Face alignment across large poses: a 3D solution. In: IEEE Conference on Computer Vision and Pattern Recognition (2016)
34. Zou, H., Hastie, T.: Regularization and variable selection via the elastic net. J. Roy. Stat. Soc.: Ser. B (Stat. Methodol.) **67**(2), 301–320 (2005)

Smart Security and Surveillance System in Laboratories Using Machine Learning

Ashwini Patil, Krupali Shetty, Shweta Hinge, G. Tejaswini,
V. Anni Shinay, Suneeta V. Budihal$^{(\boxtimes)}$, Nalini Iyer, and C. Sujata

KLE Technological University, Hubballi, Karnataka, India
suneeta_vb@kletech.ac.in

Abstract. The paper proposes to design and develop a smart authentication system in laboratory as a part of security and surveillance. To address the unauthorized entry in the laboratory, a smart alert system is designed and developed. The authentic entry to any laboratory will reduce the student response to hazards and accidents, risks to acceptable levels. The proposed methodology uses face detection and recognition techniques for the student authentication. Based on the results, the attendance is updated in the attendance data base if the authorized users enter the laboratory else the details will be sent to the course instructors through the registered mails. The authentic student is also verified for wearing the personal protective equipment during the entry to the laboratory. By this, we can reduce the vandalism occurring in laboratories and maintain the integrity.

Keywords: Security and video surveillance · Face recognition · Haar cascade · Open face · Alert system · Machine learning.3382

1 Introduction

In today's world, security is a major concern in all fields. With growing technology, the need for complex, digitalized, smart security and safety is a challenge. Surveillance is a system developed to monitor activities, behavior, or other moving information in order to influence, assist, direct, or save people. It comprises of the observation from a distance with electronic equipment or interception of electronically transmitted signals. From mechanical to electrical equipment, students and faculty, laboratories suffer a wide range of safety hazards, so it is crucial to highlight the importance of laboratory safety. The smart security is the main requirement everywhere. Injuries in labs are caused mainly due to negligence and lack of a system to monitor the safety measures. Many a times hazardous accidents in laboratories can be prevented by wearing appropriate Personal Protective Equipment (PPE).

Ignorance of hazards and crimes in areas like research centers, college laboratories [1] have increased in late years and is to be resolved. That is why it is so important to make sure that only authentic individuals have access to identified areas of the lab to maintain integrity. Students working in laboratory often forget or neglect to wear the protective measures given to them. This has resulted in increased number of accidents, even risking their life to death. In addition to this, monitoring the entry of person at the

S. M. Thampi et al. (Eds.): SoMMA 2020, CCIS 1366, pp. 15–28, 2021.
https://doi.org/10.1007/978-981-16-0419-5_2

entrance of laboratory also play a vital role in security area. The paper [2] discusses about object detection. Increased capacity of software and hardware, drives object detection technology. In this work, the author has developed algorithm for the detection of multiple objects based on Open CV. In paper [3] face recognition system is developed using Automatic Facial Expression Recognition System (AFERS). In the first phase Active Appearance Model (AAM) is used. For AFER Euclidean distance method is preferred. Based on the value of Euclidean distance output is decided and the efficiency of this method for face recognition is around 70%.

In paper [4] the author emphasizes on multiple object detection using Open CV library. There are algorithms for object detection and recognition but the accuracy and processing time are very important aspects to obtain correct results. In this paper, author uses an Open CV library to perform object detection. This method stores the features of training samples and compares the input with these stored features to detect objects. Multiple objects can be detected using this method but the efficiency of this method reduces as the number of objects to be detected increases. In paper [5] SIFT (Scale Invariant Feature Transform) is used to detect and track objects. After performing all these four steps on training sample features of objects are obtained in the form of vectors and these features are later used for comparison with the input image. Euclidean distance is calculated between the object to SIFT features and the input SIFT features, and value is used compute the position of the matched object. This algorithm can be used to similar objects in two different images. This algorithm is efficient as it considers the special features of the object for detection.

In paper [6] author explains about face recognition depending on information theory method of encoding-decoding. PCA method is used by Eigen face algorithm for image recognition. It is mainly to diminish the dimensionality of input features. Neural network method is more efficient compared to normal face detection using Open CV libraries. The paper [7] is to develop a solution for monitoring specifically a human hand and it's properties. The presently available solutions require special hardware for functioning such as depth sensor. But in this paper author uses a camera to obtain the properties of the object. Here the designed system processes data in real time, where data are read from locally stored systems or the connected device like camera.

The paper [8] introduces to a new method of object detection YOLO (You Only Look Once). This method treats object detection as regression problem to associate class probabilities and spatially separated bounding boxes. In a single evaluation single NN predicts bounding boxes and class probabilities directly from complete images. Processing rate of this method is 45 frames per second. This algorithm is more efficient in terms of accuracy compared to all other methods of object detection. This method will be more useful for multiple objects detection. In paper [9] static object recognition is done using Haar Cascade classifier. In paper [10] the attendance system development, using face recognition technique is explained. There are many face recognition algorithms like Eigen face, Fisher face, LBPH (Local Binary Pattern Histogram). Eigen face algorithm is used to develop attendance system. This algorithm is more efficient compared to Fisher face. The efficiency in attendance system is 70–90%. In paper [11] the author speaks about LBPH method of face recognition. This algorithm can recognize both front and side face. LBPH is a very simple yet very efficient algorithm which labels the pixels of an image by considering the threshold of the neighborhood of each pixel and considers the result as a binary number. The recognition rate of this algorithm reduces during illumination diversity classification and expression variation.

To solve this problem MLBPH (Median Local Binary Pattern Histogram) was introduced. This algorithm is more efficient in terms of accuracy in recognizing compared to other face recognition algorithms. From the literature survey we conclude that Haar Cascade is better algorithm for face detection, LBPH for face recognition and SIFT [12] is suitable for object detection. Paper [13] uses home automation through DIP algorithms, which gives an outline for automatic system to control, secure, with the help of Internet of Things (IoT). Image analysis is carried out to detect, recognize and match the captured image with the authenticated people dataset. If the image captured does not match, then an alert signal is sent to the owner of the house. In paper [14, 15] KNN technique which holds good for license plate reading. The concept of Tesseract-OCR is used for character recognition. Security of system has become important [16] and [17].

1.1 Identified Objectives Are Listed as Follows

- To detect and recognize multiple faces of students for providing authentication for registered students in the database and update the attendance.
- To monitor the dress code (apron, shoes) followed by the student at the entrance.
- To detect PPE worn by student working in machine zone.
- To send an email/SMS to the course instructor when the safety measures are violated.

The paper is sequenced such that Sect. 2 explains design for the student authentication system. It involves the functional block diagram, final design of the system. In the Sect. 3, implementation details are discussed. The obtained results are shown in the Sect. 4. In Sect. 5 the conclusions are drawn with for the proposed authentication system.

2 Proposed Framework to Detect the Authorized Students

In Fig. 1, design of laboratory authentication system is an integration of two sub systems, in which the first subsystem is authentication which includes the registration of student where in the student's images are captured by the camera and stored as the dataset. Whenever the student enters the lab, he is validated using face recognition algorithm. If the student entering the lab is not recognized by the system, there will be an indication through beep alert that the person is not allowed inside. In this module, Haar Cascade classifier is used for detection of faces.

Open face algorithm is used for face recognition. The second important part of this design is object detection wherein the system checks if the student is wearing the PPE according to the requirement in this module. If the student is wearing the PPEs the device detects them and is allowed to enter the laboratory. If the PPEs are not detected then the system gives a voice alert to that student. The algorithm used in this module is mobile net SSD which is most efficient way to detect objects at a faster rate. Figure 2

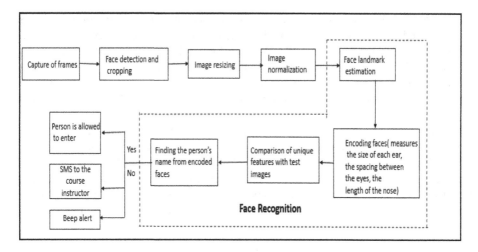

Fig. 1. Functional block diagram for laboratory student authentication system

shows the authentication of the student. When the student enters the laboratory, the frames from IP camera are captured. It involves face detection and cropping, image resizing, image normalization, face landmark estimation and encoding of faces. The resultant image from multiple face detection schemes is resized using nearest neighbor interpolation method with definite output size. One of the important challenges here is illumination variation and is addressed by image normalization. Comparison of unique features of trained images with test images is done to recognize the student name. According to the result of comparison, the student is either allowed to enter the laboratory or is denied with a beep alert and SMS to the course instructor. The object

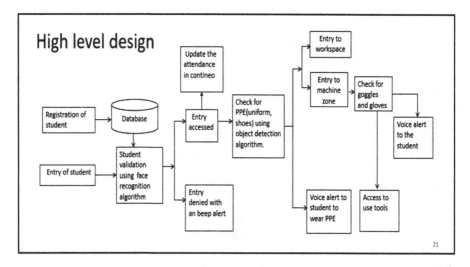

Fig. 2. Block diagram for face detection and recognition.

detection block diagram shown in Fig. 3 explains the steps to detect multiple objects. Initially the frames are extracted from live video stream through IP camera. In order to detect and recognize the PPE (apron and shoes), the images (test images) are sent through the trained mobile net SSD model. The result of the recognition is given through bounding boxes and labeling with accuracy on the objects detected in the images.

The accuracy of recognition determines whether the PPE is present in the image and accordingly the student is allowed to enter the lab else voice alert is given, cautioning them to follow the safety measures. The Table 1 contains the specifications required for face detection and recognition. For face detection and recognition, the algorithm used is open face. The required operating system is ubuntu 16.04. The number of training images taken are 400 for 40 different people of one class. SVM model classifier is used to classify the objects with 98–99% accuracy.

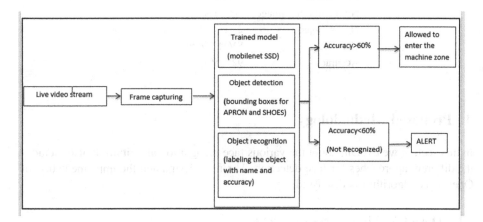

Fig. 3. Block diagram for object detection

2.1 Specifications Required for Laboratory Authentication System

The Table 2 shows the specifications for object detection. The algorithm used is MobileNet SSD which requires Anaconda platform. The libraries used are Tensorflow, Protobuf. VGG Net architecture is used for implementation. There are 2 objects with training images of 500 per class. This algorithm brings accuracy of 95%.

Table 1. Specifications for face detection and recognition

Algorithm	Open Face
Platform	Anaconda
Libraries	Dlib, Torch
Architecture	Facenet
No. of training images	400
No. of objects	40
Classifier	SVM Model
Accuracy	98–99%

Table 2. Specifications for object detection.

Algorithm	Open Face
Platform	Anaconda
Libraries	Protobuf, Tensorflow
Architecture	VGGnet
No. of training images	500/class
No. of objects	2
Classifier	SVM Model
Accuracy	92–95%

3   Proposed Methodology

In this section we explain about the various face recognition algorithm. It also includes the different approaches for face detection. The final design and the implementation of Open Face algorithm is discussed.

3.1   Open CV- Eigen Faces Algorithm

Open Face algorithm is discussed. Here we make use of Eigen Face recognizer. It considers all training images as a whole and extract the relevant components and discards the remaining. These important features are termed as principal components. It concentrates on the features that represent all the faces of all the people in training data. However, Eigen Faces algorithm considers illumination as an important feature, lights and shadows are picked up by Eigen Faces, which classifies them as representing a face.

3.2   LBPH Algorithm

Following are the steps involved in the implementation of LBPH algorithm:

- Choosing the parameters (Radius, Neighbors, Grid X, Grid Y)
- Training the algorithm

- Applying LBP operation
- Extracting histograms
- Histogram comparison for face recognition.

Open Face is the most advanced algorithm with an accuracy of 98%–99% in each test. It is observed that Open Face algorithm works well for different environmental conditions. The results of tests have a different environment between the training and test sets. These tests were performed with two pictures per subject in the test set. Open Face is constant and keeps an accuracy of 100%. This concerned only Fisher faces. The others stayed the same or had an improvement when this factor became bigger. The two algorithms with a statistical approach were better than LBPH. LBPH had the worst results with less than 50% when it was tested for different environment. A consistent gap between Open Face and the other algorithms can be noticed.

Open Face is a common face recognition library having various application. Towards exploring transient and mobile face recognition, was created as a general-purpose library, offering higher accuracy compared to prior open source projects. Uniform embeddings for face recognition and clustering Open Face besides being an open source, is used for development of model focused on real time face recognition on mobile devices.

Working of HOG for face detection is explained as follows. The image that is captured from the IP camera is converted into black and white and each pixel is compared with surrounding pixels. Vectors are drawn in the direction of the darker pixel thereby generating a gradient. This image is then converted into 16×16 pixel with gradients pointing in major direction only and generating the HOG pattern. Now to detect face the obtained HOG pattern is compared with already trained bunch of HOG pattern using the support vector machine. The faces are normalized by Open CVs Affine transformation. This image is then reduced to 96×96 pixels image and given to the trained NN. If matched the face is detected. Training of images is done by passing 500k images from two public datasets: a: CASIA-Web Face comprising 10,574 individuals with a total of 494,413 images b: Face Scrub comprising 531 individuals with a total of 06,862 images who are public figures. This helps us achieve the common facial embeddings which would be difficult over smaller dataset training. 126 facial embeddings that represent a generic face are generated. Next OpenFace uses Googles FaceNet architecture for feature extraction.

3.3 Object Detection

The combination of SSD (Single Shot Detector) architecture and Mobilenet feature extractor model is used in the implementation of detecting apron and shoes. This method achieves a good balance amongst speed and accuracy. It runs a CNN layer on input image only once and calculates a feature map. Then a small 32 sized convolution kernel is run on this feature map to predict the bounding boxes and classification probability. The steps involved in implementation of this method are as follows:

1. Gathering a dataset:
2. Creating bounding boxes:
3. Converting CSV _les to TFRecord format:

4. Choosing a model:
5. Retraining the model with custom data:
6. Using the retrained model to detect object:

3.4   Alert System Design

An alert system plays an important role in security and surveillance. The methodology and implementation details of alert system are explained in this chapter. The different types of alerts used in the implementation of smart student authentication system are also mentioned. The alert system is mainly used in the following cases: When an unknown (not registered) student enters the laboratory, when the student violates the safety rules. The section also includes the flow chart of alert system. The different forms of alert are Beep alert, Message alert, Voice alert.

The alert system works when the person does not follow the safety rules. The block diagram in Fig. 4 explains the generation of beep by the system. Beep generates simple tones on the speaker. The beep is synchronous and alterable. The frequency of the sound in hertz must be in the range of 37 to 32, 767. The duration of the sound in 3 ms.

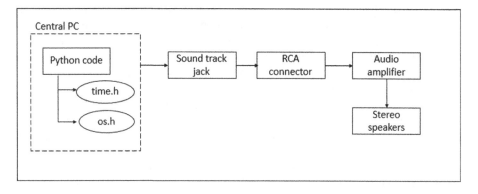

Fig. 4. Alert system implementation

The system produces a standard beep sound through the computer speaker. An RCA connector also called as a phono connector is a type of electrical connector commonly used to carry audio and video signals. Input to this is a set of jacks. In this application the input is sound track jack. Audio amplifier usually has audio input with RCA connectors, or optical input, or headphone-jack audio input because the audio output from a laptop's built-in speakers is usually low. A power amplifier is required to get a high volume which is the audio amplifier. In stereo speakers more channels are used. We can use two different channels for two speakers. This is used to create directionality, perspective, space to generate beep.

4 Results and Discussions

The results of face detection and the object detection are discussed in this chapter. The platform used for implementation is Anaconda.

4.1 Face Recognition Results

The face recognition is done through the IP camera. Face detection is performed prior to face recognition. Different test cases are considered for validating student authentication. The Fig. 5 shows the face recognition of two students at a time. The name of the student is shown below the bounding box along with the confidence score. The confidence score is around 92–97%. The Fig. 5 shows the face recognition of 6 students at a time. It recognizes all the students with high accuracy. The maximum number of students that can be recognized with maximum accuracy is ten. The unknown student who has not registered in the database is indicated as unknown and the facial image of that particular student is stored in a folder. To differentiate between known and unknown student, the bounding box for unknown is red in color.

Fig. 5. Recognition of 5 students at a time (Color figure online)

The Fig. 6 shows face recognition of five students at a time. Here three students are registered in the database. Therefore, they are recognized and allowed to enter inside. The accuracy of the recognition is the confidence score shown. The two unknown students are recognized and displayed as unknown. These people have not registered in the database. The unknown people are not allowed to enter inside. To notify this a beep alert is generated informing unknown person present. A mail is sent to the respective course instructor regarding the entry of unknown student into the laboratory. The ideal condition is ten students at a time. That is ten students can be recognized properly with the given camera specifications and distance from the camera. Figure 7 shows the face recognition of ten students at a time. The names of recognized nine students are displayed on the terminal. The unknown student in the frame is shown with red bounding box.

Fig. 6. Result of three known and two unknown students at time (Color figure online)

Fig. 7. Ideal condition of face detection and recognition in the lab using the camera to detects students at a time with 7 students registered and 1 student not registered with names. (Color figure online)

Fig. 8. Personal protective Equipment Apron detection (Color figure online)

4.2 Object Detection Results

The object detection includes the detection of apron and shoes. The person who has worn apron and shoes is allowed to enter the laboratory. A voice alert to wear apron is generated if a student violates the safety measures.

The Fig. 8 shows the apron detection of a student. The apron worn by a student is recognized with a green bounding box on which the corresponding accuracy is displayed. After apron and shoes are detected, the student is allowed to enter the laboratory. Sometimes the detection of blue color dress which is not apron is observed. But the difference is the accuracy. The accuracy is less than 50% when it is not apron. So, by keeping threshold, the further actions are taken. When the person has not worn apron, a voice alert is generated.

The shoes detection is also an important part of protective equipment detection. There are different varieties of shoes. So, shoes detection becomes tedious. The Fig. 9 shows the shoes detection of a person entering the laboratory. Figure shows 2 types of shoes detection. The percentage of detection is high i.e., more than 80% when it is exact shoes. This percentage is less (less than 50%) when the person has worn any other types of footwear.

Fig. 9. Shoes detection

The Fig. 10 shows 3 persons entering the laboratory. Here one person has not worn the apron whereas 2 people have worn the apron. These 2 people are detected with the confidence score and are allowed to enter the laboratory. The 3rd person who is not wearing the apron is not detected and is not allowed to enter inside. A voice alert is generated to wear the apron.

4.3   Updation of Attendance

When the student entering the laboratory is recognized and his USN is present in the database, his attendance is updated in the attendance database. The Fig. 11 shows the updation of attendance in the excel sheet. The student is marked as present if he is recognized. In the figure, attendance of three students is displayed as present who has entered the laboratory during the period.

Fig. 10. Person entering laboratory at a time (Color figure online)

4.4   Alert Message Results

A beep alert is given when a student has not registered in database but enters the lab. Similarly, a voice alert is given when a student has not worn the protective equipment. Figure 12 shows the mail being sent. The mail informing that unknown student has entered the lab is sent to the respective mail id of the course instructor when unknown student enters the laboratory.

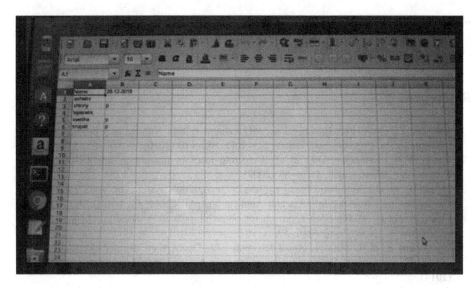

Fig. 11. Attendance updation

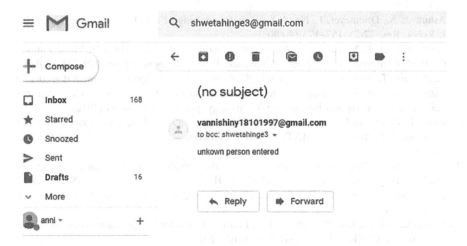

Fig. 12. Snapshot of a mail sent to the concerned authorities.

5 Conclusion

The laboratory authentication system is successfully implemented. Different algorithms were tried and the best suited algorithm is used. The face detection is successfully done using Haar Cascade algorithm. The face recognition is done using open face algorithm. To handle the increased databases HOG algorithm is the best detector in terms of speed and reliability. When the image is affected by illumination, HOG algorithm provides accurate face detection results. The algorithm used for object detection is MobileNet SSD. The efficiency is close to real-time performance. The main features on which the output depends is on the light intensity, distance of student from the webcam and the surroundings where the dataset is created. An accuracy of 97% is observed for Open face algorithm.

References

1. Takashi, Y., et al.: Introduction of security camera system with privacy protection into a residential area. Procedia-Soc. Behav. Sci. **2**(1), 105–110 (2010)
2. Yang, M.-H., Kriegman, D.J., et al.: Detecting faces in images: a survey. IEEE Trans. Pattern Anal. Mach. Intell. **1**, 34–58 (2002)
3. Mliki, H., et al.: Automatic facial expression recognition system. In: ACS International Conference on Computer Systems and Applications (AICCSA), pp. 1–4. IEEE (2013)
4. Chang, L., et al.: A Bayesian approach for object classification based on clusters of SIFT local features. Expert Syst. Appl. **39**(2), 1679–1686 (2012)
5. Guennouni, S., et al.: Multiple object detection using OpenCV on an embedded platform. In: 3rd IEEE International Colloquium in Information Science and Technology, pp. 374–377 (2014)
6. Agarwal, M., et al.: Face recognition using principle component analysis, eigenface and neural network. In: International Conference on Signal Acquisition and Processing, pp. 310–314 (2010)
7. Ashutosh, S., Driemeyer, J., Ng, A.Y.: Robotic grasping of novel objects using vision. Int. J. Robot. Res. **27**(2), 157–173 (2008)
8. Redmon, J., et al.: You only look once: unified, real-time object detection. In: Proceedings of the IEEE Conference on Computer Vision and Pattern Recognition, pp. 779–788 (2016)
9. Santhanam, T., Sumathi, C.P., Gomathi, S.: A survey of techniques for human detection in static images. In: Proceedings of the Second International Conference on Computational Science, Engineering and Information Technology, pp. 328–336. ACM (2012)
10. Rhio, S., Harefa, J., Chowanda, A.: Unlock screen application design using face expression on Android smartphone. In: MATEC Web of Conferences, vol. 54, p. 05001. EDP Sciences (2016)
11. Xie, Z., Liu, G., Fang, Z.: Face recognition based on combination of human perception and local binary pattern. In: Zhang, Y., Zhou, Z.-H., Zhang, C., Li, Y. (eds.) IScIDE 2011. LNCS, vol. 7202, pp. 365–373. Springer, Heidelberg (2012). https://doi.org/10.1007/978-3-642-31919-8_47
12. Wang, X., Bai, X., Liu, W., Latecki, L.J.: Feature context for image classification and object detection. In: CVPR 2011, pp. 961–968. IEEE (2011)
13. Dorothy, A.B., Kumar, S.B.R., Sharmila, J.J.: IoT based home security through digital image processing algorithms 2017. In: WCCCT, Tiruchirappalli, pp. 20–23 (2017)
14. Pavaskar, S., Budihal, S.: Real-time vehicle-type categorization and character extraction from the license plates. In: Mallick, P.K., Balas, V.E., Bhoi, A.K., Zobaa, A.F. (eds.) Cognitive Informatics and Soft Computing. AISC, vol. 768, pp. 557–565. Springer, Singapore (2019). https://doi.org/10.1007/978-981-13-0617-4_54
15. Suneeta, V.B., et al.: Facial expression recognition using supervised learning. In: Computational Vision and Bio-Inspired Computing. ICCVBIC 2019. Advances in Intelligent Systems and Computing, vol. 1108, pp. 275–285 (2019)
16. Karan, B.V., et al.: Distributed denial of service attacks detection system for OpenStack-based private cloud. Proc. Comput. Sci. **167**, 2297–2307 (2020)
17. Virupakshar, K.B., et al.: Detection of DDoS attacks in software defined networks. In: 3rd International Conference on CSITSS, Bengaluru, India, pp. 265–270 (2018)

Deep Neural Networks with Multi-class SVM for Recognition of Cross-Spectral Iris Images

Mulagala Sandhya[1]([⊠]), Ujas Rudani[1], Dilip Kumar Vallabhadas[1],
Mulagala Dileep[2], Sriramulu Bojjagani[3], Sravya Pallantla[4],
and P. D. S. S. Lakshmi Kumari[5]

[1] Computer Science and Engineering, National Institute of Technology, Warangal,
Warangal, India
msandhya@nitw.ac.in, ujasrudani111@gmail.com, dilip.kumar218@gmail.com
[2] Electronics and Communications Engineering, Vishnu Institute of Technology,
Bhimavaram, India
dileepecevit@gmail.com
[3] Computer Science and Engineering, SRM University-AP, Amaravati,
Amaravati, Andhra Pradesh, India
sriramulubojjagani@gmail.com
[4] Computer Science and Engineering, GVP College of Engineering,
Visakhapatnam, India
sravyapallantla@gvpce.ac.in
[5] Information Technology, SRKR Engineering College, Bhimavaram, India
divyapannasa@gmail.com

Abstract. Iris recognition technologies applied to produce comprehensive and correct biometric identification of people in numerous large-scale data of humans. Additionally, the iris is stable over time, i.e., iris biometric knowledge offers links between biometric characteristics and people. The e-business and e-governance require more machine-driven iris recognition. It has millions of iris images that are in near-infrared illumination. It is used for people's identity. A variety of applications for surveillance and e-business will embody iris pictures that are unit non-heritable below visible illumination. The self-learned iris features are created by the convolution neural network (CNN), give more accuracy than handcrafted feature iris recognition. In this paper, a modified iris recognition system is introduced using deep learning techniques along with multi-class SVM for matching. We use the Poly-U database, which is from 209 subjects. CNN with softmax cross-entropy loss gives the most accurate matching of testing images. This method gives better results in terms of EER. We analyzed the proposed architecture on other publicly available databases through various experiments.

Keywords: CNN · Feature extraction · Deep learning · Iriscode · Hough transform · Rubber sheet model

© Springer Nature Singapore Pte Ltd. 2021
S. M. Thampi et al. (Eds.): SoMMA 2020, CCIS 1366, pp. 29–41, 2021.
https://doi.org/10.1007/978-981-16-0419-5_3

1   Introduction

Biometrics can be used to recognize an individual by detecting physical or behavioral human features digitally and they are also accessible to services, devices, or records. Types of these biometric signatures such as iris, fingerprints, speech, or cadence texting are uniquely distinct as such identifiers to ensure better identification of the human [1]. Nowadays, a smartphone screen can be unlocked with facial recognition, weather updates with the help of Siri, or log in an online bank account by detecting the fingerprint of that bank account holder are the real-time examples of biometrics. We are more concerned about the authenticity and privacy of our identity with the usage of more technology. Iris is the most effective because of its high performance and accuracy. Even though an individual cannot forget or lose his/her biometric, if we store the biometric templates in some database they are vulnerable to so many security and privacy attacks [2]. The cross-spectral iris detection provides rich knowledge about the human iris by using specific spectral bands. Base on the past literature survey of cross-spectral iris detection, feature-based approaches, which are not reliable for more accurate results to changes in parameters such as spatial conditions and positions for iris extraction and iris image acquisition, results in performance degradation of iris recognition in the extraction process [3]. The structure of the iris under specific spectral lighting is considered to look differently. Generic systems for recognizing iris include 4 modules as given in Fig. 1, (1)Image Acquisition of iris (2) Segmentation and Normalization (3) Extraction of features (4) Matching and Recognition.

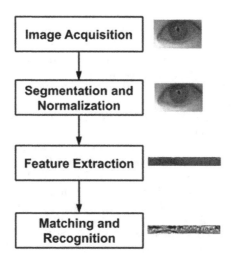

Fig. 1. Iris recognition system

High-quality NIR images are needed by image acquisition to provide an accurate identity, while most existing implementations allow subjects to comply entirely with the program. In pre-processing, the outer portion and pupil are detected. The surrounding portions of the iris pattern like eyelids, eyelashes, or mirrors are identified as unnecessary sections and retained in the noise masks of the background. With the aid of CNN, the iris structure is extracted as a required extraction function. The training model is paired with one extracted attribute from the test picture.

The usages of cross-spectral iris technologies have increased rapidly in the past few years. Cross-spectral iris recognition is used for iris detection in a particular range, such as near-infrared (NIR) iris recognition based on wavelength and visible (VIS) iris recognition based on wavelength. A cross-spectral region occupies different spectrums to gain more information regarding the human iris for better recognition. Cross-spectral iris recognition is used in many biometric systems, like visas and biometric passports, Personal Identification Card Schemes such as PAN Card, Aadhar Card, Driving License, and e-commerce applications. In iris recognition, corneal reflection may be affected in the VIS spectrum. Highlighted are light-colored irises and barely noticeable are dark-colored irises [4]. Detection of iris representations in both the VIS and NIR spectra within the same range is simpler than detection. Since cross spectra are commonly utilized and aimed in commercial implementation [5], NIR-VIS cross-spectral domain work gained attention.

The rest of the paper is organized as follows: Sect. 2 gives a survey on recent literature in cross-spectral iris recognition, Sect. 3 gives step by step explanation of the proposed method, Sect. 4 provides experimental analysis and discussion on results. The conclusion is given in Sect. 5.

2 Related Work

Recent research in the recognition domain has been investigated that iris recognition with iris matching of cross-spectral is much more complex than that of matching a single wavelength, i.e., visible to the visible iris signal or near-infrared to near-infrared iris. The previous research provides many examples of successful usage of CNN in the classification of images [6], hand-written character recognition [7], and face recognition [8]. An implementation by using CNN for periocular recognition [9], iris recognition [10], and iris image segmentation [11] and the identification of false iris images [12] have also been accomplished by other recent specialized researchers in commercial applications. Modern ocular recognition has implemented more precise learning characteristics for user authentication, such as pose or gender. Hence, more complex biometric recognition issues are explored, such as cross-spectral iris matching, to discover the pervasive capabilities of deep learning architectures. For effective iris detection, the iris images are obtained by using the VIS and also under the NIR with more accurate results than that of single illumination. This approach is generally introduced as more demanding and appealing than the multi-researchers matching cross-sensor iris. Kuo Wang and Ajay Kumar [13] used discrete hashing for iris recognition. Early attempts extensively examined the knowledge quality accessible from iris photos obtained under specific ranges and suggested incorporating

32   M. Sandhya et al.

these complementary details to boost matching precision with that accessible from traditional iris detection under NIR. The efficiency deterioration of similar iris images acquired from various resolutions or two separate sensors [14] was also noted in the literature. Bowyer et al. [15] implemented deterioration variables such as dilation of the eyes, contact lenses, and aging of the prototype, are influenced by the corresponding consistency, and contribute to the less effective delivery of matches in biometrics. Ramaiah et al. [16] suggested advanced cross-spectral iris detection utilizing bi-spectral processing, finding NIR images of VIS for iris photographs, then comparing those NIR images projected to certain NIR images in the gallery database. Markov random fields (MRF) is implemented as a more precise and accurate framework to overcome the cross-spectral iris matching disadvantages.

3 Proposed Method

The flow diagram of our method is given in Fig. 2. As given in this figure we have two phases in our model. First is the offline training phase. In the training phase, we trained our model using CNN. The second phase of the model is the testing phase that will match the user image with the trained model. In the end, the match score is generated to decide whether the given image is imposter or genuine. Each block in this diagram uses CNN to represent a step in the recognition of cross-spectral irises. The major difference between the proposed work and the work in [13] is the use of Multi-class SVM for matching as shown in the last block of Fig. 2.

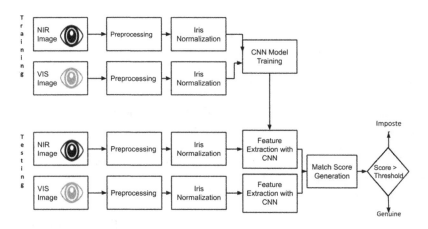

Fig. 2. Flow diagram of proposed method

The first block in the flow diagram illustrates the iris database we used which is PolyU's bi-spectral iris database. The next block is pre-processing and normalization which are the main phases of iris picture processing. The preprocessing

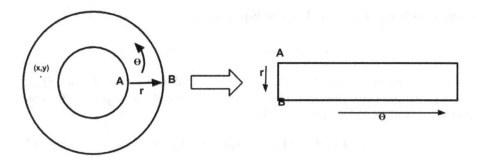

Fig. 3. Rubber sheet model

of the iris image will first define the distorted circular outer borders of the pupil and the iris in a picture of an eye. Photos captured under defined conditions should be obtained with sufficient lighting, distance stated, and other criteria, photographs of the highest standard. The iris picture not only includes iris but also certain unwanted portions of the eyelid, eyelash, pupil, and sclera. In some instances, there may be chances of specular reflections that corrupt iris patterns within the desired iris region. The angle between frame and eye and the external light levels often influences the intensity of the iris. So we have to separate and remove the unwanted noise and find the circular iris field. The fundamental operations involved in pre-processing the iris when collecting the characteristics are iris position, iris normalization, and development [13]. The next step is Iris localization where the area of interest is derived in the initial stages by isolating iris texture, i.e., circular iris areas. Two simple operations include finding the iris; then, detecting eyelids, and detecting boundaries. There are some undesired portions around the iris, which are detected with occlusion by eyelashes and eyelids. The next task is to define the internal and external boundaries of the iris image. For segmentation of Iris boundaries, Canny edge detection and Hough transform are used. Dimensions of eye photographs derived from various sources are distinctive owing to the expansion of iris with specific light intensity rates. The inconsistency resulting from different viewing distances, camera rotation, eye rotation, etc. and it will change the resolution of the iris. It also changes the actual distance between the limbus and pupil boundary. The iris images must therefore be produced with constant dimensions. Under the different conditions of two iris, images may have the same characteristic. The size of the iris area is not a constant, because it is a doughnut-shaped structure. To solve these challenges, we need to normalize iris images. We used, rubber sheet model invented by Daugman [17], as in Fig. 3.

The rubber sheet model is a linear model. This Daugman's model is applicable to each pixel of the desired iris image. In this model (r, θ) is a pair of real coordinates, where r is within [0, 1] and θ is within $[0, 2\pi]$. The transformation of cartesian coordinates (x, y) of pixel values to the non concentric polar coordinates (r, θ) of pixel values is derived using this model. The mapping of the desired iris image $I(x, y)$ is shown in Eqs. 1 and 2.

$$I\Big(x\left(r,\theta\right),y\left(r,\theta\right)\Big) \to I\left(r,\theta\right) \tag{1}$$

where pupil boundary points $(x_p(\theta), y_p(\theta))$ are combined by $\mathrm{x}(r,\theta)$ and $\mathrm{y}(r,\theta)$. $(x_s(\theta), y_s(\theta))$ indicates the outer perimeter of the desired iris. $(x_p(\theta), y_p(\theta))$ consists of a set of boundary points of the pupil.

$$x\left(r,\theta\right) = (1-r)*x_p(\theta) + r*x_s(\theta) \tag{2}$$

where, the pixel value of iris image is $I(x, y)$. The original coordinates of iris image is (x, y). The non-concentric polar coordinates of iris image is (r, θ), and corresponding (x_p, y_p) coordinates indicate the pupil and iris boundaries at θ deviation. Hence, using the above normalization method we get a normalized form of the iris image as in Fig. 4.

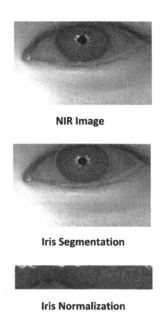

NIR Image

Iris Segmentation

Iris Normalization

Fig. 4. Normalization of an Iris image

Cross entropy loss is used as a loss function of CNN. It will calculate the loss of the trained model. The architecture of deep learning like CNN has self-learned capabilities. The CNN operating in our system is similar to AlexNet and is seen in Fig. 5. The network has three layers of convolution, two fully connected layers (FCs), and three layers of pooling. There is a nonlinear activation function. Before the Rectified Linear Unit (ReLU), a pooling layer and the first fully

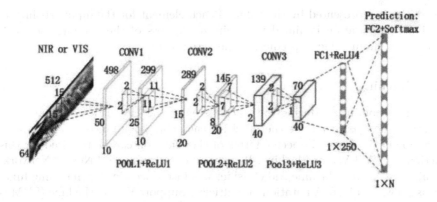

Fig. 5. Softmax cross-entropy loss in CNN taken from [13]

connected layers are used. The classification task is achieved at the last fully connected layer.

The ith channel output y^i is calculated by a convolutional layer using Eq. 3. In this equation, x^j input of jth from the last layer, convolutional kernel is known as $w^i j$, while $b^i j$ is the neuron bias.

$$y^i = \sum_j \left(b^{ij} + w^{ij} * x^i \right) \tag{3}$$

We use a max pooling to extract maximum value for each layer. It will reduce the size of input for the next process. The ReLU is used as an Activation function. ReLU gives only non negative values. ReLU is defined in Eq. 4.

$$y^i = max(y^i, 0) \tag{4}$$

The Fully Connected (FC) layer will give the output vector and all the other nodes in the layer are connected to this node. Equation 5 refers to the output vector obtained.

$$y^i = b^i + \sum_j w^{ij} * x^i \tag{5}$$

The weight of the network is initialized randomly. The randomly initialized weight will generate variation in the neurons. Error is calculated by the softmax cross entropy. The normalized error is measured between the original/actual value and our prediction value as given in Eq. 6.

$$1/N \sum_{n=1}^{N} H(p_n, l_n) = -1/N[y_n log\hat{y}_n + (1 - y_n)log(1 - \hat{y}_n] \tag{6}$$

where the number of classes is indicated as N, ground truth value is as l_n and p_n is the predicted value. The output vector size is $1*N$. The class label prediction probability is represented by the value of each element for the input iris image. The back propagation is aimed to minimize the loss of the training model to achieve maximum value of predicting the actual class.

3.1 Matching

Matching is conducted during the testing step of the biometric reconnaissance program. The classifier finds the label for each corresponding test image after extraction of the feature. Specific forms of classification can be required for this function, e.g. Aid Vector Machine, Regression of Softmax, and Neural Network. A multiclass Vector Machine Aid classifier was introduced in this matching function as shown in Fig. 6. A notation of multiclass Support Vector Machine (SVM is given as: The set of iris training data is denoted as $(x_1, y_1), (x_2, y_2), \ldots, (x_n, y_n)$. The proposed matching is classified into two different classes. Where $y_i \in -1, 1$ and the feature vector is denoted as $x_i \in R^d$.

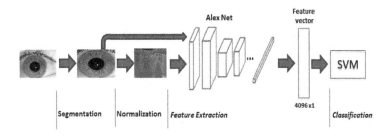

Fig. 6. Using multi class SVM for matching

Algorithm 1 is used to classify the testing images with trained model as given below. Classification is done using the SVM.

For the collection of data with M groups, the multi-class SVM can be used, we have to train M number of binary classifiers that can separate every class from all other groups, then take the class which gives greater margin (one-vs-all).

4 Experimental Results and Analysis

A publicly available database of cross-spectral iris images in the different spectrums is obtained from 209 subjects. The bi-spectral iris collection of PolyU contains 418 classes of bi-spectral photographs collected from 209 subjects. There are 15 instances in each spectrum. Photos from two spectra were obtained in this collection concurrently. There are a total of 12,540 iris images ($209 \times 22 \times 215$). The measurements of the initial images are 640480 pixels. A publicly available iris recognition algorithm is used to get various segments of iris pictures accurately in this iris recognition implementation. The size of each of the standardized and

---

Algorithm 1: Implementation of Pre-trained CNN for Feature Extraction and the SVM algorithm for Feature Classification

---

Result: The accuracy of recognition
Input: Input iris images

1. Load input images with its labels
2. Divide every category into the same number of images
3. Load trained CNN
4. Pre-process input images For CNN
5. Divide the sets of the data into testing and training
6. Feature extraction from the layers of CNN
7. Generation of training labels from the training data sets
8. Train a multiclass SVM classifier using trained features
9. Feature extraction from the test data sets
10. Test set label prediction using a trained classifier
11. Get the known test data set labels
12. Obtain the results using a confusion matrix
13. Find confusion matrix in percentage
14. Display the mean accuracy

---

iris images using a segmentation algorithm is 512664 pixels. Sample NIR and VIS iris images of the database in different preprocessing steps of the iris recognition experiment are shown in Fig. 7. This database has a low-quality sample of images. Some of them are considered as a representative sample of images from the iris databases as shown in Fig. 8.

For the experiment analysis, CNN from Softmax is employed as a feature extractor with cross-entropy loss. The vectors of features are classified from this iris recognition experiment. All the function vectors are a binary vector of 1000 bits. The comparative matching results are obtained for better performance evaluation using the common IrisCode method. There are various layers in this convolutional neural network. The self-learned features of CNN are generated from different corners, other textures, and edges. The accuracy and loss of the trained model during the train iris dataset are given in Fig. 9. The accuracy of the model is increased while epochs are increasing.

The metrics used to analyze the performance of the proposed method are:

Genuine Acceptance Rate (GAR): It is the measure by which the system accepts genuine iris templates in the total number of iris templates tested.

False Rejection Rate (FRR): It is the measure by which a genuine iris template on the total number of iris templates tested is falsely refused as shown in Eq. (7). FRR can also be represented using GAR i.e. GAR = 1–FRR. GAR stands for a genuine acceptance rate.

$$FRR = \frac{Number\ of\ false\ rejections}{Number\ of\ identification\ attempts} \tag{7}$$

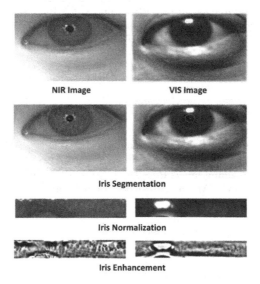

NIR Image   **VIS Image**

Iris Segmentation

Iris Normalization

Iris Enhancement

Fig. 7. Pre-processing steps of PolyU Bi-Spectral iris image

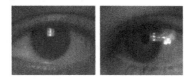

Fig. 8. Poor quality images from PolyU iris database

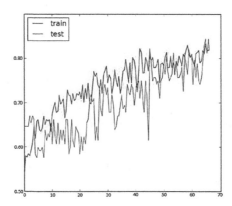

Fig. 9. Training and testing accuracy of the proposed CNN

False Acceptance Rate (FAR): It is the measure by which a false iris template on the total number of iris templates tested is wrongly accepted as shown in Eq. (8).

$$FAR = \frac{Number\ of\ false\ acceptances}{Number\ of\ identification\ attempts} \tag{8}$$

Equal Error Rate (EER): It is the error value obtained when the values of FRR and FAR equal. Using Genuine Score Distribution as well as Imposter Score Distribution, the performance measures are calculated. The matching results are compared with other approaches such as MRF approach [18] and the IrisCode approach [19]. The summary of the matching results in terms of the equal error rate is shown in Table 1.

Table 1. An analysis of comparative results of EER

Approach	EER
CNN with multi-class SVM	9.38%
MRF	24.50%
Iris Code	30.81%

Table 2. The iris recognition accuracy of different iris databases

Database	after segmentation	after normalization
PolyU Bi-Spectral	78%	78.33%
CASIA-Iris-V1	76%	65%
CASIA-Iris-Thousand	76%	76.6%
CASIA-Iris-Interval	68%	66.6%

Table 2 gives the accuracy of the proposed iris recognition method on the databases listed. From the table it is observed that, the accuracy after normalized is slightly decreased as compared to the accuracy after segmentation. It says that the proposed CNN can capture more discriminative textures of iris in the segmentation than normalization.

5 Conclusion

This work utilizes deep neural neural networks for the cross-spectral iris detection. We experimented with iris recognition, utilizing PolyU cross-spectral iris repository. The accuracy in our trained model is resulting in a 9.38% EER. Further, we used a multi class SVM classifier to achieve the recognition task on iris images. The segmented and normalized iris image is given to CNN as input. The results proved that the accuracy is deteriorated after normalization compared to segmentation.

References

1. Bowyer, K.W., Hollingsworth, K., Flynn, P.J.: Image understanding for iris biometrics: a survey. Comput. Vis. Image Underst. **110**(2), 281–307 (2008)
2. Sandhya, M., Prasad, M.V.N.K.: Biometric template protection: a systematic literature review of approaches and modalities. In: Jiang, R., Al-maadeed, S., Bouridane, A., Crookes, D., Beghdadi, A. (eds.) Biometric Security and Privacy. SPST, pp. 323–370. Springer, Cham (2017). https://doi.org/10.1007/978-3-319-47301-7_14
3. Nguyen, K., Fookes, C., Jillela, R., Sridharan, S., Ross, A.: Long range iris recognition: a survey. Pattern Recogn. **72**, 123–143 (2017)
4. Hosseini, M.S., Araabi, B.N., Soltanian-Zadeh, H.: Pigment melanin: pattern for iris recognition. IEEE Trans. Instrum. Meas. **59**, 792–804 (2010)
5. Zuo, J., Nicolo, F., Schmid, N.A.: Cross spectral iris matching based on predictive image mapping. In: Proceedings of the International Conference on Biometrics: Theory, Applications, and Systems (BTAS), pp. 1–5 (2010)
6. Krizhevsky, A., Sutskever, I., Hinton, G.E.: ImageNet classification with deep convolutional neural networks. In: Proceedings of International Conference on Advances in Neural Information Processing Systems, pp. 1097–1105 (2012)
7. Zhang, J., et al.: Watch, attend and parse: an end-to-end neural network-based approach to handwritten mathematical expression recognition. Pattern Recogn. **71**, 196–206 (2017)
8. Li, Y., Wang, G., Nie, L., Wang, Q., Tan, W.: Distance metric optimization driven convolutional neural network for age invariant face recognition. Pattern Recogn. **75**, 51–62 (2018)
9. Zhao, Z., Kumar, A.: Accurate periocular recognition under less constrained environment using semantics-assisted convolutional neural network. IEEE Trans. Inf. Forensics Secur. **12**(5), 1017–1030 (2017)
10. Gangwar, A., Joshi, A.: DeepIrisNet: deep iris representation with applications in iris recognition and cross-sensor iris recognition. In: Proceedings of International Conference on Image Processing (ICIP), pp. 2301–2305 (2016)
11. Liu, N., Li, H., Zhang, M., Liu, J., Sun, Z., Tan, T.: Accurate iris segmentation in non-cooperative environments using fully convolutional networks. In: Proceedings of International Conference on Biometrics (ICB), pp. 1–8 (2016)
12. Menotti, D., et al.: Deep representations for iris, face, and fingerprint spoofing detection. Trans. Inf. Forensics Secur. **10**(4), 864–879 (2014)
13. Wang, K., Kumar, A.: Cross-spectral iris recognition using CNN and supervised discrete hashing. Pattern Recogn. **86**, 85–98 (2019)
14. Liu, N., Zhang, M., Li, H., Sun, Z., Tan, T.: Deepiris: learning pairwise filter bank for heterogeneous iris verification. Pattern Recogn. Lett. **82**, 154–161 (2016)
15. Bowyer, K.W., Baker, S.E., Hentz, A., Hollingsworth, K., Peters, T., Flynn, P.J.: Factors that degrade the match distribution in iris biometrics. Identity Inf. Soc. **2**(3), 327–343 (2009)

16. Ramaiah, N.P., Kumar, A.: Advancing cross-spectral iris recognition research using bi-spectral imaging. In: Singh, R., Vatsa, M., Majumdar, A., Kumar, A. (eds.) Machine Intelligence and Signal Processing. AISC, vol. 390, pp. 1–10. Springer, New Delhi (2016). https://doi.org/10.1007/978-81-322-2625-3_1
17. Daugman, J.: The importance of being random: statistical principles of iris recognition. Pattern Recogn. **36**(2), 279–291 (2003)
18. Ramaiah, N.P., Kumar, A.: Towards more accurate iris recognition using cross-spectral matching. IEEE Trans. of Image Process. **26**(1), 208–221 (2017)
19. Masek, L., Kovesi, P.: Matlab Source Code for a Biometric Identification System Based on Iris Patterns, 2(4). The School of Computer Science and Software Engineering, The University of Western Australia (2003)

Gaze Fusion-Deep Neural Network Model for Glaucoma Detection

Sajitha Krishnan[1]([✉]), J. Amudha[1], and Sushma Tejwani[2]

[1] Department of Computer Science and Engineering, Amrita School
of Engineering, Bengaluru, Amrita Vishwa Vidyapeetham, Bangalore, India
{k_sajitha,j_amudha}@blr.amrita.edu
[2] Narayana Nethralaya, Bommasandra, Bengaluru, India

Abstract. The proposed system, Gaze Fusion - Deep Neural Network Model (GFDM) has utilized transfer learning approach to discriminate subject's eye tracking data in the form of fusion map into two classes: glaucoma and normal. We have fed eye tracking data in the form of fusion maps of different participants to Deep Neural Network (DNN) model which is pretrained with ImageNet weights. The experimental results of the GFDM show that fusion map dissimilar to pretrained model's dataset can give better understanding of glaucoma. The model also show the part of the screen where participants has the difficulty in viewing. GFDM has compared with traditional machine learning models such as Support Vector Classifier, Decision Tree classifier and ensemble classifier and shown that the proposed model outperforms other classifiers. The model has Area Under ROC Curve (AUC) score 0.75. The average sensitivity of correctly identifying glaucoma patients is 100% with specificity value 83%.

Keyword: Transfer learning · Glaucoma · Fusion map · Eye tracking · Deep neural network

1 Introduction

Glaucoma is a class of eye conditions that affect blindness due to the damage in optic nerve. The damage of optic nerve is caused due to the increase of pressure in the eye. This affects eyes' visual field and leads to blindness, if untreated. The diagnosis of glaucoma includes structural glaucoma test that includes Tonometry (the inner eye pressure), Ophthalmoscopy (the shape and color of the optic nerve), Gonioscopy (the angle in the eye where the iris meets the cornea), Pachymetry (thickness of the cornea), Optical Coherence Tomography (OCT) (structural form of optic nerve) and functional glaucoma test - Perimetry (visual field test). The progression of glaucoma is monitored by analysing structural and functional change using OCT and perimetry respectively. The expense of the machine and lack of expertise in rural areas hinders the understanding of the progression of disease. Researchers have developed less expensive open source softwares to screen glaucoma. But there is a limitation of development of end to end system utilizing machine learning models to perform the classification of glaucoma

© Springer Nature Singapore Pte Ltd. 2021
S. M. Thampi et al. (Eds.): SoMMA 2020, CCIS 1366, pp. 42–53, 2021.
https://doi.org/10.1007/978-981-16-0419-5_4

and normal. The advancement of deep learning has shown amazing performance in image classification. In clinical research, creation of tremendous eye tracking data for a particular task is difficult and so building deep learning model from the scratch based on existing small dataset is difficult.

Transfer learning is an approach of utilizing knowledge in the form of architecture, weights and features that is learnt in one domain (source domain) and transfer in a working or different domain. It is believed to progress in general Artificial Intelligence. Generally in pretrained model, the input or image is fed to the convolution base. The convolution base is the sequence of convolutional and pooling layers that extract features of the image. The decision of training on the number of convolution layers in convolution base is based on the size and similarity of the dataset with that of pretrained model's dataset. It extract features and the classifier identifies discriminative features that is learnt at the convolution base and outputs the number of classes. The advantage of the method is that common knowledge of features learnt in large benchmark dataset can be transferred to the working domain.

Data scientists have presented transfer learning into four quadrants based on size of the dataset of working domain and similarity with the dataset of source domain. The Fig. 1 represents matrix based on dataset size and similarity and decision map on using pretrained models. Quadrant I is the case when we have large dataset in working domain and it is different from pretrained model's dataset. In that situation we can train the whole architecture based on the image in the working domain. The low level, middle level and high level features are learnt from the images and classifier is applied based on the images of the working domain. Quadrant II is the situation when we have large dataset in working domain and it is similar to the pretrained model's dataset. Since the low level features are common knowledge in all kinds of images, the knowlege can be transferred from pretrained model to the working domain. In the case of Quadrant III, when small dataset of the working domain is different from pretrained model's dataset, finetuning has to be done in deeper layers of the convolution base and rest of the layers are frozen. In the case of quadrant IV, if we have small dataset and similar to the pretrained model, convolution base is used just as feature extractor. The feature vector from the frozen convolution base is fed to the classifier. The advancement of transfer learning reduces computational effort of choosing handcrafted features and makes classification, segmentation and modelling of visual attention easier [1].

The proposed work explore strategy in quadrant III, where eye tracking parameters of participants are extracted from raw data and visualized in the form of fusion map. The Deep Neural Network (DNN) is pretrained with ImageNet which is different from fusion map. The low-level features of fusion map must be same as that of ImageNet but middle-level and high-level features are extracted by finetuning the deeper layers of VGG-16 and finally feature map of fusion map is fed to the classifier.

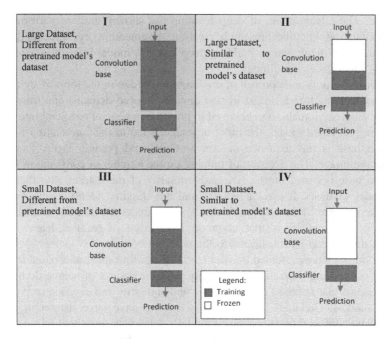

Fig. 1. Matrix and strategy of choosing pretrained model based on size-similarity of dataset

2 Related Works

The functional change of glaucoma is identified using Visual Field Perimetry. The output of the machine called visual field report helps the doctors to understand the progression of visual field loss. The perimetry test is not feasible to all age groups of patients [2]. Researchers are focusing on new techniques on developing screening test. Murray et al. [3] designed a visual field diagnostic test for all age groups, but the model only tells whether patient has seen/not seen the test point. The methodology has not included automatic recognition of glaucoma. In Jones et al. [4] work, the author has designed glaucoma screening test in portable equipment which estimates seen/not seen test point. In this work also, automatic recognition of glaucoma is missing.

There is a large room in automatic recognition of glaucoma using eye tracking and deep learning. In healthcare sectors, the advancement of deep learning helps in understanding the patterns from plenty of sample images and diagnose disease. One example for this approach is computer aided diagnosis for prediction and classification of prostate cancer and non-cancer [5]. The dataset used is expert annotations of tumor done in 444 MRI images and the architecture used is patch-based VGG-Net (Visual Geometry Group) followed quadrant I strategy. VGGNet is a Deep Neural Network (DNN) which has achieved Imagenet classification challenge 2014, and is popular till now [6]. Another example for the same strategy is transfer learning of VGG-16 to understand visual attention of autism spectrum disorder in adults using eye gaze data of 39 subjects' fixation on 100 images selected from MIT saliency benchmark based on fischer score on eye gaze features [7]. The highlight of this quadrant I strategy is that although existing architecture has been used by the author the model is trained from the scratch. The architecture is known as SALICON architecture consisting of two VGG-16 network and dense layers are removed. The last convolution layers form feature vectors which is given to SVM classifier. Inception DNN model pretrained on ImageNet is designed for modelling visual search behavior of experts in mammogram images [8] and follows quadrant III strategy. In the model for strabismus recognition, the author used pretrained model VGG-S model pretrained on ImageNet and outputs two classes from the last layer of CNN [9] which follows quadrant IV strategy. In Stember et al. Work, U-Net model is used to segment lesions in MRI images [10].

The RCNN architecture that is pretrained using COCO dataset is used to segment cup shaped optical disc in fundus images in Glaucoviz system [11]. Image segmentation is also done using U-Net model in Guo et al. work[12]. In Wu et al. Transfer learning model is created for labelling optic disc cup in fundus images and thus manual annotation is reduced [13]. In Yin et al. LeNet-5 CNN model is designed to classify nationalities based on raw data and scanpath of eye gaze data [14]. In Rafi et al. Work, the transfer learning approach is also done to track eye using iTracker model pretrained with GazeCapture dataset to measure cognitive impairement of alzheimers' participants [15]. All the existing works use Convolution Neural Networks (CNN) as a powerful feature extractor to diagnose disease. A transfer learning approach on ResNet-50 model on fundus images is used for detecting early and advanced glaucoma [17].

In the Gaze Fusion-Deep Neural Network Model (GFDM), eye tracking data in the form of fusion map are fed to the model that is pretrained with ImageNet dataset and classifies into glaucoma and normal. The fusion map of the glaucoma participants show the visual field loss in top left, top right, bottom right and bottom left quadrants of the screen. The GFDM also demonstrates how transfer learning can be applied in small dataset.

The next sections of paper are organized as follows. Section 2 describes the materials and method for discrimination of glaucoma and normal. Section 3 describes the results and discussion of the approach. Section 4 shows the conclusion of the paper.

3 Materials and Methods

3.1 Participants

All participants recruited in the study have undergone visual perimetry test using Humphrey Field Analyzer (HFA) 24-2. Twelve participants diagnosed as glaucoma after standard test such as clinical evaluation, visual field test and imaging techniques and sixteen age-related normal participants are recruited. There is no constraint on gender and all participants have normal or corrected vision. In visual field report, glaucoma participants have Glaucoma Hemifield Test (GHT) value 'outside normal limits' in one of the eyes and other eye has mild, moderate and severe in their Visual Field Index (VFI).

3.2 Apparatus

After the visual field perimetry test, participants share the copy of visual field report to the eye tracking experimenter, from which clinical measures such as Mean Deviation (MD), Pattern Standard Deviation (PSD), Visual Field İndex (VFI) and Glaucoma Hemifield Test (GHT) are noted. The overview of the eye tracking experiment are shown in the Fig. 2.

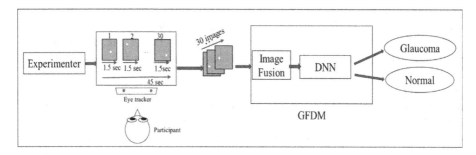

Fig. 2. Overview of the experiment

The eye tracker Eyetribe 30 Hz with accuracy 0.5° and spatial resolution 0.1° which is non-invasive is attached with the screen. Initially participants have to undergo calibration where a set of 9 points are displayed one by one anywhere on the screen. Participants have to follow the dot to get Pupil-Corneal Reflex (PCR) of the eye. If the calibration is not perfect, it has to be repeated. Participants have to sit 50 cm from the laptop screen. The eye tracking experimenter asked the participants to view the image displayed in the screen monocularly. In order to understand the visual field loss in each eye, the participants has to close one eye and view images with the other eye. To avoid the inclination of the results, a set of participants are asked to do the experiment with the right eye first and then the left eye and in case of other set of participants, the other way round. The image is a single dot displayed in the four quadrants: top left (TL), top right (TR), bottom right (BR) and bottom left (BL) within the calibration screen for 1.5 s. Minimum of seven dots are placed in each quadrant and a dot is placed at the centre of the image. The dots are displayed randomly anywhere in the screen. The trial time is sufficient inorder to grab the attention only on target point. The background is in gray color and radius of the single dot is 12 pixels. There is no response required from the participants' side.

The eye tracker that provides raw data is fed to the open source software OGAMA. It can calculate fixation event (gaze samples that are still in the position of the screen at certain point of time) [16]. At the end of the experiment, the customized program will generate fusion map of 30 images. The fusion map generated for 56 eyes of total 28 participants are stored in the database. These labelled fusion maps are fed to the deep learning model which is based on quadrant III strategy. The classifier finds the discriminative features in the fusion maps and classifies into glaucoma and normal. The system has also tried probabilistic, decision tree classifier, ensemble classifiers and Deep Neural Networks (DNN) with Gradient Boosting classifier (XGBoost) to extract features and classification. The Gaze Fusion-Deep Neural Network Model has compared with seven machine learning classifiers and DNN with Support Vector Classifier (SVC) and proven that DNN with XGBoost outperforms other classifiers.

3.3 Fusion Map

The thirty images are designed to understand whether participants can view the target point anywhere on the screen. The customized program, Gaze Fusion-Deep Neural Network Model will generate fusion map of 30 images. A fusion map is an image of size 1366 × 768 pixels generated by performing XOR operation on thirty images. This fusion image is analyzed in four quadrants: top left (TL), top right (TR), bottom right (BR) and bottom left (BL). The X co-ordinate of fusion image is divided along 683 pixels and its Y co-ordinate is divided along 384 pixels and each target point is within each quadrant. At the end of the experiment, the software calculates average fixation position made by each eye of the participant at each target point. Thus, the dataset includes 56 fixation data of 28 participants, since each participant view the image monocularly, i.e., dataset includes 28 participants X 2 eyes = 56 samples or eyes. The program will check whether participant has fixated the target point of the image. The program calculates the Euclidean distance, d between average fixation position of the eye, X^f and target point, X^T using the formula in the Eq. 1.

$$d = \sqrt{(x^T - x^f)^2 + (y^T - y^f)^2} \tag{1}$$

where (x^T, y^T) is the target point, X^T in the image and (x^f, y^f) is the average fixation position, X^f of the participant. If the Euclidean distance is within a threshold i.e., 100 pixels (the value is fixed after the pilot study), the participant has seen the target point, i.e., hit, otherwise the participant has not seen the target point, i.e. miss. The hit and miss of each trial (image) are recorded for each participant's eye. The hit is marked in red color and miss is marked in black color on the fusion image. Thus, the program generates fusion map for left and right eye of each participant, i.e. 56 fusion maps. If any target point in the image is not visible by the participant, this shows that the participant has difficulty in viewing that part (quadrant) of the screen. The trial time 1.5 s is enough for the participants to make sudden response to the target point in the stimulus [3, 4]. The workflow of the image fusion step is shown in the Fig. 3.

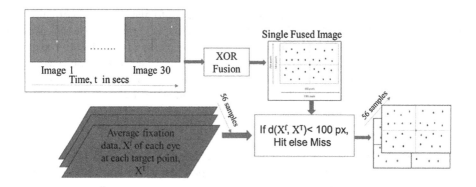

Fig. 3. Flow diagram of image fusion process

3.4 Deep Neural Networks (DNN)

The overview of the proposed architecture is shown in the Fig. 4. The dataset containing fusion map of 56 eyes is fed to the Deep Neural Network (DNN). The feature map of each image is convolved with kernel and activation map is applied to generate feature map of each fusion map. The convolution at layer l is expressed in the Eq. 2.

$$x_j^l = f\left(\sum_{i \varepsilon M_j} x_i^{l-1} * k_{ij}^l + b_j^l\right) \tag{2}$$

where M_j denotes set of input images of size $224 \times 224 \times 3$ with padding 'same', k_{ij}^l is the kernel applied on map input i and b_j^l is the additive bias. The deep learning model is implemented in Python 3.7 language in open source library Keras with TensorFlow as backend. The input dataset is split according to training-testing 60%–20% using train_test_split() function in scikit-learn library. The layers unshaded are frozen which includes 13 layers from VGG-16 [6] and layers unshaded are trained based on the fusion map which is the dataset of the proposed or working domain. To reduce overfitting, we include dropout regularization rate of 0.2. The features learnt in convolution base are flattened and is transferred to two dense layers with 1000-dimension size each. Support Vector Classifier (SVC) and eXtreme Gradient Boost (XGBoost) classifier are used in classification. In training and testing phase, XGBoost outperforms well than SVC classifier. XGBoost can handle complex dataset, since it can handle non-linear relationships and perform feature selection automatically. L1 and L2 regularization can optimize the classification and avoid overfitting. The portable and fast algorithm can perform well than SVC.

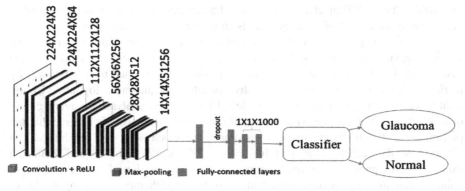

Fig. 4. Overview of the proposed DNN architecture

4 Results and Discussion

Twenty eight participants recruited in the study had undergone visual perimetry test using Humphrey Field Analyzer (HFA) 24. The mean (standard deviation) age of normal and glaucoma participants was 47.3 and 49.5 respectively. The eye tracking data of participants includes fixation data which is further used to generate fusion map. The fixation of participants can be statically represented as heat map. Heat map is the static visualization showing fixation of participants. The sample heat map of right eye of glaucoma participant (Sub_9) and left eye of normal participant (Sub_31) are shown in the Fig. 5.

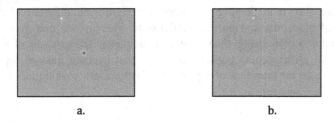

Fig. 5. Heat map of participants. a) Heat map of Sub_9 glaucoma participant b) Heat map of Sub_31 normal participant

The target point is in the top right quadrant of the screen. The red spot shows the fixation of the participant. The heat map of the glaucoma participant shows that the participant is not able to fixate the target point. The heat map of the normal participant shows that the participant can view the top of the screen. The hit or miss of the gaze data is estimated based on the Euclidean Distance between average fixation position (x, y) of each trial and the target point in the image. If the Euclidean Distance is within the threshold value of 100 pixels, it is considered as hit and otherwise it is considered as miss. The average miss of 30 target points in images are also calculated.

The fusion map is generated at the end of the experiment. To understand their difficulty in viewing the part of the screen, hit and miss of 30 points are marked on the fusion map. For each eye, hit is denoted by marking red color and miss is denoted by marking black color. The fusion map is divided into four quadrants: top left (TL), top right (TR), bottom right (BR) and bottom left (BL). We have analysed the average miss over all trials (30 target points) and also miss in each quadrants. We can see that the performance of participants in right quadrants are worse than left quadrants. The Fig. 6 show the sample images of fusion map of normal (Sub_11) and glaucoma (Sub_10) participants. The normal participant, Sub_11 has viewed most of the target points, where as the glaucoma participant, Sub_10 has difficulty in viewing the lower quadrants (i.e., BR and BL) of the screen.

a.   b.

Fig. 6. Fusion map of participants. a) Fusion map of normal participant Sub_11 b) Fusion map of glaucoma participant Sub_10

The group comparisons are done based on two-sample t test. The fusion map and p-value between normal and glaucoma is shown in the Table 1. The bar graphs of the participants are shown in the Fig. 7. There is a significant difference between the performance of glaucoma and normal participants. We can see that average miss is higher in glaucoma participants than normal participants. The analysis of the miss on the quadrants of all glaucoma participants show that average miss of top right and bottom right are larger than that of top left and bottom left. p-value less than 0.05 is shown in boldface manner.

Table 1. Mean and standard deviation (in parenthesis) and p-value of average miss between normal and glaucoma participants.

Measures	Normal Group(n = 32)	Glaucoma Group (n = 24)	p-value
Average miss	0.17(0.24)	0.78(0.28)	$\mathbf{1.0 \times 10^{-10}}$
Miss in TL	0.16(0.24)	0.75(0.34)	$\mathbf{1.07 \times 10^{-8}}$
Miss in TR	0.18(0.28)	0.80(0.30)	$\mathbf{8.58 \times 10^{-10}}$
Miss in BR	0.17(0.25)	0.80(0.26)	$\mathbf{5.01 \times 10^{-12}}$
Miss in BL	0.17(0.28)	0.76(0.28)	$\mathbf{4.25 \times 10^{-10}}$

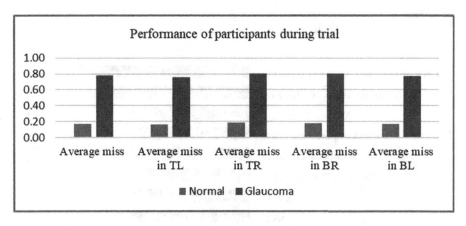

Fig. 7. Bar graphs of average miss and average miss in four quadrants of participants

The Gaze Fusion-Deep Neural Network Model has used probabilistic, suppport vector, decision tree classifier and ensemble classifiers to automatically recognize features and classify between glaucoma and normal. These classifiers fail to extract discriminative features from fusion map. The existing works have shown that convolution neural networks are good feature extractors. Inspired from existing deep learning architectures that are successfully applied in different clinical data, we propose an approach in which fusion map of participants are fed to GFDM model. The feature vector of fusion map learnt from CNN is fed to linear Support Vector Classifier (SVC). The accuracy of CNN with SVC classifier is 0.75. To improve the accuracy, an ensemble classifier XGBoost classifier is used in CNN that learns discriminative features and outputs into two classes: glaucoma and normal. The accuracy of CNN with XGBoost is 0.88 and AUC (Area Under ROC Curve) score is 0.75. For CNN model with XGBoost classifier, the detection rate of glaucoma and normal is 100% and 83% respectively. The proposed model shows Positive Predictive Value (PPV) 60% and Negative Predictive Value (NPV) 100%. The F1- score of normal and glaucoma of different models used are shown in the Fig. 8. The AUC.

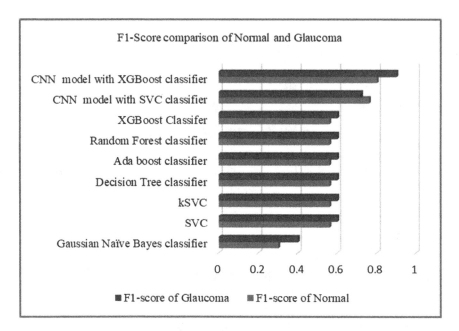

Fig. 8. F1- score of different models

5   Conclusion

The Gaze Fusion-Deep Neural Network Model (GFDM) is DNN model with XGBoost classifier that can recognize glaucoma using eye tracking data in the form of fusion map. The fusion map divided in four quadrants, show the part of the screen that the glaucoma participants have difficulty in viewing the target point. The accuracy of the model is 87.5% while the sensitivity and specificity are 100% and 83% respectively. The GFDM has used transfer learning approach with ImageNet weights to extract features and the results are promising. The model is written in open source software which is portable in any system.

References

1. Kavikuil, K., Amudha, J.: Leveraging deep learning for anomaly detection in video surveillance. Adv. Intell. Syst. Comput. **815**, 239–247 (2019)
2. Crabb, D.P., Smith, N.D., Zhu, H.: What's on TV? Detecting age-related neurodegenerative eye disease using eye movement scanpath. Front. Aging Neurosci. **6**, 312 (2014)
3. Murray, I.C., et al.: Detection and characterisation of visual field defects using Saccadic Vector Optokinetic Perimetry in children with brain tumours. Eye (Lond) **32**(10), 1563–1573 (2018)
4. Jones, P.R., Smith, N.D., Bi, W., Crabb, D.P.: Portable perimetry using eye-tracking on a tablet computer—a feasibility assessment. Trans. Vis. Sci. Tech. **8**(1), 17 (2019)

5. Tsehay, Y.K., et al.: Convolutional neural network based deep-learning architecture for prostate cancer detection on multiparametric magnetic resonance images. In: Proceedings of SPIE 1013 Medical Imaging Computer-Aided Diagnosis, 1013405 (2017)
6. Krizhevsky, A., Sutskever, I., Hinton, G.E.: ImageNet classification with deep convolutional neural networks. Commun. ACM **60**(6), 84–90 (2017)
7. Ming, J., Zhao, Q.: Learning visual attention to identify people with autism spectrum disorder. IEEE International Conference on Computer Vision (ICCV) **5**(3), 512–519 (2017)
8. Mall, S., et al.: Modeling visual search behavior of breast radiologists using a deep convolution neural network. J. Med. Imaging **5**(3), 035502 (2018)
9. Chen, Z., Fu, H., Lo, W.-L., Chi, Z.: Strabismus recognition using eye-tracking data and convolutional neural networks. J. Healthcare Eng. 7692198 (2018)
10. Stember, J.N., et al.: Eye tracking for deep learning segmentation using convolutional neural networks. J. Digit. Imaging **32**, 597–604 (2019)
11. Palakvangsa-Na-Ayudhya, S., et al.: GlaucoVIZ: Assisting System for Early Glaucoma Detection Using Mask R-CNN, ECTI-CON 2020. IEEE (2020)
12. Guo, F., et al.: A mobile app for Glaucoma diagnosis and its possible clinical applications. BMC Med. Inform. Decis. Making **20**(Suppl. 3), 128 (2020)
13. Wu, J., et al.: Leveraging undiagnosed data for glaucoma classication with teacher-student learning. Comput. Vis. Pattern Recogn. (2020)
14. Yin, Y., et al.: Classification of eye tracking data using a convolutional neural network. In: 17th IEEE International Conference on Machine Learning and Applications (ICMLA), pp. 530–535 (2018)
15. Haque, R.U., et al.: Deep convolutional neural networks and transfer learning for measuring cognitive impairment using eye-tracking in a distributed tablet-based environment. IEEE Trans. Bio-med, Eng (2020)
16. Chandrika, K.R., Amudha, J., Sudarsan, S.D.: Recognizing eye tracking traits for source code review. In: 22nd IEEE International Conference on Emerging Technologies and Factory Automation 2017, vol. 9, pp. 1–8. IEEE Xplore (2017)
17. Serener, A., Serte, S.: Transfer learning for early and advanced glaucoma detection with convolutional neural networks. In: 2019 Medical Technologies Congress (TIPTEKNO), pp. 1–4 (2019)

Deep Learning Based Stable and Unstable Candle Flame Detection

Amir Khan[1](✉) and Mohammad Samar Ansari[1,2]

[1] Aligarh Muslim University, Aligarh, India
amiramu10@gmail.com
[2] Software Research Institute, Athlone Institute of Technology, Athlone, Ireland
mdsamar@gmail.com

Abstract. This paper presents a deep learning based solution for identification of normal and abnormal candle flames, controlled and uncontrolled flames. Candle flames affected by external factors like wind, improper combustion of fuel etc. Proposed CNN based deep neural network can successfully classify the stable and unstable candle flame with an accuracy of 67% for generated test set and an accuracy of 83% for random images taken from open source on internet.

Keywords: Stable flame · Unstable flame · Deep learning

1 Introduction

Candle is one of the oldest illumination sources used by humans. Scientific study of candle flame is not new and dates backs to early civilization. Candles due to its availability and not being costly make them center of attraction for research. A domestic candle is an example of diffusion flame. Heat of the flame is utilized to melt the wax on the body of the candle and this molten wax is acquired by the wick through capillary rise and the fuel evaporates from the wick to maintain the flame. A candle flame is itself a closed surface and a stable flame has an axis-symmetric shape while the unstable flame may or may not be axis-symmetric. Candle flame differs from any other random fire as it reaches to steady state very soon. Candle though primarily the source of light but also an important element of decoration. According to Mintel (2013), total U.S. retail sales for candle products are 3.14 billion [1]. It has been estimated by National Fire Protection Association (NFPA), fire department in US has received 7900 calls annually to extinguish the fire at homes caused by candles for the period of 2013–2017 while the minor fires are unreported. An estimated average death toll due to fires is 80 while the number of injured persons are 720 along with the damages to property of worth $268 million. NFPA also pointed that home candles were the reason for the fire when some burnable substances were kept very close to candles [2]. NFPA has suggested many safety measures for candles

Supported by University Women's Polytechnic, Aligarh Muslim University.

ⓒ Springer Nature Singapore Pte Ltd. 2021
S. M. Thampi et al. (Eds.): SoMMA 2020, CCIS 1366, pp. 54–62, 2021.
https://doi.org/10.1007/978-981-16-0419-5_5

but all of them are manual and involves human intervention, and one of them is to keep candles 1 ft away from everything flammable/likely to catch fire, which requires an empty surrounding of 2 ft diameter circle along with an added cost of rigid base or candle holder. As we all know carelessness of humans are inevitable. So, detecting an unstable flame can be the first step of precautionary measures. In addition, this information provides the efficiency of fuel consumption. A stable flame represents efficient fuel consumption, and provides pleasant aesthetic sense when used for decoration. Who would deny the importance of candle light dinner with your love? Ambience around the candle can be controlled in order to keep the flame stable and steady making the perfect shape. This study presents the classification of stable and unstable candle flame using the deep learning. This study is the first of its' kind in this direction using deep learning. Primarily, this classification is useful at houses, religious places like churches etc., as a first precautionary measure. NFPA recorded that there were on average 22 fire accidents daily and Christmas and Christmas were the most accident reporting days [2].

2   Related Work

Faraday [10] in his lectures explained the science behind the working of candles. Despite being ubiquitously present, systematically structured investigation of candle has not started very early but couldn't be left for long and ultimately attracted the researchers. Kosdon et al. [10] experimented the first known nearly organised experiment for studying the candle through observing the burning candle on a erected cylindrical surface. However, this study happened to be simpler as they approximated cylinder as a flat surface while the flame near the wick was three dimensional. Alsairafi et al. [6] modeled the fuel rise to wick i.e., capillary phenomena and dynamics of flame. Flame of Candle is an instance of diffusion flame and several researchers explored different features of diffusion flames. Ballester et al. [7] reviewed the existing techniques for diagnosis and control of practical flames. These techniques include various kinds of flames of fuels like bio-fuels, fossil fuels, gasoline, and various ratio of fuels and oxygen etc., and various techniques like flame spectroscopy, flame imaging, pressure fluctuation etc. have been used to study flames. Laminar smoke point of the candle flames has been explored by Allan et al. [5] by varying the diameters of the wick and the lenghts of candles for different type of waxes. Sundeland et al. [17] analyzed and measured the shape of the candle flames for different size candles and Roper laminar burner model for flame height has been used. Riley [14] used the flame sheet model proposed by Burke-Schumann to model the reaction zone of the candle flame while ignoring all other combustion processes which limits the scope of this study. The combustion of candles exhibits various dynamic characteristics and the flickering of group of candles have attracted many researchers. Hamins et al. [11] studied the burning behavior of candles and characterized the candle flame and developed the model for candle burning behavior. Buckmaster [8] proposed the theoretical explanation for the flickering, or oscillation of large diffusion flame and suggested an infinite candle paradigm to understand this phenomenon. Moreover, it is well known that diffusion flames flicker over frequency range of 10–20 Hz. Chen et al. [9] studied the characteristics related to phase and frequency of oscillation for candle flames. They bonded several candles and studied the effect on flame frequency by considering the arrangement of candles, number and asymmetry of oscillators. They observed that the frequency slowly reduces with the count of candles when considering isolated oscillators and when two oscillators are coupled, switching between anti-phase and in-phase synchronization takes place. Wang et al. [18] studied the features of burning candle flame at pressures lower than atmosphere and also performed the scaling analysis to elucidate the dependence on pressure.

Field of machine learning research has found new and powerful sub-area famously known as Deep Learning (DL) or hierarchical learning. Deep learning is one of the most promising field being utilized to classify several task. From past multiple years DL is affecting myriads of applications in various fields of study like medical science, astronomy, market analysis etc. DL can perform classification better than any other existing techniques. One of the most utilized and chosen fundamental network is Convolutional Neural Network (CNN) of DL. Unlike the feed forward neural network, DL uses deep networks and one of the most used deep network is Convolutional Neural Network (CNN). Many researchers have exploited the enormous power of CNNs for classification task which were not possible, so accurately, by any other existing methods. DL has also been used to study the flame/fire extensively [3–5,13,16]. Muhammad et al. [13] have designed CNN for the early detection of fire during surveillance for effective disaster management. They have achieved an accuracy better than any of the presently available methods and two diverse datasets. Adedotune et al. [4] proposed an end-to-end deep selective autoencoder approach for the predicting instabilities in combustion process using the hi-speed flame video for an industrial combustor. Their proposed deep network can accurately identify the slight instability parameters as the combustion process changes state from stable to unstable. Li et al. [12] developed DL-based prediction model predicting the NOX radical emission from a biomass fires combustion process; developed model has been compared with the existing other machine learning based model and it has been demonstrated that DL-based model has surpassed all the existing models. Abdurakipov et al. [3] utilized CNN to monitor the flame regimes and achieved an accuracy of 98% for regime classification. Sarkar et al. [16] proposed a dynamic data dependent method where a huge number of sequential gray scale images are used to study the time-dependent variation of the combustion system for prior detection of instability at different working conditions by using deep neural network with Symbolic Time Series Analysis.

3   Dataset Details

In this study the data has been generated by a high resolution camera and for different types of candle. Different size and color candles of paraffin wax with

Fig. 1. Sample images

different background have been used for dataset generation. Some of the images were captured on complete dark room while some of images captured in the light of an incandescent LED bulb of 12 W. These different combinations have been used to generate a widely diverse data for training and testing. Captured images are of size 3024 × 4032 at a shutter speed of 2 s. Stable flame images have been captured for controlled environment where there was almost no flow of air in any direction, even the observer kept a mask on his face while taking the snapshots. Flame has been made unstable by giving blows from the mouth of various amplitude and from various directions and angles. In both the cases different distances from the candle have been maintained while capturing the images. To facilitate further research on this topic, the authors have open-sourced the candle flames dataset[1]. Some randomly selected images from the collected dataset are shown in Fig. 1.

---

[1] http://tiny.cc/ut0dlz.

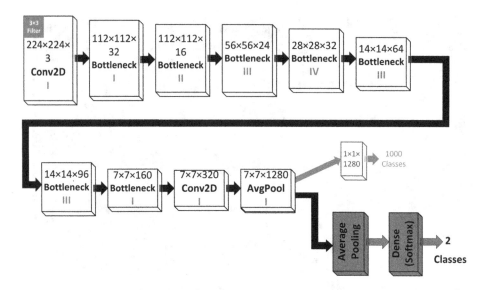

Fig. 2. Proposed architecture of the deep learning model used in this work. The greyed-out blocks show the layer(s) removed from the MobileNet$V2$ model, and the orange blocks show the added layer(s). Numbers in green denote the number of times the block is repeated. Detailed information about the internals of the various layers (except the ones added in this proposal, shown in orange), strides, and expansion factors can be obtained from [15]. (Color figure online)

4   Proposed Model

The age of high performance DL models for CV started with AlexNet in 2012. It was followed by better models like VGG, ResNet, Xception, and MobileNet (Table 1).

Table 1. Details of the DL model.

Parameter	Value	Parameter	Value
Validation Split	0.20	Optimizer	Adam
Epochs	200	Activation (Output Layer)	Softmax
Batch Size	20	Loss parameter	Binary crossentropy
Learning rate	0.001	Trainable parameters	2,230,277
Decay	0.00002	Non-trainable parameters	34,112

MobileNet was proposed as a DL model which is capable of AlexNet-like performance with a significantly reduced model size ($\sim$21 MB size, 4.2 million parameters). More recently, MobileNet$V2$ was proposed which is able to provide the same performance as MobileNet with even smaller model size ($\sim$13 MB size, 3.4 million parameters) [15].

The original MobileNet *V2* was proposed for classifying 1000 image classes in light of the ImageNet challenge[2]. However, for the purpose of this work, we are interested in only 2 classes of images: normal candle flame, and abnormal candle flame. Therefore, suitable modifications in the original MobileNet *V2* need to be incorporated to make the model amenable for the task at hand. Toward that end, we froze the parameters of the initial layers in MobileNet *V2* and removed the last layer from the original model. Subsequently, we added an average pooling layer and a dense layer with 2 outputs (equal to the number of classes to be assigned) and Softmax activation at the output. The modified model is presented in Fig. 2, which results in a model size of 26.2 MB on disk with 2,264,389 parameters.

The proposed network was implemented in Keras which is a high-level neural network API capable of running on top of the deep learning framework TensorFlow™. The MobileNet *V2* model, with the modifications described above, was trained on the images from the train dataset (3,940 training samples with 20% of the training samples used for validation). The MobileNet *V2* weights, for all layers excluding the output layer, were initialized using the pre-trained weights for the ImageNet dataset, as available from Keras[3]. The model was compiled with the `Adam` optimizer using the `Binary Crossentropy` loss function, and `Accuracy` was used as the metric to monitor the training of the model. The model was trained for 200 epochs with a batch size of 20, and learning rate set to 0.001.

5 Results

The trained model was used to perform inference on a test dataset of 272 images comprising of images from the same 2 classes as the train dataset. The classification performance of the model was adjudged based on the accuracy of the classes assigned to the test images by the model. Overall, it was found that for the 272 test images, the model was able to correctly identify the correct class for approximately 67% of the test images. Figure 3 presents some sample test results on images for the 2 categories. Figure 3(a) depicts an example of a 'normal' candle flame image taken from the test dataset, and it can be seen that the model identifies it correctly with more than 90% certainty. Figure 3(b) presents an image of a normal candle flame taken from the internet, and the trained model successfully identifies it as such with almost 100% certainty. Similarly, for the case of two 'abnormal' candle flame images (one from the test dataset shown in Fig. 3(c), one randomly taken off the internet shown in Fig. 3(d)), the model correctly identifies both of the images as belonging to the abnormal candle flame image class.

Furthermore, analysis was performed to ascertain the classification performance of the model for random candle images taken off the Internet. For such images (30 in number), the classification accuracy was found to be 83%.

---

[2] http://www.image-net.org/challenges/LSVRC/.
[3] https://keras.io/applications/#mobilenetv2.

Fig. 3. Example results on some sample images from the test dataset as well as images taken from the Internet

The estimated probabilities of the 2 classes averaged over all the test samples of the respective classes are presented as the Confusion Matrix for a 2-class classifier, in Fig. 4. As can be seen from Fig. 4.

6   Limitations and Future Work

This work is limited in the sense that it proposes a classifier for the type of flame of candles. Scope of the work can be extended by providing the methods to control the environment to keep the flame stable, an efficient state for fuel consumption and gracious decoration sense. Furthermore, deep learning may also be utilized to study the flickering/ oscillation of candle in particular and any other diffusion flame in general.

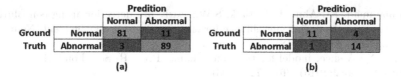

Fig. 4. Confusion matrix for the test results

7 Conclusion

Proposed work is first of its kind for the study of candle flame. Many researchers have applied deep learning in the diagnostic/prognostic of combustion process to study the flame behavior for various combustor at different conditions. This work can be utilized for the precautionary measures to be taken in case of candle flame instability. Proposed work can be integrated with the CCTV cameras and can sound the alarm when it founds substantial instability which may cause fire or may burn the nearby materials.

References

1. Candle-us-august 2013. https://store.mintel.com/candles-us-august-2013. Accessed 12 Mar 2019
2. Candles. https://www.nfpa.org/Public-Education/Fire-causes-and-risks/Top-fire-causes/Candles. Accessed 12 Mar 2019
3. Abdurakipov, S., Gobyzov, O., Tokarev, M., Dulin, V.: Combustion regime monitoring by flame imaging and machine learning. Optoelectron. Instrum. Data Process. **54**(5), 513–519 (2018)
4. Akintayo, A., Lore, K.G., Sarkar, S., Sarkar, S.: Prognostics of combustion instabilities from hi-speed flame video using a deep convolutional selective autoencoder. Int. J. Prognostics Health Manag. **7**(023), 1–14 (2016)
5. Allan, K.M., Kaminski, J.R., Bertrand, J.C., Head, J., Sunderland, P.B.: Laminar smoke points of wax candles. Combust. Sci. Technol. **181**(5), 800–811 (2009)
6. Alsairafi, A., Lee, S.T., T'ien, J.S.: Modeling gravity effect on diffusion flames stabilized around a cylindrical wick saturated with liquid fuel. Combust. Sci. Technol. 176(12), 2165–2191 (2004)
7. Ballester, J., García-Armingol, T.: Diagnostic techniques for the monitoring and control of practical flames. Prog. Energy Combust. Sci. **36**(4), 375–411 (2010)
8. Buckmaster, J., Peters, N.: The infinite candle and its stability—a paradigm for flickering diffusion flames. In: Symposium (International) on Combustion, vol. 21, pp. 1829–1836. Elsevier (1988)
9. Chen, T., Guo, X., Jia, J., Xiao, J.: Frequency and phase characteristics of candle flame oscillation. Sci. Rep. **9**(1), 1–13 (2019)
10. Faraday, M.: The Chemical History of a Candle. Courier Corporation (2002)
11. Hamins, A., Bundy, M., Dillon, S.E.: Characterization of candle flames. J. Fire. Prot. Eng. **15**(4), 265–285 (2005)
12. Li, N., Lu, G., Li, X., Yan, Y.: Prediction of NOx emissions from a biomass fired combustion process based on flame radical imaging and deep learning techniques. Combust. Sci. Technol. **188**(2), 233–246 (2016)

13. Muhammad, K., Ahmad, J., Baik, S.W.: Early fire detection using convolutional neural networks during surveillance for effective disaster management. Neurocomputing **288**, 30–42 (2018)
14. Riley, N.: A sheet model for the candle flame. Proc. R. Soc. Lond. Ser. A: Math. Phys. Sci. **442**(1915), 361–372 (1993)
15. Sandler, M., Howard, A., Zhu, M., Zhmoginov, A., Chen, L.C.: MobileNetV2: inverted residuals and linear bottlenecks. In: Proceedings of the IEEE Conference on Computer Vision and Pattern Recognition, pp. 4510–4520 (2018)
16. Sarkar, S., et al.: Early detection of combustion instability from hi-speed flame images via deep learning and symbolic time series analysis. In: Annual Conference on of the Prognostics and Health Management (2015)
17. Sunderland, P., Quintiere, J., Tabaka, G., Lian, D., Chiu, C.W.: Analysis and measurement of candle flame shapes. Proc. Combust. Inst. **33**(2), 2489–2496 (2011)
18. Wang, Q., Hu, L., Palacios, A., Chung, S.H.: Burning characteristics of candle flames in sub-atmospheric pressures: an experimental study and scaling analysis. Proc. Combust. Inst. **37**(2), 2065–2072 (2019)

Emotion Recognition from Facial Expressions Using Siamese Network

Naga Venkata Sesha Saiteja Maddula, Lakshmi R. Nair,
Harshith Addepalli, and Suja Palaniswamy$^{(\boxtimes)}$

Department of Computer Science and Engineering, Amrita School
of Engineering, Amrita Vishwa Vidyapeetham, Bengaluru 560035, India
maddulasaitej@gmail.com, lakshmirajnair1@gmail.com,
addepalliharshith@gmail.com, p_suja@blr.amrita.edu

Abstract. The research on automatic emotional recognition has been increased drastically because of its significant influence on various applications such as treatment of the illness, educational practices, decision making, and the development of commercial applications. Using Machine Learning (ML) models, we have been trying to determine the emotion accurately and precisely from the facial expressions. But it requires a colossal number of resources in terms of data as well as computational power and can be time-consuming during its training. To solve these complications, meta-learning has been introduced to train a model on a variety of learning tasks, which assists the model to generalize the novel learning tasks using a restricted amount of data. In this paper, we have applied one of the meta-learning techniques and proposed a model called MLARE(Meta Learning Approach to Recognize Emotions) that recognizes emotions using our in-house developed dataset AED-2 (Amrita Emotion Dataset-2) which has 56 images of subjects expressing seven basic emotions viz., disgust, sad, fear, happy, neutral, anger, and surprise. It involves the implementation of the Siamese network which estimates the similarity between the inputs. We could achieve 90.6% of overall average accuracy in recognizing emotions with the state-of-the-art method of one-shot learning tasks using the convolutional neural network in the Siamese network.

Keywords: Emotional recognition · Meta-learning · Machine Learning · Siamese network

1 Introduction

1.1 Challenges of ML in Emotion Recognition

Emotions are generated unconsciously to the extrinsic and intrinsic events, which express some particular physiological states. Our ability to understand and control emotions play a crucial role in taking appropriate decisions and actions in life. Using ML models, researchers have been trying to determine the emotion accurately and precisely from facial expressions. Though ML could reduce the complexity in the computational problems, challenges emerge about the business application like facial emotion recognition. For instance, a simple face or emotion recognition system

© Springer Nature Singapore Pte Ltd. 2021
S. M. Thampi et al. (Eds.): SoMMA 2020, CCIS 1366, pp. 63–72, 2021.
https://doi.org/10.1007/978-981-16-0419-5_6

demands a large number of well prepared and organized images in diverse format during training. Even an accurate ML cannot create viable results on limited amounts of data, since the data has dispersed and proliferated. So if a model trained on Asian subjects, it is challenging for the model to perform well on African subjects. Also, there is a great need for storage requirements for housing all the data and require a large amount of computational power, thereby leading to a large amount of money and may turn economically infeasible at times.

The distinct methods discussed in papers [1, 2], and [3] to recognize the emotions need a good number of resources in terms of data as well as computational power. Work presented in [1] is an extension of [4] using a layer-based CNN method from the CMU Multi-PIE dataset. The proposed model called DPIIER could achieve an average accuracy of 96.55% in 3 - fold cross-validation on 7,50,000 images taken under 15 different viewpoints and 19 illumination conditions. The requirement and management of this huge amount of data to obtain acceptable performance is a laborious task. Instead of images, 4D videos consist of 60,600 frame models used in [2] to recognize emotions by analyzing surface normals and curves and multiclass Support Vector Machine(SVM) used for classification. Though the proposed algorithm could give an appreciable average recognition rate for curves and surface normal, only few emotions have the foremost recognition rate. A geometric approach proposed in [3] using BU3DFE dataset could achieve an overall accuracy of 83.3% on emotional recognition. The method proposed in [5] applied feature level fusion technique on the AED2 dataset by considering facial expression, gestures, and both in the emotional recognition system. The method could achieve a discernible result on the limited data and suggested to leverage the deep neural network for preferable performance.

The work discussed in this paper is an extension of [5] by analyzing solely facial expression using meta-learning technique and in-house dataset having limited data. We designed a model based on the Siamese network algorithm which is the state-of-the-art method in the field of emotion recognition and obtained fine accuracy.

1.2   Meta-learning

In the scenario where the data is inadequate to constrain the problem, the paradigm called Meta-Learning has great significance. Meta-Learning at an abstract level refers to the set of problem-solving strategies that involves adapting to the new environment easily and also can train with very few examples by the procedure of learning how to learn. A fine meta-learning model has to be trained over distinct learning tasks and optimized for the leading performance on the distribution of tasks, which includes the unprecedented tasks also.

The subsequent section explains the different approaches of meta-learning and the work associated with face recognition using the Siamese network which is an incentive for us to implement the Siamese network in the emotional recognition task. Section 3 elaborates the design and implementation of the proposed model which is termed as-MLARE(Meta-Learning Approach to Recognize Emotions). Experimental results comprehend in Sect. 4 followed by conclusion and future scope.

2   Related Work

2.1   Meta-learning Framework

A Meta-Learning framework consists of training tasks and testing tasks, where we learn how to learn to classify given a set of training tasks and evaluate by using a set of test tasks. Each task in the meta-learning framework is associated with a support set and a query set. The model estimates the efficiency of learning on the query set for each task during the training period. The framework uses completely distinct tasks at test time to evaluate the model.

One-shot, K-shot and few-shot are few terminologies related to meta-learning framework. The intention of few-shot learning is to train the learning model with a few training examples. If the model learns a single example of each class, it is known as one-shot Learning. We can generalise few shot learning as N-way-k-shot classification where the model learns k examples from N classes.

2.2   Approaches to Meta-learning

The classification of meta-learning approaches is quite subtle since groundbreaking algorithms are being pioneered in this field. Recent research in meta-learning like Automatic Domain Randomization [6], has been focusing on data augmentation which democratizes the deep neural network in the domain of a limited amount of data. In fact, we classify meta-learning approaches into model-based learning, metric-based learning, optimization-based learning, and data-based learning.

Metric Based Learning
In metric based learning, the model compares the data in relevant feature space to discriminate unseen classes by learning the embeddings in the training task. Koch et al. propose a Siamese network [7] discriminate against the two unseen classes while models like Matching network [8], and Prototypical network [9], etc., discriminate many unprecedented classes by exploiting the prior knowledge about similarity. The designed models in [7, 8] and [9] are based on the nearest neighbor principle, which cannot derive the correlation between the inputs if the dimension of the data is high. In this scenario, Sung et al. introduced RelationNet [10] and Allen et al. proposed an Infinite Mixture of Prototypes [11] to eradicate the issue with the high dimensionality of data. The model in [11] is an extension of the prototypical network in [9] since it sets the model capacity in an adaptive manner based on the complexity of data. Metric based algorithms are computationally fast and maintain a fine learning consistency in most of the cases.

Model-Based Learning
The fundamental idea of model-based learning is fast parameterization for rapid generalization on the new task by training limited data. Santoro et al. proposed Memory Augmented Neural Networks in [12] by combining Neural Turing Machine(NTM) and Long-short-Term-memory(LSTM) with external memory to keep unassailable details or knowledge obtained from the training tasks and use this knowledge during deduction. Meta networks in [13] also use external memory with fast and slow weight for the

rapid generalization. Though the architecture of the models is complex, it maintains a very high learning capacity.

Optimization-Based Learning

The objective of Optimization-based learning algorithms is to optimize the procedure of acquiring task-specific parameters to show the finest performance. Finn et al. introduced Model-Agnostic Meta-Learning (MAML) in [14], to train the initial parameters of the model so that model can achieve optimal fast learning on the novel tasks by updating the parameters in a few gradient steps. One of the main challenges related to MAML is that it requires a deep neural network architecture to get a fine gradient update. Kim et al. came up with Auto-Meta in [15] to solve this issue by selecting optimal architecture for MAML. Another limitation of the MAML is the unreliability in the second order optimization method. The algorithms like Meta-SGD [16], Alpha-MAML [17], etc. can eradicate the aforementioned problem. The optimization-based models have high learning capacity as well as good learning consistency. But models are computationally expensive since they require the second-order optimization method.

Data-Based Learning

Meta-learning algorithms in the data space allow the model to expand and enhance the correlation between the data by creating diverse data. For instance, Automatic Domain Randomization (ADR) [6] that controls the distribution of the training data in simulation and assists the neural network to generalize to the limited real-world data.

2.3   Siamese Network and One-Shot Learning

Siamese network is another type of neural network that employs a different way to triage inputs based on the similarity. In general, a neural network demands a colossal number of data to build the model which shows good performance. But if the data is inadequate to constrain the problem like signature verification [18], it is impossible to obtain many copies of data samples per person. So, this kind of one-shot learning problem is the principle behind designing the Siamese network, consisting of two symmetrical neural networks with the same parameters. The symmetrical networks joined at the end using an energy function as shown in Fig. 1.

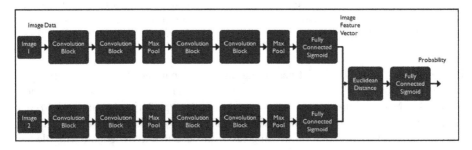

Fig. 1. Siamese network architecture

This energy function serves as the distance function which scrutinizes whether two inputs are in the same class or not. [19, 20] and [21] gives the insight about the Siamese network architecture to implement in the emotional recognition task.

In the classical face recognition system, there are 3 modules Viz face detection, face alignment, and face recognition. The paper [19] ignored the face alignment part to reduce the complexity of programming. The authors adopt cascade classification based on Haar features to detect the faces and use the convolutional Siamese network to recognize the face. This network trains layer by layer gives 92% accuracy on the ORL face database. The model estimates a high value if the sampled image and candidate image are in the same class otherwise it gives a low value. The authors in [20] demonstrate the ability of CNN to deal with the issues in recognizing the face in unconstrained nature. The authors made a slight modification in the architecture of the Siamese network by replacing the cost function with a simple Multi-Layer Perceptron classifier. The dataset CelebFaces Attributes Dataset(CelebA) used for the modeling has more than 200 celebrity images and covers clutter and pose variations. Images that come under the same class are known as genuine pairs, and images of two discrete people are called impostor pairs. The CNN model with the Siamese network gave an accuracy of 85.74% on the CelebA dataset.

In [21], the authors proposed a method to detect face liveliness through 2 stages called offline training stage and online testing stage. During the training period, the authors feed pairwise images in the database to the Siamese network. The pairwise images can be actual images or one hoax and one real image also. If the model estimates the two images are actual, then that images are known as a positive pair or else, it is called a negative pair. In the testing time, the face recognizer in the model identifies the test images and extracts the identity information of the client. Followed by retrieving the actual face image and the test images feed to the Siamese network for the face liveness detection. Euclidean distance used to compare the feature space of the input images in the model. If two images are real face images, it shows the values of 1 otherwise 0. The convolutional neural networks in the model are basically Alex Net architecture that consists of 5 convolutional layers and 3 pooling layers. It is important to note that the aforementioned methods in [19, 20] and [21] require a handful images to obtain viable results. Instead of classifying, Siamese Network demonstrates to differentiate the images by learning similarity functions.

3 Approach

3.1 Dataset and Preprocessing

We have used an in-house dataset named Amrita Emotion Dataset-2 (AED-2) [5] comprising 7 classes where each class represents a specific emotion which includes Anger, Sad, Happy, Disgust, Surprise, Neutral, and Fear. The number of objects posed for this dataset are 8 and hence 56 images in total. A few sample images of AED-2 dataset is shown in Fig. 2. Since the size of the images are different from each other, we converted each image into a 256 × 256 grayscale format i.e. the portable gray map (.pgm). Thus, the model needs to be trained only on these images to classify and identify the emotion.

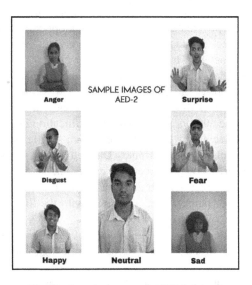

Fig. 2. Sample image of AED-2 dataset

3.2 Experimental Setup

One of the implementation challenges faced with the implementation of meta-learning is that there are no available libraries for implementing the algorithms. All the implementations need to be carried out from scratch which is time-consuming and also difficult in carrying out the operations efficiently. The implementation framework is similar to that of neural networks. The Fig. 3 shows the framework of activities that are needed to be carried out for the implementation of the project. In the preprocessing step we cropped the images only for the region of interest and converted into uniform size (256 * 256) for faster processing. In the next step we are converting the images into a grayscale format(.pgm) to manage the data in a simple and convenient manner.

Fig. 3. Block diagram for the implementation of MLARE model

To enhance the performance of the predictive model, python converts the images into NumPy arrays in the format of [height, width, channel]. To explicate the buffer as a one-dimensional array, the image has been converted to NumPy array using np. frombuffer. Once the conversion of data into a numpy array is done the next step is the generation of data. The Siamese network takes data in the form pairs(genuine and imposter). Initially, the function reads the images (img1, img2) from the same directory as shown in Fig. 4 and stores them in the x_genuine array and assigns y_genuine to 1. Subsequently, the same function reads the images (img1, img2) from the different directory as shown in Fig. 5 and stores them in the x_imposter pair and assigns y_imposter to 0.

Fig. 4. Example of Genuine pairs   **Fig. 5.** Example of Imposter pair

Finally, it is required to concatenate both x_imposter, x_genuine to X and y_imposter, y_genuine to Y. Each time this function is executed it generates 112 genuine pairs and 112 imposter pairs which determine the batch size of 224 data points.

MLARE model comprised of 2 convolutional layers with 32 number of filters and kernel_size 3. Border_mode has been assigned as 'valid' to get an output that is smaller than the input. The parameter, dim_ordering given as 'th', since we used TensorFlow as backend. In MLARE rectified linear unit (ReLU) is used as an activation function in hidden layers and max-pooling of size 2X2 followed by a flat layer with an activation function of the sigmoid. After designing the model, feed the image pair to the neural network, which transforms these images into feature vectors. Then the feature vectors, featvec_a, and featvec_b feed to the similarity function to estimate the resemblance between the two input images. In the MLARE model, Euclidean distance is used as the similarity or energy function. Rather than generating all the data at once here we are using batch training for every iteration or epoch. The function has been called to generate data and to feed into the network to train. Number of epochs is set to 15 and Root Mean Square Propagation(RMS prop) is used for optimization. RMS prop is one of the gradient optimization algorithms that take away the need to adjust the learning rate and does it automatically. Binary cross-entropy loss function(BCE) is used along with sigmoid activations as the cost function to achieve better accuracy.

4   Results and Analysis

After carrying out 420 epochs, the training loss becomes less and accuracy reaches about 94.26% and with this, we stop training the model. The next step is validating the proposed model. So to validate the model we created one batch of data points again by calling the get_data function. It is observed that the validation set gives an accuracy of about 93.75% on the test batch generated for data. So this is the ability of the MLARE model to discriminate the images by learning similarity functions. The subsequent step is to determine the label of the image. For that, we take a test image for which the label needs to be specified, and then an image from each of the classes(anger, neutral, sad, etc.) will be drawn to compare the feature space of the test image and other images. For whichever images it matches more or is close that is the label associated with the image. The authors in [5] proposed two methods to recognize emotions. In the earliest approach, emotions are recognized by considering facial expression and gestures independently. In the next approach, authors combined the features extracted from gestures and facial expression to recognize emotions. The overall average accuracy to recognize emotions from the facial expression in [5] is 86% while that of using the MLARE model is 90.6%. A comparison of the performance of the two models is pictorially represented in Fig. 6.

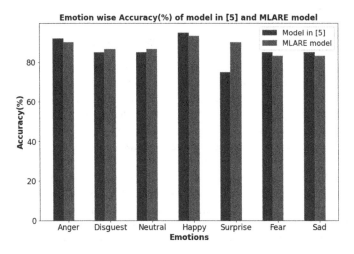

Fig. 6. Bar chart represents the emotion-wise accuracy of two models

We could observe that the MLARE model executed better than the model used in [5] on all emotions and give an extraordinary result on the 'Surprise' emotion. Both of the models could obtain the highest accuracy in 'Happy' emotion as compared to other emotions. It is evident that we could improve the overall average accuracy to recognize emotions from facial expression by enhancing the ability of the MLARE model to differentiate the images.

Figure 6, we can observe that emotions like anger and happiness results in relatively high accuracy as compared to others. In the real world, anger and happiness are the most essential emotions to recognize the feelings of others in a communication. Since the model, even if it is machine learning or meta-learning it actually tries to emulate the human cognitive functions. That is the reason why most of the models show high performance in these aforementioned emotions.

5 Conclusion and Future Scope

In this paper, we have introduced a model called MLARE consisting of two CNNs, for emotional recognition using an in-house dataset and achieved an encouraging performance on the limited data. Along with recognizing emotion from an image, the MLARE is learning similarity functions and manifesting how similar the two images are. In this model, we have chosen BCE+ sigmoid function as the loss function since we use pairs of training data. The MLARE can be modified by changing the loss function to triplet function in future work.

Through data augmentation methods, we can generate more data images from the given 56 images in the different formats to increase the diversity for the training model. Normally simple transformations like cropping, padding and horizontal flipping are used in data augmentation. Further, we can attempt the state-of-the-art methods in data augmentation- like Population-Based Augmentation(PBA) or AutoAugment, to enhance the learning ability of the MLARE on emotional recognition tasks.

Acknowledgement. We express our sincere gratitude to Mr. Pranav B. Sreedhar, for his constant support extended towards this work. His suggestions and exceptional knowledge in the field of meta-learning helped us to explore meta-learning and to complete the work successfully. We are indebted to Chiranjiv, Pranav, Ronak, Sailakshmi, Srilakshmi, Vinayak, Vasuman, and Srivathsan for expressing the required emotions for the dataset and we are thankful to Anupam for coordinating the dataset preparation.

References

1. Palaniswamy, S., Suchitra: A robust pose & illumination invariant emotion recognition from facial images using deep learning for human-machine interface. In: 4th International Conference on Computational Systems and Information Technology for Sustainable Solutions (CSITSS), Bengaluru, India, pp. 1–6 (2019)
2. Sai Prathusha, S., Suja, P., Tripathi, S., Louis, L.: Emotion recognition from facial expressions of 4D videos using curves and surface normals. In: Basu, A., Das, S., Horain, P., Bhattacharya, S. (eds.) IHCI 2016. LNCS, vol. 10127, pp. 51–64. Springer, Cham (2017). https://doi.org/10.1007/978-3-319-52503-7_5
3. Swetha, K.M., Suja, P.: A geometric approach for recognizing emotions from 3D images with pose variations. In: International Conference on Smart Technologies for Smart Nation (SmartTechCon), pp. 805–809. IEEE (2017)
4. Suja, P., Tripathi, S.: Emotion recognition from facial expressions using images with pose, illumination and age variations for human-computer/robot interaction. J. ICT Res. Appl. **12** (1), 14–34 (2018)
5. Keshari, T., Palaniswamy, S.: Emotion recognition using feature-level fusion of facial expressions and body gestures. In: 2019 4th International Conference on Communication and Electronics Systems, Coimbatore, TamilNadu, India, pp. 1184–1189 (2019)
6. Akkaya, I., et al.: Solving Rubik's cube with a robot hand. arXiv preprint arXiv:1910.07113 (2019)
7. Koch, G., Zemel, R., Salakhutdinov, R.: Siamese neural networks for one-shot image recognition. In: ICML Deep Learning Workshop (2015)

8. Vinyals, O., Blundell, C., Lillicrap, T., Kavukcuoglu, K., Wierstra, D.: Matching networks for one shot learning. In: Proceedings of the 30th International Conference on Neural Information Processing Systems (NIPS 2016), pp. 3637–3645. Curran Associates Inc., Red Hook (2016)

9. Snell, J., Swersky, K., Zemel, R.: Prototypical networks for few-shot learning. In: Proceedings of the 31st International Conference on Neural Information Processing Systems (NIPS 2017), pp. 4080–4090. Curran Associates Inc., Red Hook (2017)

10. Sung, F., Yang, Y., Zhang, L., Xiang, T., Torr, P.H., Hospedales, T.M.: Learning to compare: relation network for few-shot learning. In: Computer Vision and Pattern Recognition (CVPR), pp. 1199–1208 (2018)

11. Allen, K.R., Shelhamer, E., Shin, H., Tenenbaum, J.B.: Infinite mixture prototypes for few-shot learning. arXiv preprint arXiv:1902.04552 (2019)

12. Santoro, A., Bartunov, S., Botvinick, M., Wierstra, D., Lillicrap, T.: Meta-learning with memory-augmented neural networks. In: Proceedings of the 33rd International Conference on International Conference on Machine Learning, ICML 2016, vol. 48, pp. 1842–1850. JMLR.org (2016)

13. Munkhdalai, T., Yu, H.: Meta networks. In: Proceedings of the 34th International Conference on Machine Learning, ICML 2017, vol. 70, pp. 2554–2563. JMLR.org (2017)

14. Finn, C., Abbeel, P., Levine, S.: Model-agnostic meta-learning for fast adaptation of deep networks. In: Proceedings of the 34th International Conference on Machine Learning, ICML 2017, vol. 70, pp. 1126–1135. JMLR.org (2017)

15. Kim, J., et al.: Auto-meta: automated gradient based meta learner search. arXiv preprint arXiv:1806.06927 (2018)

16. Li, Z., Zhou, F., Chen, F., Li, H.: Meta-SGD: learning to learn quickly for few-shot learning. arXiv preprint arXiv:1707.09835 (2017)

17. Behl, H.S., Baydin, A.G., Torr, P.H.S.: Alpha MAML: adaptive model-agnostic meta-learning. arXiv preprint arXiv:1905.07435 (2019)

18. Bromley, J., Guyon, I., LeCun, Y., Säckinger, E., Shah, R.: Signature verification using a "siamese" time delay neural network. In: Advances in Neural Information Processing Systems, pp. 737–744 (1994)

19. Wu, H., Xu, Z., Zhang, J., Yan, W., Ma, X.: Face recognition based on convolution siamese networks. In: 10th International Congress on Image and Signal Processing, BioMedical Engineering and Informatics (CISP-BMEI), Shanghai, pp. 1–5 (2017) https://doi.org/10.1109/CISP-BMEI.2017.8302003

20. Bukovčiková, Z., Sopiak, D., Oravec, M., Pavlovičová, J.: Face verification using convolutional neural networks with Siamese architecture. In: International Symposium ELMAR, Zadar, pp. 205–208 (2017). https://doi.org/10.23919/ELMAR.2017.8124469

21. Hao, H., Pei, M., Zhao, M.: Face liveness detection based on client identity using siamese network. In: Lin, Z., et al. (eds.) PRCV 2019. LNCS, vol. 11857, pp. 172–180. Springer, Cham (2019). https://doi.org/10.1007/978-3-030-31654-9_15

Activity Modeling of Individuals in Domestic Households Using Fuzzy Logic

Sristi Ram Dyuthi² and Shahid Mehraj Shah¹⁽✉⁾

¹ Communication Control and Learning Lab, Department of Electronics
and Communication Engineering, National Institute of Technology, Srinagar,
Srinagar, Jammu and Kashmir, India
shahidshah@nitsri.net
² Department of ECE, University of California San Diego, San Diego, USA
http://shahidshah.weebly.com

Abstract. A model which predicts the activities of each individual in
a household is developed. This model is used to simulate the activities
of 25,000 households in a town in Kerala (a state in southern region of
India). A fuzzy-logic based approach is used to estimate the probabilities
of an individual to be in a particular state/activity. Then an optimization problem is formulated to compute the activity transitions. Further,
the activity transitions of the individuals within a house are tied in an
appropriate way. These activity transitions are then used to simulate a
Markov chain of the activities for a sample set of households in a town
in Kerala.

Keywords: Fuzzy logic · Activity modelling · Optimization · Markov
chain

1 Introduction

Energy is the lifeline of economic development. It is therefore essential to reduce
wastage of energy and to utilize the available energy resources efficiently. Residential energy usage is a significant fraction of the total energy usage footprint.
According to some estimations, the residential sector constitutes between 16%
to 50% of the global energy demand across countries [1]. In this paper, we take
a case of one kerela state located in south India. Households in a town in Kerala are being provided with comparisons and interpretations on how they are
consuming electricity along with their electricity bill. These comparisons and
interpretations are based on the estimated consumption of energy by each appliance type (cooling, heating, ovens, lighting, etc.,). This estimation is done by
using the information from activity modeling and disaggregation of electricity
consumption associated with the activities. In this paper, we have been studying
and implementing a household centric activity model for each household in the
town. Figure 1 gives an overview of the activity model.

© Springer Nature Singapore Pte Ltd. 2021
S. M. Thampi et al. (Eds.): SoMMA 2020, CCIS 1366, pp. 73–87, 2021.
https://doi.org/10.1007/978-981-16-0419-5_7

Related Work

Fuzzy logic based activity modeling has been extensively studied in literature. In [1] the daily activity of transport is modeled using fuzzy logic. A case study based on one city of Italy is studied in [2] where bottom-up approach based of inferences made via fuzzy logic system is used for estimation of starting probability of particular appliance. Genetic algorithm based optimization for energy usage analysis of residential buildings is studied in [3] for various European cities. In [4], the authors have proposed Fuzzy logic based modeling of behavior of consumer to characterize the activation profile of various appliances and use this analysis for simulation of demand side management policies. Fuzzy logic forecasting for saving electricity bills by integrating photo voltaic cells with conventional electrical energy source is studied in [5]. Energy efficient Fuzzy logic based algorithm is proposed in [6] where the authors relate physical and economic factors with the behavior of consumer. User behavior with respect to usage of lighting sources is modeled using Fuzzy logic in [7], where the authors propose Fuzzy logic based algorithm to predict the pattern of behavior of user towards switching on/off the lights.

We also note that activity pattern analysis is also studied in the context of transportation in [8–10] and [11].

Our Contribution

In this work, we take a different approach. We use the survey data from the houses taken from the area of Aluva of Kerala, and develop activity model using Fuzzy logic. We then use constrained optimization to obtain stationary probabilities of doing particular activities at time resolution of one hour. The rest of the paper is organizes as follows. In Sect. 2 we propose the model and the Fuzzy logic based activity prediction technique, then in Sect. 3 we propose optimization based method to find probabilities of activities, then in Sect. 4 we present the simulation results and finally we conclude the paper.

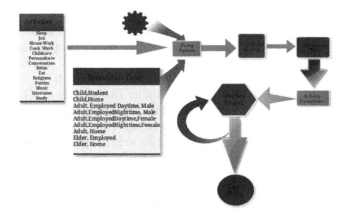

Fig. 1. Overview of activity model

2   Methodology

The activity transitions of an individual have been modeled using Markov Chains. Activity transition is defined as the probability of an individual to be in a particular state or activity, given the individual's previous state or activity. The individuals are categorized into 9 types which are listed in Table 1. This categorization is based on the individual's gender, age, occupation. Activities are tabulated in Table 2. Activity transitions of individuals are computed in two steps. In the first step, the probability of an individual doing a particular activity is computed. In second step, an optimization problem is formulated to compute activity transitions.

Table 1. Types of individuals.

S. No.	Type of individual
1	Child, Student
2	Child, Stay at home
3	Adult, Employed daytime, Male
4	Adult, Employed nighttime, Male
5	Adult, Employed daytime, Female
6	Adult, Employed nighttime, female
7	Adult, Stay at home
8	Elder, Employed
9	Elder, Stay at home

Table 2. Types of activities.

S. No.	Type of activity
1	Job
2	House work
3	Cook/Wash
4	Gardening
5	Childcare
6	Dress/Personalcare
7	Sleep
8	Conversation
9	Relax
10	Eat
11	Religious activities
12	Parties
13	Music
14	Television
15	Study

2.1 Fuzzy-Logic Based Approach

The probability of an individual doing a particular activity is computed using fuzzy-logic based approach. Fuzzy-logic is a widely used technique to deal with problem of fuzziness. A fuzzy-logic system need two kinds of inputs

1. Static inputs like membership functions of inputs, membership functions of outputs, fuzzy rules. These are fixed for a given fuzzy system.
2. Dynamic inputs over which the fuzzy system has to be applied and the output has to be generated.

In context of our work, each type of individual is designed with a specific fuzzy-logic system for a weekday and weekend. Each fuzzy-logic system has a single input, 15 outputs and 360 fuzzy rules. Time of the day is the input to the fuzzy-logic system. The membership function (mf) of input is shown in the Fig. 2. Each output corresponds to an activity listed in Table 2. Each output of this fuzzy-logic system is classified into 5 levels - Very low (VL), low (L), moderate (M), high (H) and very high (VH). Membership function of the output is computed from the set of values assigned to these 5 categories as shown in Table 3. This table lists the crisp values which are used to define the membership functions of all activities of type 1 individual on a weekday. The mapping from crisp values to the membership functions is done as follows.

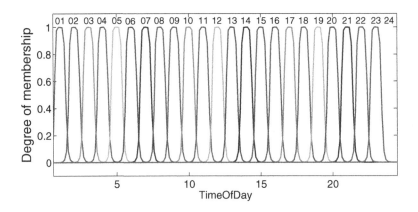

Fig. 2. Input membership function

1. Range of the output is in between 0 and 'VH' value
2. Membership function of VL is a trapezoidal function with the parameters [0, 0, VL, (VL+L)/2].
3. Membership function of L is a triangular function with the parameters [(VL+L)/2, L, (L+M)/2].
4. Membership function of M is a triangular function with the parameters [(L+M)/2, M, (M+H)/2].

Table 3. Crisp values to define the mf of type 1 individual on a weekday

Type 1, weekday	VL	L	M	H	VH
Job	0.0001	0.01	0.6	0.8	0.96
Housework	0.0001	0.01	0.02	0.2	0.3
CookWash	0.0001	0.01	0.02	0.2	0.3
Gardening	0.0001	0.01	0.1	0.2	0.3
Childcare	0.0001	0.0001	0.1	0.2	0.3
Personalcare	0.0001	0.01	0.25	0.4	0.5
Sleep	0.001	0.1	0.3	0.7	0.9
Conversation	0.001	0.01	0.05	0.1	0.2
Relax	0.001	0.01	0.05	0.1	0.2
Eat	0.001	0.04	0.24	0.45	0.6
Religious	0.0001	0.01	0.1	0.2	0.3
Parties	0.0001	0.01	0.1	0.15	0.3
Music	0.0001	0.01	0.05	0.1	0.2
Television	0.0001	0.01	0.05	0.1	0.2
Study	0.0001	0.01	0.2	0.3	0.5

5. Membership function of H is a triangular function with the parameters [(M+H)/2, H, (H+VH)/2].
6. Membership function of VH is a triangular function with the parameters [(H+VH)/2, VH, 1].
   Here VL, L, M, H, VH represent the values of cell at the corresponding columns in the table.

The membership functions of an individual of type 1 doing an activity 1 on a weekday are shown in Fig. 3. Our interest is to compute the probabilities of doing each activity at a one hour time resolution. So the crisp input to the fuzzy system is [1, 2, 3 ... 24].

A fuzzy-logic based approach involves three steps: Fuzzification, Inference, Defuzzification. In fuzzification, all the input values are fuzzified based on fuzzy membership functions. In inference, all applicable rules in the rule base are executed to compute the fuzzy output function. In defuzzification, the fuzzy output function is defuzzified to give a crisp output.

Fuzzification. In fuzzification crisp inputs are converted to fuzzified inputs. Fuzzified input is defined as the extent to which crisp input belongs to each of the fuzzy sets. This fuzzified input value is computed from the membership function. The value of each of the membership functions at the given crisp input value is called fuzzified input. At 10:00AM, the value of each of the membership function is listed in the Table 4 and the membership functions are shown in Fig. 4.

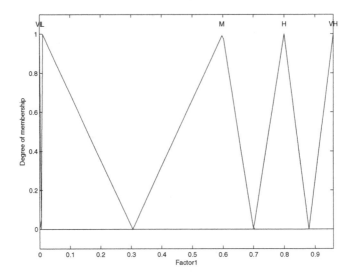

Fig. 3. The membership functions of an individual of type 1 doing an activity 1 on a weekday

Table 4. At 10:00AM, the value of each of the membership function is listed

Type of mf	1	2	3	4	5	6	7	8
Membership Value	3.4e−10	7.8e−10	1.9e−09	5.8e−09	2.0e−08	1.0e−07	7.5e−07	1.2e−05
Type of mf	9	10	11	12	13	14	15	16
Membership Value	0.0016	1.0	0.0016	1.2e−05	7.5e−07	1.0e−07	2.0e−08	5.8e−09
Type of mf	17	18	19	20	21	22	23	24
Membership Value	1.9e−09	7.8e−10	3.4e−10	1.6e−10	8.4e−11	4.5e−11	2.6e−11	1.5e−11

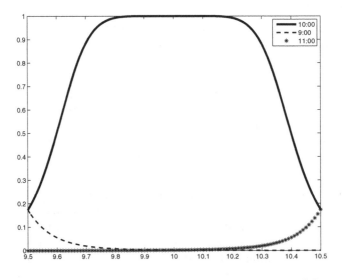

Fig. 4. The input membership functions verses time of day

Inference. As mentioned earlier, all applicable rules in the rule base are executed to compute the fuzzy output function in this step. This involves three steps

1. Apply fuzzy operator
2. Implication Method
3. Aggreagation Method

Apply Fuzzy Operator. Input is a two or more membership values and the output is a single truth value. Fuzzy operator is applied among these multiple inputs. There are two types of fuzzy operators - And, Or. In Mamdani fuzzy inference, 'and' operator corresponds to minimum and 'or' operator corresponds to maximum. This means that while executing the antecedent in the fuzzy rules, when an 'and' operator is used among the input variables, minimum of the input variables is taken. When an 'or' operator is used among the input variables, maximum of the input variables is taken. As our fuzzy-logic system has only a single input, this step has no role to play.

Implication Method. Input is a single truth value from the antecedent of each fuzzy rule. Output is a truncated or scaled version of consequent of each fuzzy rule. There are two standard methods in this step - AND method, Product method. In AND method, output is the minimum of membership function from the consequent and single truth value from the antecedent. This will be the truncated version of membership function from the consequent. In the product method, output is the product of membership function from the consequent and single truth value from the antecedent. This will be the scaled version of membership function from the consequent. Apart from these, any other method can also be defined. In our work, AND method is used for implication.

Illustration: This method is explained in detail for a specific case of type 1 individual. In this illustration, input is the value of the membership functions at 10:00AM which are listed in the Table 4. From this table, it can be observed that the contribution from the membership functions away from 10:00AM are almost negligible. So for the convenience, the membership function values other those which are adjacent to 10:00 AM (i.e. 9:00AM and 11:00AM) are neglected. Our goal in this illustration is limited to obtain the truncated version of consequent of the fuzzy rule set for output 1. The complete fuzzy rule set for a type 1 individual on a weekday is shown in the Table 5. As we have only three membership functions(9:00AM, 10:00AM, 11:00AM) that are contributing significantly, evaluating the following three rules will be sufficient. This is because the output of the AND method would anyways end up with a value close to zero for the remaining membership functions. The three rules are

1. If time of day is 09:00AM, then output 1 is H
2. If time of day is 10:00AM, then output 1 is VH
3. If time of day is 11:00AM, then output 1 is VH

Table 5. Fuzzy rule set of type 1 individual on a weekday.

Type1,WD	1	2	3	4	5	6	7	8	9	10	11	12	13	14	15	16	17	18	19	20	21	22	23	24
Job	VL	VL	VL	VL	VL	L	L	M	H	VH	VH	VH	H	VH	VH	VH	H	M	L	L	L	VL	VL	VL
HouseWrk	VL	VL	VL	VL	VL	L	VL	VL	VL	VL	VL	VL	VL	VL	VL	VL	VL	L	L	L	L	VL	VL	VL
CookWash	VL	VL	VL	VL	VL	L	VL	VL	VL	VL	VL	VL	VL	VL	VL	VL	VL	L	L	L	VL	VL	VL	L
Gardening	VL	VL	VL	VL	VL	VL	VL	VL	VL	VL	VL	VL	VL	VL	VL	VL	VL	VL	VL	VL	VL	VL	VL	VL
Childcare	VL	VL	VL	VL	VL	VL	VL	VL	VL	VL	VL	VL	VL	VL	VL	VL	VL	VL	VL	VL	VL	VL	VL	VL
Personalcare	VL	VL	VL	VL	VL	VL	H	H	M	L	VL	VL	VL	VL	VL	VL	VL	M	V	V	VL	VL	VL	VL
Sleep	VH	VH	VH	VH	VH	H	H	M	L	VL	VL	VL	VL	VL	VL	VL	VL	VL	VL	M	H	H	H
Conversation	VL	VL	VL	VL	VL	VL	VL	VL	VL	VL	VL	VL	VL	VL	VL	VL	H	VH	VH	VH	M	L	L	VL
Relax	VL	VL	VL	VL	VL	VL	L	L	L	L	L	L	M	L	L	L	M	VH	VH	M	M	M	L	L
Eat	VL	VL	VL	VL	VL	L	M	VH	M	L	VL	L	M	L	VL	VH	H	M	L	VL
Religious	VL	VL	VL	VL	VL	VL	L	L	VL	VL	VL	VL	VL	VL	VL	VL	M	M	L	VL	VL	VL	VL
Parties	VL	VL	VL	VL	VL	VL	VL	VL	VL	VL	VL	VL	VL	VL	VL	VL	H	H	M	M	L	VL	VL
Music	VL	VL	VL	VL	VL	VL	VL	VL	VL	VL	VL	VL	VL	VL	VL	L	M	M	M	L	VL	VL	VL
Television	VL	VL	VL	VL	VL	VL	VL	VL	VL	VL	VL	VL	VL	VL	VL	L	M	M	M	L	VL	VL	VL
Study	VL	VL	VL	VL	L	M	L	L	L	VL	VL	VL	VL	VL	VL	VL	L	H	M	H	M	L	L

Rule 1 is illustrated in the Fig. 5. The output from the antecedent of this rule is 0.0016. The membership function of the consequent is shown in the Fig. 5. Therefore output will be the minimum of 0.0016 and the membership function of the consequent.

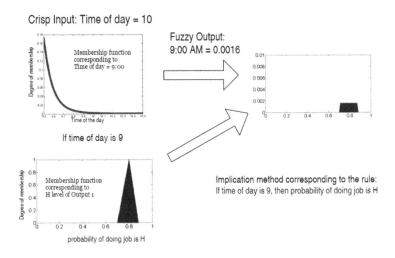

Fig. 5. Illustration of the implication method to the rule: If time of day is 09:00AM, then output 1(Probability of doing activity 1) is H

Rule 2 is illustrated in the Fig. 6. The output from the antecedent of this rule is 1.0. The membership function of the consequent is shown in the Fig. 6. Therefore output will be the minimum of 1.0 and the membership function of the consequent.

Rule 3 is illustrated in the Fig. 7. The output from the antecedent of this rule is 0.0016. The membership function of the consequent is shown in the Fig. 7.

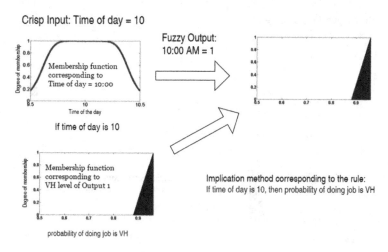

Fig. 6. Illustration of the implication method to the rule: If time of day is 10:00AM, then output 1(Probability of doing activity 1) is VH

Therefore output will be the minimum of 0.0016 and the membership function of the consequent.

Aggregation Method. Input is the output of the implication method for each fuzzy rule i.e. a fuzzy set from each fuzzy rule. Output is a single fuzzy set. As long as the aggregation method is commutative, the order in which rules are executed is unimportant [2]. Some of the standard aggregation methods are max (maximum), probor (probabilistic OR), sum. In max method, output is the maximum of each rule's output set. In probor method, output is the probabilistic OR of each rule's output set. Probabilistic OR of two elements is defined as follows.

$$probor(a, b) = a + b - ab \qquad (1)$$

In sum method, output is the summation of each rule's output set. In our work, max method is used for aggregation. Output of the aggregation method for the example illustrated in implication method is as shown in the Fig. 8.

Defuzzification. The input for the defuzzification process is a fuzzy set (the aggregate output fuzzy set) and the output is a single number [2]. Some of the standard methods for defuzzification are

1. Centroid - x-coordinate of the centroid of the fuzzy set is the output.
2. Bisector - the x-coordinate of the vertical line which bisects the fuzzy set area is the output.
3. middle of maximum - average of the maximum value of the fuzzy set is the output.
4. largest of maximum - largest of the maximum value of the fuzzy set is the output.

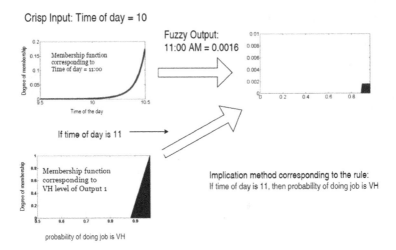

Fig. 7. Illustration of the implication method to the rule: If time of day is 11:00AM, then output 1(Probability of doing activity 1) is VH

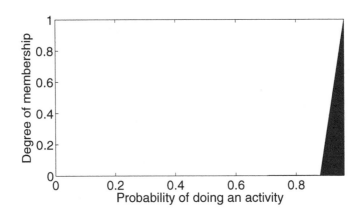

Fig. 8. Output of the aggregation method for a example discussed in implication method

5. smallest of the maximum - smallest of the maximum value of the fuzzy set is the output.

In our work, centroid method is used for defuzzification. The x-coordinate of the centroid of the fuzzy set obtained in the aggregation method is computed as follows.

$$<x> = \frac{Total\ moment}{Total\ area} \tag{2}$$

$$Total\ area = Area\ of\ trapezium + Area\ of\ triangle \tag{3}$$

$$\text{Area of trapezium} = \frac{1}{2}(0.0016)(0.18 + 0.179712) = 0.00028777$$

$$\text{Area of triangle} = \frac{1}{2}(base)(height) = \frac{1}{2}(0.08)(1) = 0.04$$

Substituting (4) and (5) in (3), we get, therefore Total area = 0.04028777

$$\text{Total moment} = \int_a^b xf(x)dx = moment\ of\ trapezium + moment\ of\ triangle$$

$$\text{moment of trapezium} = \int_{0.7}^{0.88} xf(x)dx$$

approximating f(x) = 0.0016,

$$\text{moment of trapezium} = \int_{0.7}^{0.88} 0.0016xdx$$

$$\text{moment of trapezium} = 0.00012 \tag{4}$$

$$\text{moment of triangle} = \int_{0.88}^{0.96} xf(x)dx, \quad \text{where } f(x) = \frac{x - 0.88}{0.88}. \tag{5}$$

$$moment\ of\ trapezium = 0.037333 \tag{6}$$

Substituting (8) and (9) in (7), we get

$$Total\ moment = 0.037897 \tag{7}$$

Substituting (6) and (10) in (2), we get

$$<x> = 0.94065 \tag{8}$$

therefore the probability of a type 1 individual doing an activity 1 at 10:00AM is 0.94065. Same procedure is followed for all types of combinations of individuals and activities and the probabilities are computed. The probability of doing a each activity on a weekday which is computed from this fuzzy logic system verses the time of the day for a type 1 individual is illustrated in Fig. 9.

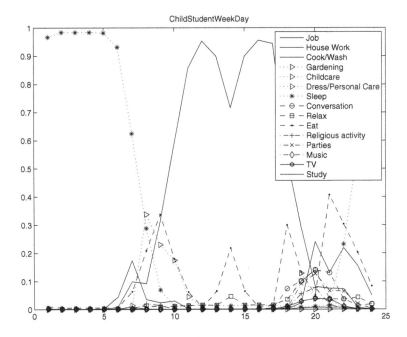

Fig. 9. The probability of doing a each activity on a weekday which is computed from the developed fuzzy logic system verses the time of the day for a type 1 individual

3   Optimization

We now have the stationary probabilities of doing activities at a time resolution of one hour for all individual types. These probabilities are used to compute activity transitions. Let $\Pi_j(t)$ be the probability of doing an activity j at time t and

$$\Pi(t) = [\Pi_1(t), \Pi_2(t), \Pi_3(t), ..., \Pi_N(t)], \tag{9}$$

where N is the number of activities. Now, our goal is to compute a matrix

$$P = [P_{ij}]_{i,j=1,2,3,...,N} \tag{10}$$

such that

$$\Pi(t + \Delta t) = P * \Pi(t), \tag{11}$$

given $\Pi(t)$ and $\Pi(t+\Delta t)$. To solve this underdetermined equation, the following optimization problem is formulated.

$$\arg\min_P \| P \|_2 \tag{12}$$

Subject to:

$$\Pi(t + \Delta t) = P * \Pi(t) \tag{13}$$

$$\sum_{i=0}^{N} P_{ij} = 1 \ \forall j = 1, 2, 3, ..., N \tag{14}$$

$$0 \le T_{ij} \le 1 \ \forall i, j = 1, 2, 3, ..., N \tag{15}$$

The solution to this optimization problem gives the activity transitions. A look up table of these activity transitions is formed.

3.1 Mapping the Survey Data to Individual Types

The survey data has the following family information.

1. Number of children (Age ≤ 18)
2. Number of adults (Age ≥ 18 and ≤ 60)
3. Number of elders (Age ≥ 60)

On a typical weekday, number of people staying at home during
4. 6:00AM - 10:00AM
5. 10:00AM - 5:00PM
6. 5:00PM - 10:00PM

The following rules have been followed in mapping the survey data to individual types.

1. Check the number of people staying at home during 10:00AM - 5:00PM and assign them to individuals of type 9, type 7, type 2 in this priority order
2. Subtract the maximum of the number of people staying at home during 6:00AM - 10:00AM, 10:00AM - 5:00PM and 5:00PM - 10PM from the total number of family members to get the number the individuals of type 4 and type 6. Assign them in almost equal number.
3. Subtracting the number of type 2 individuals from number of children gives the number of type 1 individuals
4. Subtracting the number of type 4, type 6, type 7 individuals from number of adults gives the total number of type 3 and type 5 individuals. Assign them in almost equal number.
5. Subtracting the number of type 9 individuals from number of elders gives the number of type 8 individuals.

4 Simulation of Household Activities

Family information collected from the survey is mapped to the individual type as discussed in Sect. 2.3. The Markov chain of the activities of all individuals are initialized with an activity 7 (sleep) at 1:00AM. The appropriate activity transitions of individuals are taken from the look up table formed after solving the optimization problem which is discussed in Sect. 2.2. These activity transitions are weighed based on the present activities of family members. To be more precise, let $P_{ij}(t)$ be the probability of an individual to make a transition from state i to state j. Let k be the number of family members who are presently in the state j. Then $(1 + k)$ is the weight assigned to this transtion. After assigning weights to all the transitions, the activity transitions are renormalized. With these new activity transitions, the next states are predicted. This procedure is looped to get the states for two months duration, at one hour time resolution.

Apart from the family information, appliance information is also provided in the survey data. Appliance information consists of some basic information like specifications of the appliance (example: ac-capacity, ac-rating, tv-size, etc.,), average number of usage hours of the appliance, appliance count, etc., From this information, average number of usage hours of television is taken to tune the parameters. Once the states of all individuals in a household are computed as described above, the average number of usage hours of tv is computed. If this is not in agreement with the appliance information from the survey data, weight which is equal to the ratio between calculated tv usage hours and experimental data from the survey is assigned at different time intervals based on individual type. The individuals of type 1, 3, 5, 8 are weighed during 6:00PM to 10:00PM. The individuals of type 2, 7, 9 are weighed during 10:00AM to 10:00PM. The individuals of type 4, 6 are weighed during 10:00AM to 5:00PM. Activity transitions are re-computed from these weighted stationary probabilities using optimization as discussed in Sect. 2.2. States of the individuals are re-simulated with these new activity transitions.

5   Conclusion and Future Work

We presented a model to simulate the activities of a household. Activity transitions are computed from the probabilities obtained through fuzzy-logic based approach. These activity transitions and the family information that were collected from the survey are collectively used to simulate the activities. Further, parameters of the fuzzy-logic system are tuned using appliance information. The activities are re simulated.

These activities will further be mapped to the appliances and duration of usage to enable estimation of electricity consumption for each appliance type.

6   Software Environment

Fuzzy-logic system is developed on MATLAB2013a, using the inbuilt fuzzy logic toolbox. Modules for optimization and simulation of the activities are developed in python2.7. PyOpt package is used for optimization. An inbuilt function - SLSQP (Sequential least squares quadratic programming) from the PyOpt package is used to obtain the activity transitions from stationary probabilities of activities.

Acknowledgement. The author would like to thank TEQIP-III for the support for this project. Part of the work was carried out when the author was project associate at IISc Bangalore. The data was obtained from KSEB under the joint project of IISc

Bangalore and Clytics Pvt. Ltd. Their support and permission to use the data is highly acknowledged.

References

1. Olaru, D., Smith, B.: Modelling daily activity schedules with fuzzy logic. In: Proceedings of the 10th International Conference in Travel Behaviour Research, Switzerland. Citeseer (2003)
2. Ciabattoni, L., Grisostomi, M., Ippoliti, G., Longhi, S.: A fuzzy logic tool for household electrical consumption modeling. In: 39th Annual Conference of the IEEE Industrial Electronics Society, IECON 2013, pp. 8022–8027. IEEE (2013)
3. Salata, F., Ciancio, V., Dell'Olmo, J., Golasi, I., Palusci, O., Coppi, M.: Effects of local conditions on the multi-variable and multi-objective energy optimization of residential buildings using genetic algorithms. Appl. Energy 260, 114289 (2020)
4. Zúñiga, K., Castilla, I., Aguilar, R.: Using fuzzy logic to model the behavior of residential electrical utility customers. Appl. Energy 115, 384–393 (2014)
5. Ciabattoni, L., Grisostomi, M., Ippoliti, G., Pagnotta, D.P., Foresi, G., Longhi, S.: Residential energy monitoring and management based on fuzzy logic. In: 2015 IEEE International Conference on Consumer Electronics (ICCE), pp. 536–539. IEEE (2015)
6. Spandagos, C., Ng, T.L.: Fuzzy model of residential energy decision-making considering behavioral economic concepts. Appl. Energy 213, 611–625 (2018)
7. Cılasun Kunduracı, A., Kazanasmaz, Z.T.: Fuzzy logic model for the categorization of manual lighting control behaviour patterns based on daylight illuminance and interior layout. Indoor Built Environ. 28(5), 584–598 (2019)
8. Srinivasan, S., Bhat, C.R.: Modeling household interactions in daily in-home and out-of-home maintenance activity participation. Transportation 32(5), 523–544 (2005)
9. Fu, X., Lam, W.H., Xiong, Y.: Modelling intra-household interactions in household's activity-travel scheduling behaviour. Transportmetrica A: Transp. Sci. 12(7), 612–628 (2016)
10. Bradley, M., Vovsha, P.: A model for joint choice of daily activity pattern types of household members. Transportation 32(5), 545–571 (2005)
11. Gärling, T., Kwan, M.-P., Golledge, R.G.: Computational-process modelling of household activity scheduling. Transp. Res. Part B: Methodol. 28(5), 355–364 (1994)

Stock Price Prediction Using Machine Learning and LSTM-Based Deep Learning Models

Sidra Mehtab, Jaydip Sen[✉], and Abhishek Dutta

Department of Data Science and Artificial Intelligence, Praxis Business School,
Bakrahat Road, P.O. Rasapunja, Off Thakurpukur Road, Kolkata 700104, India
smehtab@acm.org, jaydip@praxis.ac.in,
duttaabhishek0601@gmail.com

Abstract. Prediction of stock prices has been an important area of research for a long time. While supporters of the *efficient market hypothesis* believe that it is impossible to predict stock prices accurately, there are formal propositions demonstrating that accurate modeling and designing of appropriate variables may lead to models using which stock prices and stock price movement patterns can be very accurately predicted. Researchers have also worked on technical analysis of stocks with a goal of identifying patterns in the stock price movements using advanced data mining techniques. In this work, we propose an approach of hybrid modeling for stock price prediction building different machine learning and deep learning-based models. For the purpose of our study, we have used NIFTY 50 index values of the National Stock Exchange (NSE) of India, during the period December 29, 2014 till July 31, 2020. We have built eight regression models using the training data that consisted of NIFTY 50 index records from December 29, 2014 till December 28, 2018. Using these regression models, we predicted the *open* values of NIFTY 50 for the period December 31, 2018 till July 31, 2020. We, then, augment the predictive power of our forecasting framework by building four deep learning-based regression models using long-and short-term memory (LSTM) networks with a novel approach of walk-forward validation. Using the grid-searching technique, the hyperparameters of the LSTM models are optimized so that it is ensured that validation losses stabilize with the increasing number of epochs, and the convergence of the validation accuracy is achieved. We exploit the power of LSTM regression models in forecasting the future NIFTY 50 *open* values using four different models that differ in their architecture and in the structure of their input data. Extensive results are presented on various metrics for all the regression models. The results clearly indicate that the LSTM-based univariate model that uses one-week prior data as input for predicting the next week's *open* value of the NIFTY 50 time series is the most accurate model.

Keywords: Stock price prediction · Regression · Long and short-term memory network · Walk-forward validation · Multivariate time series

© Springer Nature Singapore Pte Ltd. 2021
S. M. Thampi et al. (Eds.): SoMMA 2020, CCIS 1366, pp. 88–106, 2021.
https://doi.org/10.1007/978-981-16-0419-5_8

1 Introduction

Prediction of future movement of stock prices has been an area that attracted the attention of the researchers over a long period of time. While those who support the school of thought of the *efficient market hypothesis* believe that it is impossible to predict stock prices accurately, there are formal propositions demonstrating that with the choice of appropriate variable and suitable modeling, it is possible to predict the future stock prices and stock price movement patterns, with a fairly high level of accuracy. In this regard, Sen and Datta Chaudhuri demonstrated a new approach to stock price prediction using the decomposition of time series [1–3]. The authors have also proposed a granular approach of stock price prediction in a short-term forecast horizon that exploits powerful capabilities of machine learning and deep learning models [4, 5].

Mehtab and Sen present a highly robust and reliable predictive framework for stock price prediction by combining the power of text mining and natural language processing in machine learning models like regression and classification [6]. By analyzing the sentiments in the social media and utilizing the sentiment-related information in a non-linear multivariate regression model based on *self-organizing fuzzy neural networks* (SOFNN), the authors have demonstrated a high level of accuracy in predicted values of NIFTY index values. In another recent work, Mehtab and Sen presented a suite of *convolutional neural network* (CNN)-based models, for achieving a high level of accuracy and robustness in forecasting on a multivariate financial time series data [7, 8].

Researchers have proposed models on technical analysis of stock prices wherein the goal is to detect patterns in stock movements that lead to profit for the investors. For this purpose, various economic and stock price-related indicators have been proposed in the literature. Some of these indicators are: Bollinger Band, *moving average convergence divergence* (MACD), *relative strength index* (RSI), *moving average* (MA), *momentum stochastics* (MS), *meta sine wave* (MSW). In addition to these indicators, some of the well-known patterns in stock price movements like *head and shoulders*, *triangle, flag, Fibonacci fan, Andrew's pitchfork*, etc., are also considered as important indicators for investment in the stock market. These approaches provide effective visualizations to potential investors in making the right investment decisions.

The current work proposes a gamut of machine learning and deep learning-based predictive models for accurately predicting the NIFTY 50 stock price movement in NSE of India. The historical index values of NIFTY 50 for the period December 29, 2014 till December 28, 2018 have been used as the training dataset. Using the training dataset, the predictive models are built and using the models, the *open* values of the NIFTY 50 index are predicted for the test period that spanned over the time horizon December 31, 2018 till July 31, 2020. The predictive power of the models is further enhanced by introducing the powerful deep learning-based *long- and short-term memory* (LSTM) network into the predictive framework. Four LSTM models have been built in this work. The models have different architectures and different structures in their input data. While three LSTM models are based on univariate data, one model is a multivariate one. From the input data point of view, three models used the previous two weeks' data as their input for forecasting the *open* values of the NIFTY 50 time series for the next week, while one model used only one-week prior data as the input.

The contributions of this work are two-fold. First, the work presents a set of deep learning models that yields a very high level of accuracy in stock price prediction. The most accurate model in this work produces a value of 0.0311 as the ratio of *root mean square error* to the mean value of the target variable of forecasting. To the best of our knowledge, this is the highest level of accuracy yielded by a stock price prediction model on daily price forecasting. Second, the proposed models are very fast in execution. The model that was found to be the fastest in execution required a total time of 14.53 s to construct the predictive framework using 1045 records in the training dataset, and then predict on 415 records in the test dataset.

The rest of the paper is organized as follows. In Sect. 2, we explicitly define the problem at hand. Section 3 provides a brief review of the related work on stock price movement prediction. In Sect. 4, we describe our research methodology. Extensive results on the performance of the predictive models are presented in Sect. 5. This section describes the details of all the predictive models that are built in this work and the results they have produced. Finally, Sect. 6 concludes the paper.

2   Problem Statement

The goal of our work is to collect the stock price of NIFTY 50 from the NSE of India over a reasonably long period of five and half years and develop a robust forecasting framework for forecasting the NIFTY 50 index values. We hypothesize that it is possible for a machine learning or a deep learning model to learn from the features of the past movement patterns of daily NIFTY 50 index values, and these learned features can be effectively exploited in accurately forecasting the future index values of the NIFTY 50 series. In the current proposition, we have chosen a forecast horizon of one year for the machine learning models, and one week for the deep learning models and demonstrated that the future NIFTY index values can be predicted using these models with a fairly high level of accuracy. To validate our hypothesis, in our past work, we used CNN-based deep learning models to build highly accurate predictive frameworks for forecasting future NIFTY 50 index values [7]. In the present work, we follow four different approaches in building *long and short-term memory* (LSTM) network-based models in order to augment the predictive power of our forecasting models. It must be noted that in this work, we are not addressing the issues of short-term forecasting which are of interest to the intra-day traders. Instead, the propositions in this paper are relevant for medium-term investors who might be interested in a weekly forecast of the NIFTY 50 index values.

3   Related Work

The currently existing work in the literature on time series forecasting and stock price prediction can be broadly categorized in three clusters, based on the use of variables and the approach to modeling the problem. The first category of work mainly consists of models that use bivariate or multivariate regression on cross-sectional data [9–13]. Due to their inherent simplicity and invalidity of the linearity assumptions that they make, these models fail to produce highly accurate results most of the time. The propositions in the second category utilize the concepts of time series and other econometric techniques like *autoregressive integrated moving average* (ARIMA), Granger Causality Test, *autoregressive distributed lag* (ARDL), and *vector autoregression* (VAR) to forecast stock prices [14–18]. The third category of work includes learning-based propositions using machine learning, deep learning, and natural language processing [4–8, 19–23].

Except for the category of work that utilizes learning-based approaches, one of the major shortcomings of the current propositions in literature for stock price prediction is their inability to accurately predict highly dynamic and fast-changing patterns in stock price movement. In this work, we attempt to address the problem by exploiting the power of machine learning and deep learning-based models in building a very robust, reliable, and accurate framework for stock index prediction. In particular, we have used a *long-and-short-term memory* (LSTM) network-based deep learning model and studied its performance in predicting future stock index values.

4 Methodology and Model Designs

In Sect. 2, we mentioned that the goal of this work is to develop a predictive framework for forecasting the daily price movement of NIFTY 50. We collect the historical index values of NIFTY 50 for the period: December 29, 2014 till July 31, 2020 from the Yahoo Finance website [24]. The raw NIFTY 50 index values consist of the following variables: (i) *date*, (ii) *open* value of the index, (iii) *high* value of the index, (iv) *low* value of the index, (v) *close* value of the index, and (vi) *volume* of the stock traded on a given date.

We followed the approach of regression in forecasting the NIFTY 50 index values. For this purpose, we used the variable *open* as the response variable and the other variables as the predictors. We carried out some pre-processing of the data before using it in training and testing the regression models. We design the following derived variables using the *six* variables in the raw NIFTY 50 index records. These derived variables will be used for building predictive models.

The following five variables are derived and used in our forecasting models:

a) *high_norm*: it refers to the normalized values of the variable *high*. We use *min-max normalization* to normalize the values. Thus, if the maximum and the minimum values of the variable *high* are H_{max} and H_{min} respectively, then the normalized value *high_norm* is computed as: $high\_norm = (high - H_{min})/(H_{max} - H_{min})$. After the normalization operation, all values of *high_norm* lie inside the interval [0, 1].

b) *low_norm*: this normalized variable is computed from the variable *low* in a similar way as *high_norm* is computed: $low\_norm = (low - L_{min})/(L_{max} - L_{min})$. The values of *low_norm* also lie in the interval [0, 1].

c) *close_norm*: it is the normalized version of the variable *close*, and is computed as: *close_norm* = (*close* − C_{min})/(C_{max} − C_{min}). The interval in which the values of this variable lie is [0, 1].

d) *volume_norm*: this variable is the normalized value of the variable *volume*. It is computed in a similar way as *high_norm*, *low_norm*, and the *close_norm*, and its values also lie in the interval [0, 1].

e) *range_norm*: this variable is the normalized counterpart of the variable *range*. The *range* for a given index record is computed as the difference between the *high* and the *low* values for that index record. Like all other normalized variables e.g., *high_norm*, *low_norm*, or *close_norm*, the variable *range_norm* also lies in the closed interval [0, 1].

After we carry out the pre-processing and transformation of the variables on the NIFTY 50 data for the period December 29, 2014–July 31, 2020, we use the processed data for building and testing the regression models based on machine learning and deep learning.

For training the regression models, we use the data for the period December 29, 2014 (which was a Monday) till December 28, 2018 (which was a Friday). The models are then tested on the data for the period December 31, 2018 – a Monday–till July 31, 2020 – a Friday. The data is collected from the Yahoo Finance website and these are daily NIFTY 50 index values. The training dataset consisted of 1045 records that included NIFTY 50 index data for 209 weeks. On the other hand, there were 415 records in the test dataset encompassing 83 weeks. For the machine learning-based models, we used the daily data in the training set to construct the models, and then we predicted the *open* values of the NIFTY 50 index for every day in the test dataset. For building the deep learning-based LSTM models, however, we follow a different approach. The approach is called *multi-step forecasting with walk-forward validation* [25]. Following this approach, we build the models using the records in the training dataset and then deploy the model for forecasting the *open* value of the NIFTY 50 index on a weekly basis for the records in the test dataset. As soon as the week for which the last round of forecasting was made was over, the actual records for that week were included in the training dataset for the purpose of forecasting the next week's *open* values of the NIFTY 50 index. As a working week in the NSE involves five days - Monday through Friday – each round of forecasting resulted in five values corresponding to the predicted *open* values for the five days in the upcoming week.

For building the machine learning-based regression models, we considered two cases, which we discuss below.

Case I: As already been mentioned earlier, the training dataset included historical records of NIFTY 50 index values for the period December 29, 2014 till December 28, 2018. The training dataset included index values for 1045 days. In *Case I*, the performance of the models was tested in terms of the accuracy with which they could predict the *open* values for NIFTY 50 index records of the training dataset. In other words, in *Case I*, we evaluate the training performance of the machine learning-based regression models. The predictions are made on daily basis.

Case II: In this case, the predictive models are tested on the test dataset and their performance is evaluated. The test data consists of historical records of NIFTY 50 index values for the period December 31, 2018 till July 31, 2020. The performances of the models are evaluated in terms of their prediction accuracy of *open* values for each of the 415 days included in the test dataset. Hence, in *Case II*, we have evaluated the test performance of the machine learning models.

In this work, we designed and evaluated eight machine learning-based regression models. These models are: (i) *multivariate linear regression*, (ii) *multivariate adaptive regression spline* (MARS), (iii) *regression tree*, (iv) *bootstrap aggregation* (Bagging), (v) *extreme gradient boosting* (XGBoost), (vi) *random forest* (RF), (vii) *artificial neural network* (ANN), and (viii) *support vector machine* (SVM). For the purpose of evaluation of performances of these model, we use two metrics. The first metric that we use for evaluating a regression model is the value of the *product-moment correlation coefficient* between the *actual* and the *predicted* values of the *open* values of the NIFTY 50 index. The models exhibiting higher values of correlation coefficient are supposed to be more accurate. The second metric that we use for model evaluation is the ratio of the *root mean square error* (RMSE) values to the mean of the actual *open* values in the dataset. The models that yield lower values of this ratio are more accurate.

To make our forecasting framework more robust and accurate, we build some deep learning-based regression models too. In one of our previous work, we demonstrated the efficacy and effectiveness of *convolutional neural networks* (CNNs) in forecasting time series index values [7]. In this work, we have utilized the predictive power of another deep learning model – *long- and short-term memory* (LSTM) networks - in forecasting on a complex multivariate time series like the NIFTY 50 series. LSTM is a special type of *recurrent neural networks* (RNNs) – neural networks that allow feedback loops to communicate data from a node in a forward layer to a node in a backward layer [26]. In RNN networks, the output of the network at a given time slot is dependent on the input to the network in the given time slot along with the state of the network in the previous time slot. However, RNNs suffer from a problem known as *vanishing and exploding gradient problem*, in which a network either stops learning or continues to learn at a very high learning rate so that it never converges to the point of the minimum error [26]. LSTM networks overcome the problem of vanishing and exploding gradient problems by intelligently forgetting some past irrelevant information, and hence such network proves very suitable for modeling sequential data, like texts and time series. LSTM networks consist of memory cells that maintain their state information over time using memory and gating units that regulate and control information flow through them. Three types of gates are used in an LSTM network – *forget gates*, *input gates*, and the *output gates*. The forget gates are instrumental in throwing away irrelevant past information, and in remembering only that information which is relevant at the current slot. The input gates control the new information that acts as the input to the current state of the network. The old information from the forget gates and the new information from the input gates are effectively aggregated by the cell state vector. Finally, the output gates produce the output from the network at the current slot. This output can be considered as the forecasted value computed by the model for the current slot. The architecture of LSTM networks integrated with the *backpropagation through time* (BPTT) algorithm for learning the parameters provides these networks with a high degree of power in forecasting in univariate and multivariate time series [26].

We exploit the power of LSTM models in multi-step time series forecasting using a *walk-forward validation method* [25]. In this method, a model is required to make a one-week prediction, and the actual data for that week is used in the model for making the forecast for the next week. This is both realistic and practical, as in most of the real-world applications, forecast horizon longer than one week is not used.

We have used four different LSTM models in this work. The approaches vary in architectures of the models and also on the shape of the input data the models use. The four models are: (i) *LSTM model for multi-step forecasting with univariate input data of one week*, (ii) *LSTM model for multi-step forecasting with univariate input data of two weeks*, (iii) *Encoder-decoder LSTM for multi-step forecasting with univariate input data for two weeks*, and (iv) *Encoder-decoder LSTM for multi-step forecasting with multivariate input data for two weeks*. In the following, we discuss the architectural details of each model, and in Sect. 5, we present their forecasting performance.

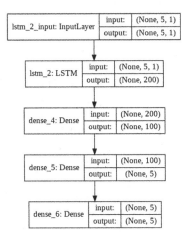

Fig. 1. The architecture of univariate LSTM model with prior one week's data as the input

The first model - univariate LSTM model with prior one week's data as the input - performs multi-step time series forecasting using only the univariate sequence of the *open* values of the NIFTY 50 time series. We train the model using the training dataset records, and then use the model to forecast the *open* values for the next week (i.e., the next five values as a week consists of five working days). The forecasting is being done in a multi-step manner with a walk-forward validation mode. The details of the design of each layer and the overall architecture of the model are as follows. The shape of the input data to the input layer of the network is (5,1) indicating that the previous five values (i.e., one week's data) of the time series are used as the input, and only one attribute of the data (i.e., the *open* value) is considered. The use of the previous one week's data for the purpose of prediction of the next week's values is realistic and practical as the immediate future values of stock prices are, in general, found to be dependent on their most recent past values. The input layer passes the data onto the LSTM layer that has 200 nodes at the output with the ReLU activation function being used in those nodes. The output of the LSTM layer is passed onto a dense layer that has 200 nodes at its input, and 100 nodes with ReLU activation function at the output. The dense layer uses *mean square error* (MSE) as the *loss function* and ADAM as the *optimizer*. The dense layer is finally connected to the output layer that is also a fully-connected layer. The output layer of the model has 100 nodes at its input and 5 nodes at the output. The 5 nodes at the output produce the forecasted values for the five days of the next week. Again, the nodes at the output layer use MSE as the *loss function* and ADAM as the *optimizer*. Figure 1 depicts the architecture of the first LSTM model, which we will refer to as LSTM#1.

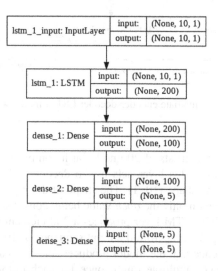

Fig. 2. The architecture of univariate LSTM model with prior two week's data as the input

The second LSTM model, which we refer to as LSTM#2, is also a univariate model that uses the previous two weeks' *open* values as the input and yields the forecast for the next five days (i.e., for the next week). The architecture and other parameters of the model remain identical to those of the first model (i.e., LSTM#1). The only change that is introduced is that the input to the model, in this case, is the previous two week's *open* values. Figure 2 depicts the architecture of the model.

The third LSTM model – encoder-decoder LSTM model with univariate data of the previous two weeks as the input - does not produce a vector sequence as its output directly, unlike the previous two models. In fact, the model consists of two sub-models: the encoder sub-model reads and encodes the input sequence, while the decoder sub-model reads the encoded input sequence, and makes a one-step prediction for each element in the output sequence. We have employed LSTM in the decoder sub-module of the model that enables the model to be aware of the values that were predicted for the prior day in the predicted output sequence and utilize that information in the prediction of its next value. Figure 3 shows the architecture of the model.

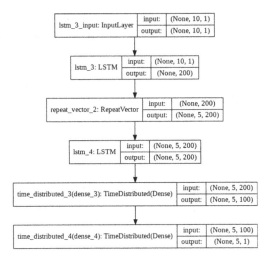

Fig. 3. The architecture of univariate encoder-decoder LSTM model with prior two weeks' data as the input

The first LSTM layer consists of 200 nodes at its output with each node having a ReLU activation function. This layer acts as the decoder sub-module that reads the input sequence having the shape (10, 1). The shape of the input data indicates that the time series is univariate with only the *open* value being considered for the previous two weeks' data as input. The LSTM layer produces a 200-element vector (one output per node) that captures deep features from the input sequence of 10 values. For each time-step in the output sequence that the model produces, the internal representation of the input sequence is repeated multiple times, once for each output sequence. The data shape form output of the repeat vector layer is (5, 200) that corresponds to the five time-stamps in the output sequence, and the 200 features being extracted by the LSTM layer working as a decoder. An additional second LSTM decoder layer performs decoding of the output sequence using its 200 units (i.e., nodes). Essentially, each of the 200 nodes will yield a value for each of the five days in a week. This represents a basis for the predicted value for each day in the output sequence. The output sequence of the second LSTM decoder is passed through a fully-connected layer that interprets each value in the output sequence before it is sent to the final output layer. Finally, the output layer produces the prediction for a single step (i.e., for a single day) at each step, not for all the five steps in a single round. The same fully connected layer and output layer are used to process each time-step provided by the decoder LSTM. This is achieved by using a *TimeDistributed wrapper* that packs the interpretation layer and the output layer in a time-synchronized manner allowing the use of wrapped layers in an identical manner for each time-step from the decoder. This feature enables the decoder LSTM and the wrapped dense layers in understanding the context of each step in the output sequence while reusing the same weights to perform the interpretation. The output of the model, in this case, is a three-dimensional vector with the same structure as the input – each output consisting of [*samples, timestamps, features*]. We have a single feature – the *open* value of the NIFTY 50 index. A single-week prediction will, therefore, have the shape [None, 5, 1]. The structure of the output of this model is thus different from the first two LSTM models, both of which were of the shape [None, 5]. While we used the ReLU activation function in the output of the two decoder LSTM layers and the *TimeDistributed Dense layer*, at the final output layer of the model, MSE and ADAM were used as the *loss function* and the *optimizer* respectively. We refer to this model as LSTM#3.

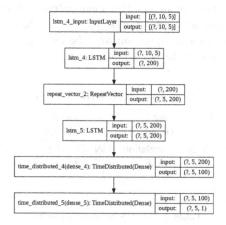

Fig. 4. The architecture of multivariate encoder-decoder LSTM model with prior two week's data as the input

The fourth and the last model of our current work is based on an encoder-decoder LSTM that uses multivariate input. In other words, instead of using a single input variable *open* as the input as it was done by the three models previously discussed, this model uses all the five variables – *open, high, low, close,* and *volume* – to forecast the value of *open*. The model is built using each one-dimensional time series corresponding to each of the input variables as a separate sequence of input. The LSTM creates an internal representation of each input sequence and combines them together before interpreting and decoding the combined representation. This model is the most complex model proposed in this work. Figure 4 shows the schematic architecture of this model, which we will refer to as LSTM#4.

5   Performance Results

This Section provides a detailed discussion on the performance results of all the predictive models that we have constructed and tested in this work. As mentioned in Sect. 4, we designed two metrics for evaluating the performance of the machine learning-based regression models. These metrics are: (i) product-moment correlation coefficient between the actual and the predicted *open* NIFTY 50 index values, and (ii) the ratio of the RMSE and the mean of the actual *open* NIFTY 50 index values in the dataset. In Tables 1, 2, 3, 4, 5, 6, 7 and 8, we have presented the performance results of the machine learning-based regression models. We have implemented all the machine learning-based regression models using R (Version 4.0.2) on Windows 10 operating system. The performances of all models in training and tests are presented. Since the test performance is the one that matters, we observe that multivariate regression, MARS, and random forest have outperformed all other models on the metric correlation coefficient among the actual and the predicted *open* values in the test dataset. However, the lowest ratio of RMSE to the mean of the actual *open* values was yielded by the multivariate regression and the random forest. Hence, on the basis of the performances of all machine learning models, we conclude that the multivariate regression and the random forest regression were the most accurate models in terms of their forecasting accuracies on the NIFTY 50 time series.

Table 1. Multivariate regression results

Stock	Case I Training Data		Case II Test Data	
NIFTY 50	Correlation	0.99	Correlation	0.99
	RMSE	0.27	RMSE	0.42

Table 2. MARS regression results

Stock	Case I Training Data		Case II Test Data	
NIFTY 50	Correlation	0.99	Correlation	0.99
	RMSE	0.42	RMSE	0.85

Table 3. Decision tree regression results

Stock	Case I Training Data		Case II Test Data	
NIFTY 50	Correlation	0.98	Correlation	0.16
	RMSE	2.52	RMSE	10.40

Table 4. Bagging regression results

Stock	Case I Training Data		Case II Test Data	
NIFTY 50	Correlation	0.99	Correlation	0.96
	RMSE	1.75	RMSE	3.72

Table 5. Boosting regression results

Stock	Case I Training Data		Case II Test Data	
NIFTY 50	Correlation	0.99	Correlation	0.98
	RMSE	0.37	RMSE	1.87

Table 6. Random forest regression results

Stock	Case I Training Data		Case II Test Data	
NIFTY 50	Correlation	0.99	Correlation	0.99
	RMSE	0.29	RMSE	0.42

Table 7. ANN regression results

Stock	Case I Training Data		Case II Test Data	
NIFTY 50	Correlation	0.67	Correlation	0.44
	RMSE	12.77	RMSE	19.31

Table 8. SVM regression results

Stock	Case I Training Data		Case II Test Data	
NIFTY 50	Correlation	0.99	Correlation	0.58
	RMSE	0.75	RMSE	8.40

We now present the performance results of the deep learning models. The details of the design of all the four models were presented in Sect. 4. The performance of each of the models is evaluated by executing it on the test data over 10 rounds. For each round, we have observed its overall RMSE value of a week, the RMSE values for the individual days in a week (i.e., Monday–Friday), the time the model took for completing its execution, and the ratio of the RMSE to the mean of the actual *open* value in the test dataset. It may be noted here that the number of records in the training and the test dataset was 1045 and 415 respectively. The mean *open* value in the test dataset was 11070.59.

We implemented all LSTM models using Python 3.7.4 on the TensorFlow 2.3.0 and Keras 2.4.3 frameworks. The models were trained on a hardware system consisting of an Intel i5-8250U processor with clock speed 1.60 GHz – 1.80 GHz, 8 GB RAM, and running 64-bit Windows 10 operating system. Table 9 presents the performance results of the LSTM#1 model. The unit of measurement for all execution time-related records is *second*. We observe that the LSTM#1 model took 18.64s on an average, and it yielded a mean value of the ratio of RMSE to the mean of the *open* values in the test dataset as 0.0311. It is also interesting to note that the mean RMSE values consistently increased from Monday through Friday. Figure 5 presents the performance results of the LSTM#1 model for round #2 presented in Table 9.

Table 9. LSTM regression results – univariate time series with previous week data as the training input (LSTM#1)

No	RMSE	Mon	Tue	Wed	Thu	Fri	Time
1	350.7	250	295	343	396	437	19.14
2	347.2	232	303	341	390	435	16.42
3	351.9	243	296	349	398	439	19.80
4	323.6	210	273	305	369	419	19.36
5	347.4	253	285	336	388	441	18.52
6	314.5	201	259	299	359	411	18.54
7	330.8	234	276	322	369	419	18.85
8	340.1	228	278	326	393	434	18.55
9	378.1	251	385	341	412	467	18.87
10	361.5	219	284	338	450	456	18.35
Mean	**344.57**	232	293	330	392	436	**18.64**
Min	314.5	201	259	299	359	411	16.42
Max	378.1	253	385	349	450	467	19.80
SD	18.47	17.9	34.5	16.7	25.8	17.0	0.899
RMSE/Mean	**0.0311**	0.02	0.03	0.03	0.04	0.04	

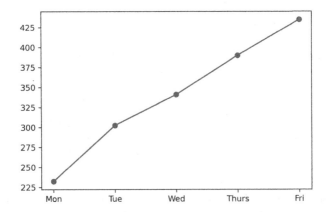

Fig. 5. Day-wise RMSE of LSTM#1 – univariate time series with one-week data as the input

Table 10 presents the performance of the deep learning regression model LSTM#2. The mean execution time for the 10 rounds of execution of the model on the same computing environment was found to be 31.44 s. This was almost two times the time needed for the execution of the LSTM#1 model. The average value the ratio of the RMSE to the mean of the actual *open* values yielded by the model was 0.0353, while the mean RMSE was 390.46. Hence, in terms of both the metrics – RMSE to mean *open* value and the mean execution time – the LSTM#2 model is found to be inferior to the LSTM#1 model.

Table 10. LSTM regression results – univariate time series with the previous two weeks' data as the training input (LSTM#2)

No	RMSE	Mon	Tue	Wed	Thu	Fri	Time
1	393.1	336	363	390	439	429	31.29
2	369.4	293	343	373	413	411	31.40
3	368.0	318	346	363	410	396	31.36
4	431.9	367	409	398	528	440	31.95
5	397.9	343	383	376	452	425	31.49
6	391.6	318	360	397	439	429	31.45
7	408.2	356	414	397	448	421	31.44
8	363.9	304	337	357	406	405	31.53
9	395.1	345	369	404	438	413	31.03
10	385.5	322	353	389	435	418	31.44
Mean	**390.46**	330	367	385	441	419	**31.44**
Min	363.9	293	337	357	406	396	31.03
Max	432	367	414	404	528	440	31.95
SD	20.5	23.2	26.6	16.4	34.7	12.9	0.23
RMSE/Mean	**0.0353**	0.03	0.03	0.03	0.04	0.04	

Unlike the LSTM#1 model, model #LSTM#2 exhibited a different behavior in its RMSE. While the RMSE values for the model LSTM#2 increased consistently from Monday till Thursday in a week, the RMSE values for Friday were found to be smaller than those for Thursday. Figure 6 presents the performance results of the LSTM#2 model for round #2 presented in Table 10.

Table 11 presents the performance results for the model LSTM#3 – the univariate encoder-decoder LSTM model. The mean time for execution of the model for 10 rounds of execution was found to be 14.53s, while the ratio of mean RMSE to the mean of the *open* values was 0.0369. Thus, while the model LSTM#3 is found to be marginally faster in execution when compared to the model LSTM#1, the latter is more accurate in its forecasting performance. The model LSTM#3 exhibited similar behavior in weekly RMSE values as the model LSTM#2. RMSE values increased from Monday till Thursday before experiencing a fall on Friday. Figure 7 presents the performance results of the model LSTM#3 for round #9 presented in Table 11.

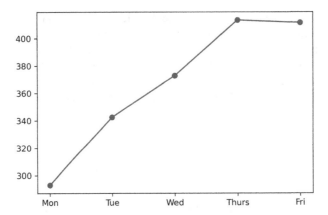

Fig. 6. Day-wise RMSE of LSTM#2 – univariate time series with previous two weeks' data as the input

Table 11. Encoder decoder LSTM regression results – univariate time series with previous two weeks' data as the training input (LSTM#3)

No	RMSE	Mon	Tue	Wed	Thu	Fri	Time
1	391.7	318	383	395	433	418	12.79
2	418.1	367	398	415	459	446	12.56
3	409.1	334	381	403	462	452	14.95
4	423.0	365	400	413	467	461	14.74
5	403.4	326	414	389	424	453	14.79
6	397.9	349	379	393	440	422	14.68
7	389.8	344	384	372	425	418	15.11
8	395.6	327	362	391	445	440	15.44
9	449.0	343	387	468	527	493	14.95
10	412.1	348	382	411	456	453	15.26
Mean	**408.97**	342	387	405	454	446	**14.53**
Min	389.8	318	362	372	424	418	12.56
Max	449.0	367	414	468	527	493	15.44
SD	17.92	16.2	14.0	25.7	29.3	22.9	1.00
RMSE/Mean	**0.0369**	0.03	0.04	0.04	0.04	0.04	

Table 12 presents the performance results of the model LSTM#4 – the *multivariate encoder-decoder LSTM model*. Figure 8 depicts the weekly RMSE values of the model for round # 7 presented in Table 12. It is evident that the model is too heavy, as it took almost five times more time for the model to execute when compared to the model LSTM#3. It is also observed that the model has yielded a much higher value for the ratio of the mean RMSE to the mean *open* values when compared with other models that we discussed earlier. It is evident that the dataset of NIFTY 50 did not exhibit multivariate characteristics and univariate models were much more accurate and

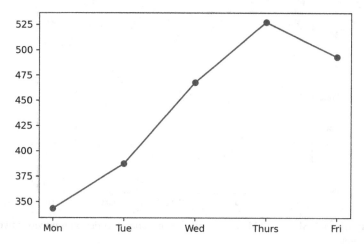

Fig. 7. Day-wise RMSE of LSTM#3 – univariate encoder-decoder with previous two weeks' data as the input

Table 12. Encoder decoder LSTM regression results – multivariate time series with previous two weeks' data as the training input (LSTM#3)

No	RMSE	Mon	Tue	Wed	Thu	Fri	Time
1	1329.8	1396	1165	949	1376	1655	72.79
2	2798.8	3253	3131	2712	2407	2369	69.01
3	2764.2	2588	2926	2761	3100	2391	79.88
4	1754.2	1402	1856	1766	1543	2114	62.76
5	1217.4	1521	1098	1045	1001	1340	59.61
6	1162.9	1421	1100	1075	920	1239	72.28
7	2485.4	2034	2108	2258	2767	3091	68.76
8	1788.6	1280	1590	1705	1962	2252	62.82
9	1451.6	1921	1317	1367	1362	1179	62.42
10	2185.6	1191	1373	1901	2601	3194	58.73
Mean	**1893.85**	1801	1766	1754	1904	2082	**66.91**
Min	1162.9	1191	1098	949	920	1179	58.73
Max	2798.8	3253	3131	2761	3100	3194	79.88
SD	1236.93	1527	1209	1351	1140	1032	0.624
RMSE/Mean	**0.1711**	0.16	0.16	0.16	0.17	0.19	

efficient in forecasting the future *open* values. At the same time, univariate models with one-week prior data input were very fast in their execution speed as well. The results clearly depict that while the deep learning regression models are much more accurate than the machine learning models, the univariate models with prior one-week data are among the most accurate and the fastest in execution. The univariate LSTM model with one-week data as the input turned out to be the most optimum model – both in terms of accuracy and execution time.

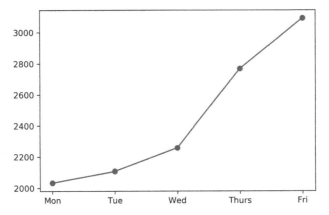

Fig. 8. Day-wise RMSE of LSTM#4 – multivariate encoder-decoder with previous two weeks' data as the input

6   Conclusion

In this paper, we have presented several approaches to prediction of stock index values its movement patterns on a weekly forecast horizon using eight machine learning, and four LSTM-based deep learning regression models. Using the daily historical data of NIFTY 50 index values during the period December 29, 2014 till July 31, 2020, we constructed, optimized, and then tested the predictive models. Data pre-processing and data wrangling operations were carried on the raw data, and a set of derived variables are created for building the models. Among all the machine learning and deep learning-based regression models, the performances of the LSTM-based deep learning regression models were found to be far too superior to that of the machine-learning-based predictive models. The study has conclusively proved our conjecture that deep learning-based models have much higher capability in extracting and learning the features of a time series data than their corresponding machine learning counterparts. It also reveals the fact that multivariate analysis is not a good idea in LSTM-based regression, as univariate models are more accurate and faster in their execution. As a future scope of work, we will investigate the possibility of using *generative adversarial networks* (GANs) in time series analysis and forecasting of stock prices.

References

1. Sen, J., Datta Chaudhuri, T.: An alternative framework for time series decomposition and forecasting and its relevance for portfolio choice - a comparative study of the Indian consumer durable and small cap sector. J. Econ. Libr. **3**(2), 303–326 (2016)
2. Sen, J., Datta Chaudhuri, T.: An investigation of the structural characteristics of the indian IT sector and the capital goods sector - an application of the R programming language in time series decomposition and forecasting. J. Insur. Financ. Manag. **1**(4), 68–132 (2016)
3. Sen, J., Datta Chaudhuri, T.: Understanding the sectors of indian economy for portfolio choice. Int. J. Bus. Forecast. Mark. Intell. **4**(2), 178–222 (2018)

4. Sen, J., Datta Chaudhuri, T.: A robust predictive model for stock price forecasting. In: Proceedings of the 5th International Conference on Business Analytics and Intelligence, Bangalore, India, 11–13 December 2017 (2017)
5. Sen, J.: Stock price prediction using machine learning and deep learning frameworks. In: Proceedings of the 6th International Conference on Business Analytics and Intelligence, Bangalore, India, 20–22 December 2018 (2018)
6. Mehtab, S., Sen, J.: A robust predictive model for stock price prediction using deep learning and natural language processing. In: Proceedings of the 7th International Conference on Business Analytics and Intelligence, Bangalore, India, 5–7 December 2019 (2019)
7. Mehtab, S., Sen, J.: Stock price prediction using convolutional neural network on a multivariate time series. In: Proceedings of the 3rd National Conference on Machine Learning and Artificial Intelligence (NCMLAI), New Delhi, India, 1 February 2020 (2020)
8. Mehtab, S., Sen, J.: A time series analysis-based stock price prediction using machine learning and deep learning models. Technical Report, No: NSHM_KOL_2020_SCA_DS_1 (2020). https://doi.org/10.13140/RG.2.2.14022.22085/2
9. Enke, D., Grauer, M., Mehdiyev, N.: Stock market prediction with multiple regression, fuzzy type-2 clustering, and neural networks. Proc. Comput. Sci. **6**, 201–206 (2011)
10. Ma, J., Liu, L.: Multivariate nonlinear analysis and prediction of shanghai stock market. Discrete Dyn. Nat. Soc. **2008**, 1–9 (2008). Article ID: 526734
11. Khan, U., et al.: A robust regression-based stock exchange forecasting and determination of correlation between stock markets. Sustainability **10**, 3702 (2018)
12. Sharma, V., Khemnar, R., Kumari, R., Mohan, B.R.: Time series with sentiment analysis for stock price prediction. In: Proceedings of the IEEE International Conference on Intelligent Communication and Computational Techniques (ICCT), Jaipur, India (2019)
13. Ivanovski, Z., Ivanovska, N., Narasanov, Z.: The regression analysis of stock returns at MSE. J. Mod. Account. Audit. **12**(4), 217–224 (2016)
14. Adebiyi, A.A., Adewumi, A.O., Ayo, C.K.: Stock price prediction using the ARIMA model. In: Proceedings of the International Conference on Computer Modelling and Simulation, Cambridge, UK, pp. 105–111 (2014)
15. Xiao, Y., Xiao, J., Liu, J., Wang, S.: A multiscale modeling approach incorporating ARIMA and ANNs for financial market volatility forecasting. J. Syst. Sci. Complex. **27**(1), 225–236 (2014). https://doi.org/10.1007/s11424-014-3305-4
16. Jammalamadaka, S.R., Qiu, J., Ning, N.: Predicting a stock portfolio with multivariate Bayesian structural time series model: do news or emotions matter? Int. J. Artif. Intell. **17**(2), 81–104 (2019)
17. Selvin, S., Vinayakumar, R., Gopalakrishnan, E.A., Menon, V.K., Soman, K.P.: Stock price prediction using LSTM, RNN, and CNN-sliding window model. In: Proceedings of the IEEE International Conference on Advances in Computing, Communications, and Informatics (ICACCI), Udupi, India, pp. 1643–1647 (2017)
18. Kim, M., Sayama, H.: Predicting stock market movements using network science: an information-theoretic approach. Appl. Netw. Sci. **2**, 1–14 (2017). Article No: 35
19. Wang, Z., Ho, S-B., Lin, Z.: Stock market prediction analysis by incorporating social and news opinion and sentiment. In: Proceedings of the IEEE International Conference on Data Mining Workshops, Singapore (2018)
20. Porshnev, A., Redkin, I., Shevchenko, A.: Machine learning in prediction of stock market indicators based on historical data and data from Twitter sentiment analysis. In: Proceedings of the IEEE International Conference on Data Mining Workshops, Dallas, TX, USA (2013)
21. Tang, J., Chen, X.: Stock market prediction based on historic prices and news titles. In: Proceedings of the International Conference on Machine Learning Technologies (ICMLT), Jinan, China, pp. 29–34 (2018)

22. Obthong, M., Tantisantiwong, N., Jeamwatthanachai, W., Wills, G.: A survey on machine learning for stock price prediction: algorithms and techniques. In: Proceedings of the 2nd International Conference on Finance, Economics, Management and IT Business, FEMIB 2020, Prague, Czech Republic, 5–6 May 2020 (2020)
23. Zhou, J., Fan, P.: Modulation format/bit rate recognition based on principal component analysis (PCA) and artificial neural networks (ANNs). OSA Continuum **2**(3), 923–937 (2019)
24. Yahoo Finance Website. https://in.finance.yahoo.com
25. Brownlee, J.: Introduction to Time Series Forecasting with Python (2019)
26. Geron, A.: Hands-on Machine Learning with Scikit-Learn Keras & Tensorflow. O'Reilly Publications, Sebastopol (2019)

An Improved Salp Swarm Algorithm Based on Adaptive β-Hill Climbing for Stock Market Prediction

Abhishek Kumar[1]([✉]) [iD], Rishesh Garg[2] [iD], Arnab Anand[3] [iD],
and Ram Sarkar[4] [iD]

[1] Department of Production Engineering, Jadavpur University, Kolkata, India
theabhi999@outlook.com
[2] Department of Mechanical Engineering, Jadavpur University, Kolkata, India
risheshg@gmail.com
[3] Department of Chemical Engineering, Jadavpur University, Kolkata, India
29arnabanand@gmail.com
[4] Department of Computer Science and Engineering, Jadavpur University,
Kolkata, India
ramjucse@gmail.com

Abstract. Stock market prediction is a tool to maximize the investor's money and minimize the risk associated with it. This paper proposes a new machine learning based model to predict the stock market price. The proposed model is an improved version of existing Salp Swarm Optimizer (SSO) which is integrated with Least Square-Support Vector Machine (LSSVM). The improved version is a hybrid meta-heuristics algorithm, which is a combination of SSO and Adaptive β-Hill Climbing (Aβ-HC) algorithm. The proposed model selects the best hyperparameters for LSSVM to avoid over fitting and local minima, and in turn increases the model's accuracy. It is evaluated on four standard and publicly available stock market datasets, and its result is compared with some popular meta-heuristic algorithms. The results show that our proposed model performs better than the existing models in most of the cases. The source code for our proposed algorithm is available in https://github.com/singhaviseq/SSA-ABHC.

Keywords: Stock market prediction · Adaptive β Hill Climbing · Salp swarm optimizer · Meta-heuristics · Optimization · Least square support vector machine

1 Introduction

Predicting the future has always been fantasy to humans and, if we can predict the stock market, then indeed we have built one of the greatest tools for wealth building. Predicting the future prices of stocks is very essential for any investor in order to decrease the risks associated with it. With the rise of technology, better

S. M. Thampi et al. (Eds.): SoMMA 2020, CCIS 1366, pp. 107–121, 2021.
https://doi.org/10.1007/978-981-16-0419-5_9

and efficient models are being developed to minimize the risks and maximize the wealth. But stock markets are quite fluctuating in nature and hence it is a challenge to predict their correct movements, hence researchers try to find best possible algorithm for the task.

One of the popular methods for predicting time-series data is ARIMA (Auto Regressive Integrated Moving Average), but it is most effective against datasets which have a seasonality or trend associated with them. Therefore, in the case of stock market data, which is generally full of nonlinearity and irregularities, this is considered as a weak model. Some other methods which have proven their nonlinear modelling capability, thus, gaining popularity among researchers are Artificial Neural Networks (ANNs) and Support Vector Machines (SVM). SVM is a supervised machine learning technique proposed by Vapnik [29] and his co-workers in 1995 whereas LS-SVM, introduced by Suykens and Vandewalle [27], is a modified version of SVM that can be used for regression, classification, and function estimation [27]. It simplifies the optimization process by using linear equations instead of quadratic equations [15].

In recent years, meta-heuristic algorithms have been popular in various domains such as real-life engineering designs [14], signal denoising [15], feature selection [11], mathematical optimization problems and many such problems. The core operations of these methods do not rely on gradient information of the objective landscape or its mathematical traits. Apart from that ease of implementation and simplicity are other factors that have made these algorithms increasingly popular among researchers. But these meta-heuristic algorithms have their own drawbacks: a delicate sensitivity to the tuning of user-defined parameters, and convergence that may not always be the global optimum [14].

In this paper, we have made an attempt to propose a machine learning model which is a hybrid of LSSVM with a recently proposed meta-heuristic algorithm called Salp Swarm Optimization (SSO) algorithm [20]. SSO has produced significantly better results compared to optimizers mentioned in the literature, when it is deployed in practice, with a series of advantages over parameters like simplicity, flexibility and effectiveness as compared to other optimizers present in the literature. However, SSO, like other swarm intelligence optimization algorithms, also suffers from some problems like population diversity, slow convergence ability and local optimum solution. As suggested by Wolpert & Macready in No-Free-Lunch Theorem [30], there is no single optimization algorithm that can work universally superior to other optimizers in terms of performance on every computation problem. This also implies, a specific optimization algorithm might outperform others over a subset of problems, but not on all types of problems. This phenomenon has motivated our study to improve SSO alongside getting better accuracy on stock market price prediction problem. To enhance the exploration ability, we have embedded a local search algorithm called Adaptive β hill climbing (Aβ-HC) [3] algorithm. The performance of LSSVM is based on the selection of three parameters A (cost penalty), ε (loss function) and γ (kernel parameter). SSO with local search is used to find the best parameter combination for LSSVM. The contributions of this paper are highlighted below:

- Application of SSO and LSSVM hybrid model for the first time to the best of our knowledge.
- Enhance the exploration ability of SSO by addition of local search called Aβ-HC.
- Validation of the proposed model on four stock market datasets.
- The proposed algorithm is compared against five meta-heuristic algorithms.

The rest of the paper is organized as follows: Sect. 2 provides a brief overview of the past meta-heuristic algorithms used on stock market prediction. Section 3 provides detailed description of proposed hybrid algorithm i.e. details on LSSVM, SSO and Aβ-HC. The proposed model and its implementation on stock market prediction are discussed in Sect. 4, Sect. 5 introduces experimental results and discussion. Finally, Sect. 5 is devoted to conclude the proposed work and provides directions for future extension of this work.

2   Literature Survey

The field of meta-heuristic algorithms is an ever-expanding field and now a new trend is on the rise that is the field of hybrid meta-heuristics algorithms. Meta-heuristic algorithms can be categorized in various ways such as single solution based or population based [9], nature inspired or non-nature inspired [8], metaphor based or non-metaphor based [1] etc. Broadly, we can group them into four categories [23]: evolutionary, swarm based, inspired by physics and related to humans.

- Evolutionary algorithms use mechanisms inspired by biological evolution, such as reproduction, mutation, recombination, and selection. It also utilizes the mutation and crossover phenomena in evolution in the form of tuneable parameters to improve upon the randomly initialized population over successive generations (iterations) and provides us with the last surviving offspring as the optimal solution. The Genetic algorithm(GA) [5], proposed in early 1970s, is one of the most famous evolutionary algorithms. Some popular evolutionary algorithms are Co-evolving algorithm, Cultural algorithm, Genetic programming, Grammatical evolution, Bio-geography based optimizer, Stochastic fractal search etc.
- Swarm based algorithms are one of the most popular categories of meta-heuristics algorithms. As defined by Bonabeau, "The emergent collective intelligence of groups of simple agents" [4] is the principal behind swarm-based algorithms. They are mainly inspired by the behaviour of social animals such as group foraging, nest-building or cooperative transportation to name a few. Every individual particle has its own unique behaviour, and the combined effect of all these particles help us to reach an optimal solution. Particle Swarm optimization (PSO) [18] is one of the oldest and one of the most popular swarm-based algorithms which follows the behaviour of birds while searching for food. Another common swarm optimizer is the Ant Colony

Optimization [6] based on the foraging behaviour of some ant species. Artificial bee colony [16], Firefly algorithm [31], are few other common swarm optimizers. Few other popular swarm-based optimizers are Shuffled frog leaping algorithm , Bacterial foraging, Crow search algorithm, Squirrel search algorithm.

- Physics based algorithms are based on physical and physics-chemical phenomena. These algorithms may take inspiration ranging from chemistry, physics, music, light etc. Simulated Annealing [19] is one the oldest and most commonly used physics-based algorithms which is based on the annealing process in material science. Another famous algorithm is Gravitational Search Algorithm [25] which is based on the interaction between mass and gravity. Ray Optimizer [17] used Snell's light refraction law to introduce a new optimization algorithm. Few other examples are: Black hole optimization , Multiverse optimizer [21], Galaxy-based Search Algorithm , Central Force Optimization.
- Human based algorithm mimics the human behaviour. Few popular human based algorithms are: Teaching-Learning-Based optimization , League championship algorithm , Society and civilization .

Meta-heuristics algorithms are commonly used in the finance domain. There have been many notable works using different types of meta-heuristics algorithms on stock market predictions like Fruit Fly optimization algorithm [7], Butterfly optimization algorithm [10], Artificial Bee Colony (ABC) [12], GA [22] etc. Now a days, to achieve greater accuracy, hybrid meta-heuristics algorithms are being used. These algorithms perform better than their original algorithms [28]. In these algorithms, one algorithm is combined with another algorithm for local search. One of the earliest hybrid meta-heuristics algorithm used GA with a local search algorithm [24]. These algorithms tend to perform better when compiled with traditional machine learning algorithms like LS-SVM and also overcame local minima and overfitting problems [13]. Another is using PSO with COM used in stock market prediction [26].

3   Present Work

3.1   Least Square Support Vector Regression

Combined with another algorithm for local search. One of the earliest hybrid meta-heuristics algorithm used GA with a local search algorithm [24].Another is using PSO with COM used in stock market prediction

LSSVM is Least Squared version of SVM in which due to the equality constraints, a set of linear functions needs to be solved rather than quadratic programming as needed in classical SVM.

Let X be $n * m$ input data matrix and y is $n * 1$ output vector. Given the training set of n data points $\{x_j, y_j\}_{j=1}^{n}$, where $x_j \in \mathbb{R}^m$,$y_j \in \mathbb{R}$. The goal of LSSVM is to construct a function $f(x) = y$, which represents the dependence of one variable over other. The equation is formulated as:

$$f(x) = w^T \phi(x) + b \tag{1}$$

where w^T and $\phi(x) : \mathbb{R}^m \to \mathbb{R}^n$ are $n*1$ column vectors and $b \in \mathbb{R}$. Using LSSVM we compute the minimization which is similar to SVM. The optimization problem and the equality constraints of LSSVM are given as follows:

$$\phi_{W,\xi,b}(W,\xi,b) = 0.5W^TW + A*0.5\xi^T \tag{2}$$

$$y_j = W^T\phi(x) + b + \xi \tag{3}$$

where $A \in \mathbb{R}^+$ is a trade-off variable between solution size and training errors and ξ is a $n*1$ vector. To minimize a given equation with given constraints, we apply Lagrange's multiplier, which gives us an equation which we can minimize without thinking about the constraints. From Eq. (2), a Lagranian is formed, and differentiating this with respect to W, ξ, b, α (where α is a Lagrangian multiplier) we obtain:

$$\begin{bmatrix} I & 0 & 0 & -S^T \\ 0 & 0 & 0 & -1^T \\ 0 & 0 & AI & -I^T \\ S & 1 & I & 0 \end{bmatrix} \begin{bmatrix} W \\ b \\ \xi \\ \alpha \end{bmatrix} = \begin{bmatrix} 0 \\ 0 \\ 0 \\ y \end{bmatrix} \tag{4}$$

where I is the identity matrix and

$$S = \left[\phi(x_1), \phi(x_2), \phi(x_3), \ldots, \phi(x_n)\right]^T \tag{5}$$

By evaluating the Eq. (4) we obtain $W = S^T\alpha$ and $A\xi = \alpha$ and here we define a kernel which helps us to map the input points to higher dimensions without adding them. Kernel $\psi = SS^T$ and $\lambda = A^{-1}$ and and these conditions lead to the following solution:

$$\begin{bmatrix} 0 & -I^T \\ 1 & \psi + \lambda I \end{bmatrix} \begin{bmatrix} b \\ \alpha \end{bmatrix} = \begin{bmatrix} 0 \\ y \end{bmatrix} \tag{6}$$

where kernel functions ψ can be as follows:

- $\qquad$ Linear Kernel: $\psi(x, x_j) = x_j^T x$ $\hfill (7)$

- $\qquad$ Polynomial Kernel of degree d : $\psi(x, x_j) = (1 + x_j^T x/A)^d$ $\hfill (8)$

- $\qquad$ RBF Kernel: $\psi(x, x_j) = exp(\|x_j^T x\|^2/\sigma^2)$ $\hfill (9)$

In this paper, we have used RBF kernel.

3.2 Salp Swarm Optimizer

SSO is a swarm based meta-heuristic algorithm which is derived from the behaviour of salps in oceans during locomotion or forging. The salps are divided into two parts, first is the leader and second is the followers. The leader at the front of the chain and rest of the followers follow the leader. There can be only one leader at a particular iteration which is the best solution found by the model up to that iteration. The position of the salps is stored in an n-dimension search space where n is the number of variables of the given problem. The position of all the salps is stored in a two-dimension matrix k. We also assume that there is a food source P_j presentThese new features or technical indicators in the search space which the salps will target. To update the leader's position the following equation is used:

$$k_j^1 = \begin{cases} P_j + d_1\Big((u_j - l_j)d_2 + l_j\Big), & d_3 \geq 0 \\ P_j - d_1\Big((u_j - l_j)d_2 + l_j\Big), & d_3 < 0 \end{cases} \tag{10}$$

where k_j^i is the position of the leader salp in the jth dimension, P_j is the position of food in the jth dimension, u_j, l_j are the upper and lower bounds of the jth dimension respectively, and d_2 and d_3 are random numbers. d_2 and d_3 are random numbers between $[0,1]$ and d_1 is the coefficient which balances between exploration and exploitation phases of the optimizer and is defined as:

$$d_1 = 2e^{-(4t/T)^2} \tag{11}$$

where t is the current iteration and T is the total number of iterations. To update the position of followers after each iteration we use Newton's law of motion:

$$k_j^i = \frac{1}{2}at^2 + v_0 t \tag{12}$$

where k_j^i is the ith follower particle in the jth dimension, and $i \geq 2$ as $i = 1$ is for the leader position which is updated by Eq. (10) , t is time, v_0 is the initial velocity, $a = \frac{v_{final}}{t}$ and $v_{final} = \frac{k-k_0}{t}$. Substituting these values in Eq. (12) and considering initial velocity $v_0 = 0$ the equation we get to update the follower salps is:

$$k_j^i = \frac{1}{2}(k_j^i + k_j^{i-1}) \tag{13}$$

Using Eqs. (10) and (13), we can update the leader and followers respectively in SSO.

3.3 Adaptive β-Hill Climbing

Aβ-HC [3] is a local search algorithm which is an adaptive version of β Hill Climbing [2], which is, actually an improved version of Hill Climbing meta-heuristic algorithm. One of the main drawbacks of the Hill Climbing algorithm is that it gets stuck in local optima. To counter this drawback, a new improved version of the existing algorithm was proposed called β-Hill Climbing. For a given solution $\Upsilon = (r_1, r_2, r_3, ..., r_n)$, β-Hill Climbing iteratively generates a better solution $\Upsilon'' = (r_1'', r_2'', r_3'', ..., r_n'')$ which is based on two operators: N-operator (neighbourhood operator) and β-operator. The N-operator first choses a random neighbour $\Upsilon' = (r_1', r_2', r_3', ..., r_n')$, of the solution Υ, which is defined by the following equation:

$$r_i' = r_i \pm U(0,1) * N \tag{14}$$

where i is integer randomly chosen between $[1, D]$, D is the dimension of the given problem, N is the maximum distance between current solution and its neighbour. The new solution r_n'' is either chosen from the above solution or is randomly chosen from the given probability value $\beta \in [0, 1]$.

$$r_i'' = \begin{cases} r_r, & \text{if } rnd \leq \beta \\ r_i', & else \end{cases} \tag{15}$$

where rnd a random number between $[0, 1]$, and r_r is a random number within the range of dimension of the problem.

Overall, β-Hill Climbing works fine but its output depends entirely on the values of N-operator and β-operator. Tuning of this hyperparameters require excessive computation power and time. To avoid tuning of hyperparameter, new model was proposed called Aβ-HC where N-operator and β-operator were defined as a function of iteration number. $N(t)$is value of N in t^{th} iteration. The value of $N(t)$ is defined as:

$$N(t) = 1 - \frac{t^{\frac{1}{H}}}{MaxItr^{\frac{1}{H}}} \tag{16}$$

where $MaxItr$ is total number of iterations, and H is a constant. The details of this calculations is present in [4].

The value of β in the tth iteration is denoted as $\beta(t)$ within a range of $[\beta_{min}, \beta_{max}]$. The equation is defined as:

$$\beta(t) = \beta_{min} + (\beta_{max} - \beta_{min}) * \frac{t}{MaxItr} \tag{17}$$

The value is updated based on the condition given in Eq. (15).

3.4   Proposed Method: SSO-AβHC

As discussed earlier, the convergence at local optima is one of the issues that troubles SSO. Swarm followers follow their leader, and there are chances that the leader may get attracted to some solution too rapidly, without sufficiently exploring the search space. This embedded drawback cannot be simply solved by increasing number of search agents (salps) or number of iterations, but local search techniques have proven to be of help in such scenarios. Its whole idea is to let a solution make improvements by searching its neighbouring solutions. In this paper, our proposed algorithm targets to improve the behaviour of SSO using AβHC, by searching the neighbourhood for better optimum solutions, rather than changing the updating mechanism of SSO. The use of AβHC is to target the improvement of exploitation abilities of followers as, it is the followers that have the largest impact on the convergence ability of solutions towards global optimum. This integration adds more strength to its exploitation ability and stops it from converging at local optima. The detailed framework of the proposed algorithm is explained in Fig. 1.

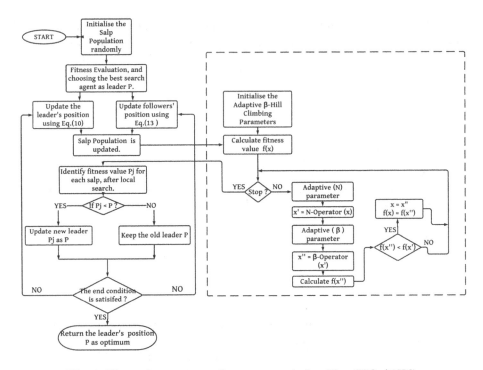

Fig. 1. The main structure of our proposed algorithm SSO-AβHC.

First, we define the parameters and generate population representing set of candidate solutions according to the given problem. Then performance of each solution is evaluated according to fitness function, the best candidate solution is selected and Local Search is performed on all the candidate solutions. Alongside, best salp among these population is set as F. Over these, the main loop is applied on all of these salps to update their positions based on Eqs. (12) and (13), and AβHC is then applied over the population to check and find better solution than the current one. At the end of every iteration of main loop, if AβHC has found any improved solutions in the nearby neighbourhood, it is updated as candidate solution. At the end, improved SSO returns the best solution F.

To get the best possible result, we need to tune our hyperparameters (A, γ) and for this purpose we use our proposed SSO-AβHC. This model helps us to find the best possible solution without getting stuck in local optima. The cost function used here is Mean Squared Error (MSE), which measures the efficiency of the model. In each iteration of our proposed model, LSSVM with "RBF" kernel is applied on solutions provided by the optimizer on training dataset, and MSE is calculated. SSO after total exploitation of search space and enhancement by AβHC algorithm, returns us with best hyperparameters to be fitted to LSSVM.

4 Results and Analysis

4.1 Dataset Description

The stock market dataset features include High, Low, Open, Close, Volume and Adj. Close. Using these features, we pre-process them and create a new set of features. These new features or technical indicators carry the trend details better than raw data and help to gain better results. The datasets used are the historical stock prices of four companies namely Adobe, Tesla, Apple and ExxonMobil. The period under consideration is from 01-01-2016 to 06-07-2020.

The technical indicators calculated on the raw dataset are:

Money Flow Index (MFI): It is a momentum indicator that measures the flow of money into and out of a security over a specified period of time. It is related to the Relative Strength Index (RSI) but incorporates volume, whereas the RSI only considers price. This indicator is also known as volume-weighted RSI.

$$MoneyFlowIndex(MFI) = 100 - \frac{100}{1 + MoneyFlowRatio} \tag{18}$$

where:

$$MoneyFlowRatio = \frac{Period\,of\,PositiveFlow}{Period\,of\,NegativeFlow} \tag{19}$$

$$TypicalPrice = \frac{High + Low + Close}{3} \tag{20}$$

Exponential Moving Average (EMA): This indicator gives exponential moving average of a field over a range of period where more recent values are given more weight compared to the older values.

$$EMA = [\alpha * TClose] + [1 - \alpha * YEMA] \tag{21}$$

where T is Today's close and Y is Yesterday's EMA.

Relative Strength Index (RSI): It is a momentum oscillator that measures the speed and change of price movements to evaluate overbought or oversold conditions in the price of a stock or other asset.

$$RSI = 100 - \frac{100}{1 + \frac{AverageGain}{AverageLoss}} \tag{22}$$

Moving Average Convergence Divergence (MACD): The MACD turns two trend-following indicators, moving averages, into a momentum oscillator by subtracting the longer moving average from the shorter one. As a result, the MACD offers the best of both worlds: trend following and momentum.

$$MACD = 0.075 * EMA(CP)(A) - 0.15 * EMA(CP)(B) \qquad (23)$$

$$SignalLine = 0.2 * EMAofMACD \qquad (24)$$

where EMA(CP)(A) and EMA(CP)(B) are the long term and short term EMA of Closing Price.

Stochastic Oscillator (SO): It is a momentum indicator that shows the location of the close relative to the high-low range over a set number of periods.

$$\%K = \left(\frac{C - L}{H - L}\right) * 100 \qquad (25)$$

where:
C = The most recent closing price
H = The highest price traded during the look-back period
L = The lowest price traded during the look-back period

4.2 Experiment Setup

The dataset is divided into two sets, 75% of which are used as the training set and the remaining data are used for validation.

The proposed algorithm is compared to some standard meta-heuristic algorithms, which are, SSO based LSSVM, ABC based LSSVM, GA based LSSVM, BOA based LSSVM and PSO based LSSVM. The predictions made by LSSVM represented Close Price for day $t + 7$ with respect to Close Price for day t. The metric used to evaluate the performance of the model is MSE.

$$MSE = \frac{1}{N} \sum_{j=1}^{N} (y_j - f_j)^2 \qquad (26)$$

where y_j and f_j denote the actual and predicted values for the j_{th} data point, respectively and N is the number of forecasting days.

5-fold cross validation is used and the average value during all runs is taken to evaluate the MSE. In order to facilitate comparative study between different optimizers, the range of parameter search space is kept constant at $[0.002, 500]$ for both the parameters. In our experiment, the number of search agents is taken to be 20 and number of iterations is 30. The computations are carried out using Python3 and graphs are plotted using Matplotlib on Google Colaboratory.

4.3 Results

Figure 2 provides a comparison of forecast of the validation data for the selected stocks between our proposed algorithm and other standard algorithms. An analysis of the model forecasts shows that the SSO-AβHC is consistently one of best performers among other algorithms in terms of prediction accuracy.

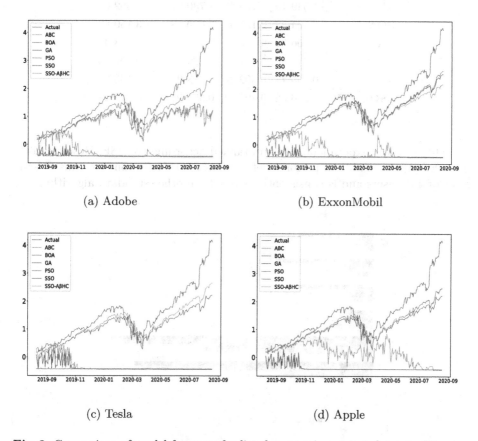

(a) Adobe   (b) ExxonMobil

(c) Tesla   (d) Apple

Fig. 2. Comparison of model forecasts for listed companies on test datasets. Here, x-axis represents time period for our test data and y-axis represents the scaled stock market prices during the time period

Figure 2c represents results of using our proposed model on "Tesla" dataset and it can be observed that SSO-AβHC is most close to the actual curve and is able to predict the stock prices with better accuracy. A consistent improvement from base optimizer, i.e. SSO is observed. A common issue encountered with some other optimizers is that the parameters returned by those have a tendency to overfit on training data, and hence, failed to generalise on the validation set, which is clearly visible in Fig. 4. Our proposed model is able to overcome this drawback and is also able to capture the sudden fluctuations in the time-series, which is evident from Fig. 2b and Fig. 2d.

Table 1. Comparison of the SSO-AβHC with other methods in terms of MSE.

	Adobe	Apple	ExxonMobil	Tesla
ABC	1.549 19	1.125 50	2.780 97	2.862 09
BOA	2.004 42	2.129 42	3.000 18	3.150 82
GA	0.506 32	0.472 53	0.339 05	0.328 45
PSO	0.271 80	0.301 65	0.409 18	0.897 23
SSO	0.255 73	0.302 48	0.418 94	1.165 00
SSO-AβHC	0.246 52	0.301 71	0.398 91	0.897 24

Table 1 shows experimental results ranked according to MSE. Results show that SSO-AβHC is able to perform better than SSO. It also outperforms GA in 2 out of 4 datasets and is consistently better than other standard algorithms.

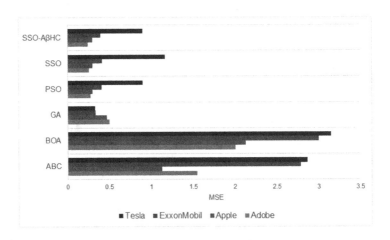

Fig. 3. Bar plot of MSEs of various methods for different datasets

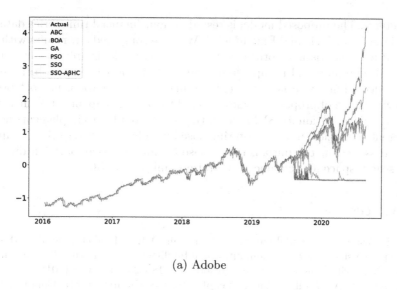

(a) Adobe

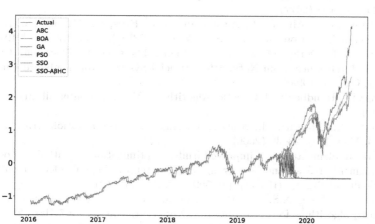

(b) Tesla

Fig. 4. Comparison of model forecasts for a) Adobe b) Apple on whole dataset, showing overfitting tendency of other performers. Here, x-axis represents time period for our test data and y-axis represents the scaled stock market prices during the time period

5   Conclusion and Future Research

This paper presents a machine learning model which is an implementation of SSO with a local search technique, called AβHC, and LSSVM for predicting 7 day-ahead trends in the stock market. The meta-heuristic is used to tune the hyper-parameters of LSSVM namely, penalty factor A and RBF kernel function width parameter γ. The proposed model is tested on four financial time series datasets of Apple, Adobe, Tesla and ExxonMobil. We have compared our results with five standard meta-heuristic algorithms. The proposed model is able to converge to the global minimum and is capable to overcome the over-fitting problem found in other algorithms, especially encountered in case of fluctuations in stock prices. The performance of proposed model is found to be more capable and efficient in parameter optimization for SVM. For future work, we plan to implement the use of different strategies such as clustering based population initialization, adaptive randomness, etc. at the initialization phase to improve its population diversity in the search space and enhance exploration abilities of SSO.

References

1. Abdel-Basset, M., Abdel-Fatah, L., Sangaiah, A.K.: Metaheuristic algorithms: a comprehensive review. In: Computational Intelligence For Multimedia Big Data on the Cloud with Engineering Applications, pp. 185–231. Elsevier (2018)
2. Al-Betar, M.A.: β-hill climbing: an exploratory local search. Neural Comput. Appl. **28**(1), 153–168 (2017)
3. Al-Betar, M.A., Aljarah, I., Awadallah, M.A., Faris, H., Mirjalili, S.: Adaptive β-hill climbing for optimization. Soft Comput. **23**(24), 13489–13512 (2019)
4. Bonabeau, E., Dorigo, M., Marco, D.D.R.D.F., Theraulaz, G., Théraulaz, G., et al.: Swarm Intelligence: from Natural to Artificial Systems. vol. 1. Oxford University Press, Oxford (1999)
5. Davis, L.: Handbook of Genetic Algorithms. VNR computer library, Samford (1991)
6. Dorigo, M., Birattari, M., Stutzle, T.: Ant colony optimization. IEEE comput. Intell. Mag. **1**(4), 28–39 (2006)
7. Du, H.: Implementation of improved fruit fly optimization algorithm in stock market segment analysis and forecasting. In: 2019 International Conference on Robots & Intelligent System (ICRIS), pp. 509–512. IEEE (2019)
8. Fister Jr, I., Yang, X.S., Fister, I., Brest, J., Fister, D.: A brief review of nature-inspired algorithms for optimization. arXiv preprint arXiv:1307.4186 (2013)
9. Gendreau, M., Potvin, J.Y.: Metaheuristics in combinatorial optimization. Ann. Oper. Res. **140**(1), 189–213 (2005)
10. Ghanbari, M., Arian, H.: Forecasting stock market with support vector regression and butterfly optimization algorithm. arXiv preprint arXiv:1905.11462 (2019)
11. Ghosh, K.K., Ahmed, S., Singh, P.K., Geem, Z.W., Sarkar, R.: Improved binary sailfish optimizer based on adaptive β-hill climbing for feature selection. IEEE Access **8**, 83548–83560 (2020)
12. Hegazy, O., Soliman, O.S., Salam, M.A.: Lssvm-abc algorithm for stock price prediction. arXiv preprint arXiv:1402.6366 (2014)
13. Hegazy, O., Soliman, O.S., Salam, M.A.: Comparative study between FPA, BA, MCS, ABC, and PSO algorithms in training and optimizing of LS-SVM for stock market prediction. Int. J. Adv. Comput. Res. **5**(18), 35–45 (2015)
14. Heidari, A.A., Mirjalili, S., Faris, H., Aljarah, I., Mafarja, M., Chen, H.: Harris hawks optimization: algorithm and applications. Fut. Gener. Comput. Syst. **97**, 849–872 (2019)

15. Hu, H., Zhang, L., Yan, H., Bai, Y., Wang, P.: Denoising and baseline drift removal method of mems hydrophone signal based on VMD and wavelet threshold processing. IEEE Access **7**, 59913–59922 (2019)
16. Karaboga, D., Basturk, B.: A powerful and efficient algorithm for numerical function optimization: artificial bee colony (abc) algorithm. J. Global Optim. **39**(3), 459–471 (2007). https://doi.org/10.1007/s10898-007-9149-x
17. Kaveh, A., Khayatazad, M.: A new meta-heuristic method: ray optimization. Comput. Struct. **112**, 283–294 (2012)
18. Kennedy, J., Eberhart, R.: Particle swarm optimization. In: Proceedings of ICNN 1995-International Conference on Neural Networks, vol. 4, pp. 1942–1948. IEEE (1995)
19. Kirkpatrick, S., Gelatt, C.D., Vecchi, M.P.: Optimization by simulated annealing. Science **220**(4598), 671–680 (1983)
20. Mirjalili, S., Gandomi, A.H., Mirjalili, S.Z., Saremi, S., Faris, H., Mirjalili, S.M.: Salp swarm algorithm: a bio-inspired optimizer for engineering design problems. Adv. Eng. Softw. **114**, 163–191 (2017)
21. Mirjalili, S., Mirjalili, S.M., Hatamlou, A.: Multi-verse optimizer: a nature-inspired algorithm for global optimization. Neural Comput. Appl. **27**(2), 495–513 (2016)
22. Nair, B.B., Mohandas, V., Sakthivel, N.: A genetic algorithm optimized decision tree-SVM based stock market trend prediction system. Int. J. Comput. Sci. Eng. **2**(9), 2981–2988 (2010)
23. Nematollahi, A.F., Rahiminejad, A., Vahidi, B.: A novel meta-heuristic optimization method based on golden ratio in nature. Soft Comput. **24**(2), 1117–1151 (2020)
24. Oh, I.S., Lee, J.S., Moon, B.R.: Hybrid genetic algorithms for feature selection. IEEE Trans. Pattern Anal. Mach. Intell. **26**(11), 1424–1437 (2004)
25. Rashedi, E., Nezamabadi-Pour, H., Saryazdi, S.: GSA: a gravitational search algorithm. Inf. Sci. **179**(13), 2232–2248 (2009)
26. Seidy, E.E.: A new particle swarm optimization based stock market prediction technique. Int. J. Adv. Comput. Sci. Appl. **7**(2), 322–327 (2016)
27. Suykens, J.A., Vandewalle, J.: Least squares support vector machine classifiers. Neural Process. Lett. **9**(3), 293–300 (1999)
28. Talbi, E.G.: A taxonomy of hybrid metaheuristics. J. Heuristics **8**(5), 541–564 (2002)
29. Vapnik, V.N.: Introduction: four periods in the research of the learning problem. In: The Nature of Statistical Learning Theory, pp. 1–15. Springer (2000). https://doi.org/10.1007/978-1-4757-3264-1_1
30. Wolpert, D.H., Macready, W.G.: No free lunch theorems for optimization. IEEE Trans. Evol. Comput. **1**(1), 67–82 (1997)
31. Yang, X.-S.: Firefly algorithms for multimodal optimization. In: Watanabe, O., Zeugmann, T. (eds.) SAGA 2009. LNCS, vol. 5792, pp. 169–178. Springer, Heidelberg (2009). https://doi.org/10.1007/978-3-642-04944-6_14

Data Driven Methods for Finding Pattern Anomalies in Food Safety

S. Anantha Krishna, Amal Soman, and Manjusha Nair[✉]

Department of Computer Science and Applications, Amrita Vishwa
Vidyapeetham, Amritapuri, Kollam, India
manjushanair@am.amrita.edu

Abstract. The indigenous part of all living organisms in the world is food. As the world population increases, the production and consumption of food also increases. Since the population progresses in a rapid manner, the productivity of the food materials may not be sufficient for feeding all the people in the world. There rises the cause of food adulteration and food fraud. Adulteration is the process of adding a foreign substance to the food material which affects the natural quality of the food. As the amount of adulterants increases, the toxicity also increases. Machine learning techniques has been used previously to auto-mate the prediction of food adulteration under normal scenarios. In this paper, we use different machine learning technique for finding food adulteration from milk data sets. This paper surveys the different concepts used in automating the detection of food adulteration and discusses the experimental results obtained by applying machine learning algorithms like Naive Bayes, Support Vector Machine (SVM), K-Nearest Neighbor (KNN), Artificial Neural networks (ANN), Linear Regression, and Ensemble methods. The accuracy of the models ranged from 79% to 89%. Ensemble method outperformed other algorithms with an accuracy of 89% and Linear Regression showed least accuracy of 79%. Artificial Neural networks showed an accuracy of almost 87%. SVM and Naïve Bayes showed accuracy 84% and 80% respectively.

Keywords: Machine learning · Food safety · Food fraud · Adulteration · Neural networks

1 Introduction

There has been a dramatic change in the food production and consumption worldwide. According to the High-level Expert forum, the world in the 21st century is not very capable of mapping the food production to food consumption, as the labor force and other natural resources are not as adequate. The demand for cereals is expected to grow by over 3 billion tons in the year 2050 in which the current need is 2.1 billion tons [1]. From these, it is clear that the production cannot meet the requirement. Hence the use of adulterants is raised significantly over the past few years. Adulteration in food mostly happens due to the unhygienic or unhealthy treatment of food items during production, storage or delivery, which is done mainly for financial benefits. Unhealthy

© Springer Nature Singapore Pte Ltd. 2021
S. M. Thampi et al. (Eds.): SoMMA 2020, CCIS 1366, pp. 122–130, 2021.
https://doi.org/10.1007/978-981-16-0419-5_10

food consumption results in an unhealthy civilization, which is a main threat in the current century for the world to face.

There has been a number of studies initiated on food safety through improved analytic and machine learning tools in detection of adulteration in food materials. There were several machine learning methods applied in previous studies, including Artificial Neural Networks (ANN), Time series analysis, SVM, Fuzzy logic etc. [2]. The main application of Artificial Neural Network was on prediction and fraud detection. It can be also seen that 90% of the tools were used to build models based on yield, concentration and quantity of food safety parameters. The current study uses similar machine learning tools to predict the presence of foreign substance in milk [3].

Machine learning algorithms like PCA, Naïve Bayes, K-nearest neighbor, Linear Discriminate Analysis, Decision Tree, ANN and Support vector machines were used previously for quality control of olive oil [4]. Similar algorithms were used previously to predict drug likeliness in compounds [5]. In the studies conducted in [4], there were two methodologies involved in the process and Artificial Neural Network (ANN) had the highest accuracy of 65.83% for the test data while Naïve Bayes had the lowest accuracy of 45.83% among the algorithms, using the first method. The test results of the second method told a different story as Naïve Bayes produced the highest accuracy with 70.83% and Linear Discriminate Analysis (LDA) had the lowest accuracy with 56.67%. When the prediction of food fraud was done using the Bayesian Network (BN) modelling approach [2], accuracy of prediction was increased to 91%. A food fraud early warning system using European Media Monitor (EMM) was used in the study along with a media monitoring system called MedISys. A similar text classification method was used to extract data from Wikipedia texts and articles in another study [6]. They used natural language processing and recurrent neural networks to establish an automated system that helped to detect the adulteration in food.

Deep learning and ensemble methods were used previously to find the adulteration in milk samples [3]. In adulteration, the milk industry tops the market, making milk and milk products as one of the highly adulterated foods. The study used Fourier Transformed Infrared Spectroscopy (FTIR) for accessing the milk quality by producing the spectral data on the samples. The compositional information is fed into the machine learning algorithms-neural networks and decision trees. The goal of the project was to perform a binary classification of raw milk and adulterated milk, and also a multi class classification of predicting the ingredient present in the adulterated sample. Using ensemble machine learning methods and Convolutional Neural Networks (CNN), the system showed an accuracy of 98.67% which was much higher than the classical learning methods in the dairy industry. In the current study, we are using six machine learning algorithms, namely, Naive Bayes, Support Vector Machines (SVM), Artificial Neural Networks (ANN), K-Nearest Neighbor (KNN), Linear Regression, and Ensemble methods to predict the presence of adulterants from milk data set.

2 Machine Learning Algorithms Used

Six different machine learning algorithms, as detailed below (Sect. 2.1 to 2.6), are used in this study. WEKA tool is used to get the statistical output of the data and helps in inspecting the data. Initially it is dome in WEKA and later the algorithms are implemented using Python language.

2.1 Naive Bayes

The Bayes classifiers are used widely in the food sectors, food supply chain, food fraud and in health sectors [7–10]. The Naive Bayes classifier follows probabilistic machine learning approaches using Bayes theorem, assuming strong, or naive, independence between the features in the feature vector. The probabilities are estimated as,

$$P(Y|X_1, X_2, \ldots X_n) = \frac{P(X_1|Y)P(X_2|Y)\ldots P(X_n|Y)P(Y)}{P(X_1).P(X_2)\ldots P(X_n)} \quad (1)$$

$P(Y|X_i)$: Posterior Probability
$P(Y)$: Prior probability of the class variable
$P(X_i|Y)$: Likelihood
$P(X_i)$: Predictor Prior Probability

This type of classifiers are proved to be successful in many real world applications with lesser training data set, irrespective of the oversimplification and assumptions of the variables. It is also defined as a classification technique based on Bayes Theorem with the assumption of the independence among the predictors. The Bayes classifiers assume the presence of a specific feature in a class is unrelated to the presence of any other feature. This model is actually easy to build and is used mostly in larger dataset.

2.2 Support Vector Machines

The Support Vector Machines (SVMs) are supervised, non-probabilistic, binary learning models with related learning algorithms that analyses data for classification purpose mostly [11, 12]. It is a discriminative classifier formally defined by a separating hyperplane. There are different hyperplanes that can classify the data, choosing the best hyperplane is the one that can distinguish the two classes with a wide separation. These created hyperplanes are used for the classification and regression. Linear and non-linear classifiers are used for transforming the feature space. The SVMs are used to solve some real-world problems like text categorization, classification of images and it is being applied in the biological and other sciences. SVMs are also used in rice yield predictions in India [13]. The machine learning technique is now widely used for the prediction of crop yield under different climate scenarios. SVM uses classification algorithm for two-group classification problems. After giving the SVM model sets of the labelled training data for reach category, they will be able to categorize new text.

2.3   Artificial Neural Network

Artificial Neural Networks are an advanced machine learning technique that works on the principle of neurons of the brain [14]. A neuron gets its input from other neurons through the synapses and dendrites and the processed information is transmitted from the soma to the next level of neurons through axons [15]. Analogues to that, there are three different layers in a simple neural network: the input layer, hidden layers and the output layer. The perceptron in the neural network receives multiple input values, say feature values of the dataset. The weighted sum of all inputs after processed by an activation function, is fed to the output layer of the neural network. Given a unit j in a hidden or output layer, the net input, I_j, to unit θj is

$$I_j = w_{ij}O_j + \theta_j \tag{2}$$

where, w_{ij} = weight of connection from unit i in the previous layer to unit j in the hidden layer, O_j = i[th] output from previous layer and θ_j = bias of unit.

ANN is the foundation of artificial intelligence which solves the problems which prove to be difficult for human or statistical standards. It also has the self-learning capabilities which allows them to get better result as more data becomes available. An ANN has a number of artificial neurons called the processing unit, which are interconnected by the nodes and these processing units are made up of input and output units.

2.4   K-Nearest Neighbor

K-Nearest neighbor algorithm is a powerful machine learning technique that is used in pattern recognition for classification and regression. It is a non-parametric method [16]. In both cases of classification and regression the input set contains K closest training examples which is placed in the feature space with the basic assumption that similar data points in the feature space are close to each other. The value of K is initialized to the chosen number of neighbors and the distance between the test data and each row of training data, is calculated. From the ordered and sorted collection of K such distances, the most frequent class is estimated as the resulting class in the algorithm. This supervised, non-parametric machine learning technique, irrespective of its simplicity, finds wide applications in the field of machine learning. Even though KNN can be used for both classification and regression predictive problems, it is more widely used in the classification problem in the industry. This algorithm fairs around all parameters of consideration and it is commonly used for its ease of interpretation and low calculation time.

2.5 Linear Regression

Regression is a term used for describing the models that examines the variable's inter-relationship. This model learns one-to-one relationships among dependent variables and one or more independent variables. If one independent variable is present, it is called simple linear regression and if more than one independent variables are present, it is referred to as multiple linear regression [17]. The main purpose of the linear regression is to predict the relationship between input variables (X) and output variables (Y).

The simple linear regression model is represented as:

$$Y = \beta_0 + \beta_1 X + \in \tag{3}$$

where β values are the bias coefficients and $\in$ represents the error term in the model. In a linear regression model for classification, the values of the coefficients are estimated from data. Then the learned model is used for predictions.

2.6 Ensemble Learning

We have discussed several machine learning methods that are used to build and predict the models. Apart from that learning model's discussed above, Ensemble method is a technique which combines multiple base models which can produce an optimal single predictive model [18]. The advantage of the ensemble learning mechanism is that the resultant classifier produces more accurate predictions than any of the single classifier used in the ensemble learning. Bagging and Bboosting methods are the two latest and most commonly used ensemble methods [19]. Bagging (Bootstrap Aggregating) works on the principle of attaining a number of base learners from bootstrap sample and trains that base learners. The bootstrap sample is generated from the training data set by sub sampling them with replacement. Boosting deals with the utilization of set of algorithms with each of its weighted average for making the weak learners stronger. Unlike the bagging mechanism, boosting builds the model with further combination of features: like after running a model it finds out what feature needs to be run next for better classification.

2.7 Dataset

This study used machine learning techniques on spectral data of milk samples, downloaded from public repository [3]. The data set contained milk samples of 1000 instances with information on different properties of milk such as whether it is raw milk, whether it contains lactose, milk urea, fat, protein, free fatty acid, solid content in the milk, somatic cell counting, casein content; freezing point of the milk, and Qvalue which shows the quality of milk. The data set is split into two parts in which the training set contained 66% of the original data and the rest is used for testing the algorithms. The dataset was carefully examined and arranged in a manner that it contains 14 parameters and these are the key factors in classifying the milk sample as raw or contaminated. The algorithms we prescribed correlates these values form the dataset and perform the analysis through training and testing the data. After the dataset is trained with parameters it then tests the data and produces the final result which shows the instances having contaminants.

3 Results and Discussion

3.1 Result Evaluation

The possible classifications of the instances were converted into 4 categories:

TP (True Positive): Both condition and prediction are true.
TN (True Negative): Both condition and prediction are false.
FP (False Positive): Here the condition is false but the prediction is true.
FN (False Negative): Here the condition is true but prediction is false.

These values are represented as a confusion matrix to compare the actual observed value to the predicted value. The true positive and true negative fields, placed on the diagonal of the table showed the correct predictions that the algorithm had made. Accuracy is the most common metric used in the result and it is formulated as:

$$Accuracy = (TP + TN)/(TP + FP + FN + TN) \tag{4}$$

Sensitivity and specificity are the other two metrics used here. Sensitivity is also called recall and specificity is also known as precision. Sensitivity deals with the percentage of correctly classified instances and specificity is the percentage of incorrectly classified instances. Sensitivity measures the proportion of actual positives correctly classified as positive. Specificity measures the exactness of the models and measures the proportion of actual negatives correctly classified as negatives.

$$Sensitivity \ or \ Recall = TP/(TP + FN) \tag{5}$$

$$Specificity \ or \ Precision = TP/(TP + FP) \tag{6}$$

3.2 Accuracy Estimates of the Algorithms

The accuracy of the models ranged from 79% to 89% (Fig. 1). Ensemble method outperformed other algorithms with an accuracy of 89% and Linear Regression with least accuracy of 79%. Artificial Neural networks showed an accuracy of almost 87%. SVM and Naïve Bayes showed accuracy 84% and 80% respectively. Thus it has been concluded that ensemble methods performed better than other classification methods used.

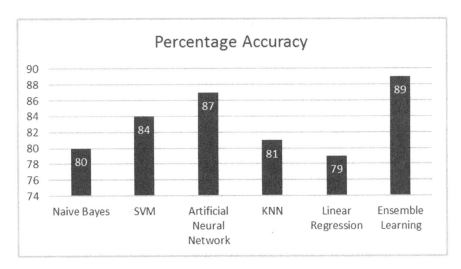

Fig. 1. Accuracy of prediction of different algorithms. Among all methods used, the Ensemble method showed highest accuracy of prediction (89%) and Linear regression showed the lowest (79%).

3.3   Sensitivity and Specificity

Since accuracy of a machine learning algorithm shows the number of correctly predicted instances from all the predictions made, and is not the only measure to evaluate the performance of algorithms, two other measures like sensitivity (recall) and specificity (precision) were also estimated from the data set and plotted (Fig. 2). Sensitivity was calculated to be maximum for ANN (84.14%) and minimum for KNN (81.37%) Specificity was calculated to the maximum for Naïve Bayes model (88.57%) and minimum for linear regression (83.81%).

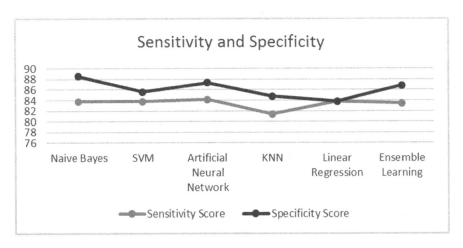

Fig. 2.   Sensitivity and specificity scores

4   Conclusion

In this paper, we used different machine learning algorithms to classify the adulterated milk data set. The Classification accuracies of the algorithms ranged from 79% to 89%, the highest being reported in the Ensemble method. The current Ensemble methods can be further improved using Random Forest and Gradient boosting regressing trees. Only binary classification is used in the models and an extended study can be used to predict the adulterant present in the milk sample [20]. Also less attention was given in this study to capture the actual data set from a region of interest or subject of interest. Future studies should also focus on how automated techniques can be used for optimal utilization of resources, in food industry. Safety can be monitored more rigorously using automated techniques such as machine learning combined with data analytics in cloud computing and block chain technologies.

References

1. Executive Summary: How to Feed the World in 2050, pp. 1–35. https://www.fao.org/
2. Bouzembrak, Y., Marvin, H.: Development of early warning systems to detect, predict and assess food fraud (2018)
3. Neto, H.A., Tavares, W.L.F., Ribeiro, D.C.S.Z., Alves, R.C.O., Leorges, M., Campos, S.V. A.: On the utilization of deep and ensemble learning to detect milk adulteration. BioData Min. **12**, 1–13 (2019)
4. Ordukaya, E., Karlik, B.: Quality control of olive oils using machine learning and electronic nose. J. Food Qual. **2017**, 1–7 (2017)
5. Ani, R., Manohar, R., Anil, G., Deepa, O.S.: Virtual screening of drug likeness using tree based ensemble classifier. Biomed. Pharmacol. J. **11**(3), 1513–1519 (2018)
6. Gou, Y.: Food adulteration detection using neural network (2016)
7. Smith, J.Q., Barons, M.J., Zhong, X.: Bayesian Networks for Food Security What and Why Bayesian Networks? Influence Diagram, no. 2009 (2013)
8. Kubade, H.M.: The overview of Bayes classification methods. Int. J. Trend Sci. Res. Dev. (IJTSRD) **2**, 2801–2802 (2018)
9. Stein, A.: Bayesian networks and food security – an introduction, no. 1996, pp. 107–116 (2001)
10. Jha, K., Doshi, A., Patel, P., Shah, M.: A comprehensive review on automation in agriculture using artificial intelligence. Artif. Intell. Agric. **2**, 1–2 (2019)
11. Kavitha, K.R., Syamili Rajendran, G., Varsha, J.: A correlation based SVM-recursive multiple feature elimination classifier for breast cancer disease using microarray. In: 2016 International Conference on Advances in Computing, Communications and Informatics (ICACCI) (2016)
12. Hastie, T., Tibshirani, R., Friedman, J.: The Elements of Statistical Learning: Data Mining, Inference, and Prediction, 2nd edn. Springer, New York (2008). p. 134
13. Armstrong, J.: Rice crop yield prediction in India using support vector machines. In: 2016 13th International Joint Conference on Computer Science and Software Engineering, no. 2010, pp. 1–5 (2016)
14. Hopfield, J.J.: Neural networks and physical systems with emergent collective computational abilities. Proc. Natl. Acad. Sci. U.S.A. **79**(8), 2554–2558 (1982)

15. Nair, M., Surya, S., Kumar, R.S., Nair, B., Diwakar, S.: Efficient simulations of spiking neurons on parallel and distributed platforms: towards large-scale modeling in computational neuroscience. In: 2015 IEEE Recent Advances in Intelligent Computational Systems, RAICS (2015)
16. Altman, N.S.: An introduction to kernel and nearest-neighbor nonparametric regression. Am. Stat. **46**(3), 175–185 (1992)
17. Yan, X.: Linear Regression Analysis: Theory and Computing, pp. 1–2. World Scientific, Singapore (2009)
18. Dietterich, T.G.: Ensemble methods in machine learning (1990)
19. Opitz, D., Maclin, R.: Popular ensemble methods: an empirical study. J. Artif. Intell. Res. **11**, 169–198 (1999)
20. Menon, R., Aswathi, P.: Document classification with hierarchically structured dictionaries . In: Berretti, S., Thampi, S.M., Dasgupta, S. (eds.) Intelligent Systems Technologies and Applications. AISC, vol. 385, pp. 387–397. Springer, Cham (2016). https://doi.org/10.1007/978-3-319-23258-4_34

Exam Seating Allocation to Prevent Malpractice Using Genetic Multi-optimization Algorithm

Madhav M. Kashyap[(✉)], S. Thejas[(✉)], C. G. Gaurav[(✉)], and K. S. Srinivas[(✉)]

Department of Computer Science and Engineering, PES University,
Bengaluru, Karnataka, India
madhavkashyap99@gmail.com, s.thejas99@gmail.com,
officialgauravcg492@gmail.com, srinivasks@pes.edu

Abstract. Despite unceasing debate about it's pros and cons, exams and standardized testing have emerged as the main mode of evaluation and comparison in our increasingly competitive world. Inevitably, some examinees attempt to illegally gain an unfair advantage over other candidates by indulging in cheating and malpractice. Even a single case of examination malpractice can destroy an Examination body's credibility and even lead to costly and time-consuming legal proceedings.

Our paper attempts to strategically allot examinees in specific seats and rooms, such as to mitigate the overall probability of malpractice. It involves examining multiple crucial factors such as subject similarity, distancing between examinees, and human field of vision to find the most optimal seating arrangement. We have exploited the property of Evolutionary Genetic Algorithms to find globally optimal or close to optimal solutions in an efficient time for this otherwise NP-complete permutation problem.

Keywords: Evolutionary computing · Genetic algorithm · Metaheuristic · Combinatorics · Permutation · Seating · Arrangement · NP hard · NP complete

1 Introduction

The main advantage of the examination system is that it provides a fair and uniform platform for all examinees to succeed. However this trust in fairness is shattered when examinees engage in malpractice in order to illegally get ahead of their peers. The most common cheating methods involved looking at other student's exam papers, arranging for someone else to take the exam, using "cheat-sheets" or other aids, and obtaining advance copies of the exam [1]. This research paper focuses on reducing/eliminating the possibility of cheating via looking at other examinee's answer scripts. This method of cheating is easily thwarted by

Supported by PES University.

a generalized seating algorithm, that can be widely adopted by any examination body. Whereas preventing other malpractice methods require more physical inspection and external countermeasures out of our control.

There is some research done on exam hall seating arrangement. However these use simple geometrical arrangements and hard constraints in order to allocate seats. The methodology adopted by [2] allots same subject examinees into the same column allowing at least one column distance between two columns having same subject examinees. A seat allocation algorithm for wedding planners [3] uses a set of restrictive boolean hard constraints to allocate seats using graph theory. As the number of subjects and students become larger and complex, the number of hard constraints become too numerous and restrictive to manually set. Although these methodologies have the advantage of being computationally fast and easy to visualize, they do not specifically solve the problem of preventing malpractice by accounting factors affecting vulnerability to malpractice.

This research paper presents a novel examination seating allocation methodology that strategically places examinees of various subjects into specific rooms and seats so as to give the least chance for examinees to cheat by copying from other examinee's answer scripts. It considers the crucial factors facilitating chance of malpractice: subject similarity, distancing between examinees, and human field of vision. We approach it with evolutionary genetic algorithms for a number of reasons. This problem is a NP-complete permutation problem. The solution search space increases exponentially with the number of seats. Genetic algorithms have been proven to work exceedingly well in efficiently finding globally optimal/near optimal solutions to NP complete problems [4–6]. Multi-objective genetic algorithms [7] consider all the malpractice factors using soft constraints rather than restrictive hard constraints.

2   Algorithm

2.1   Approach to Multi Objective Optimization

There are 2 objectives the Genetic algorithm has to solve.

1. Objective 1: Ensure that examinees with similar subjects do not sit physically close to each other.
2. Objective 2: Prevent examinees with similar subjects from being in the field of vision of each other.

This constitutes a multi objective optimization problem. The situation is challenging since we have to solve both the objectives satisfactorily, even in cases where the objectives are in conflict relative to each other. Often, the optimization of all the objectives cannot coexist in the same solution. Hence, the multi objective problem can be stated as searching for the best compromise among all the required objectives. There are 3 major approaches to solve Multi Objective optimizations [7]:

- A posteriori approach: Aims to determine the shape of the whole Pareto front, and then let a Decision Maker decide which solution to retain. A pareto set is a set of good solutions none of which are best for all objectives. Decision making algorithms then help in choosing one solution in the pareto set that seems best suited.
- A priori approach: Preferences are given at the beginning of the search process. In Weighted sum method, weights are assigned to objectives signifying it's relative importance. In Lexicographic ordering method, objectives are ranked in the order of relative importance and a single optimization problem is solved for each objective ensuring that the solution obtained for more important objectives are not worsened. In Goal Programming, a target is set for each objective and the sum of deviations of each objective from its target is minimized.
- Interactive approach: Preferences are used interactively during the optimization process, requiring a large time investment from the Decision Maker algorithm.

The a priori approach is especially useful in situations where the algorithm designer already has a realistic idea about the importance and values of the objectives. In our problem we have a clear understanding of the relative priority of the 2 objectives specified. Another advantage of the a priori approach is that a posteriori approaches have to search through a much larger set of pareto solutions causing it to be much slower.

We approach the multi-objective problem using weighted sum method for a priori articulation of preferences [8]. This method entails selecting scalar weights w_i and creating a linear combination of the objective function values. The weights w_i are positive and directly proportional to the importance of the objective relative to other objectives. The composite linear combination objective function behaves as the fitness function, which we aim to maximize. where there are k objective functions $F_i(x)$ weighed by the scalar weights w_i. Literature [8] specifies some guidelines on using the weighted sum method:

1. Guideline 1: The value of a weight must be significant relative to its corresponding objective function.
2. Guideline 2: All objective functions should be transformed and normalized such that they have similar ranges.
3. Guideline 3: Well understood preferences between objective functions, must be articulated with positive unrestricted scalar weights whose magnitude is proportional to its preference.

2.2   Functions and Terms

Subject DisSimilarity Coefficient. The subject similarity coefficient is a measure of how much 2 subject are related to each other. Each subject pair has a separate subject similarity coefficient denoted as $SubjectSimilarity_{subject1, subject2}$, abbreviated as $SS_{subj1, subj2}$. The $SS_{subj1, subj2}$ is a floating number between 0 to 1. The higher the correlation between subjects, the higher the $SS_{subj1,subj2}$ magnitude.

The corresponding Subject Dissimilarity Coefficient is $SubjectDisSimilarity_{subject1,subject2}$, abbreviated as $SD_{subj1,subj2}$. The $SD_{subj1,subj2}$ is also a floating point number between 0 to 1 inclusive. The higher the correlation between subjects, the lower the $SD_{subj1,subj2}$ magnitude.

$$SD_{subj1,subj2} = 1 - SS_{subj1,subj2} \tag{1}$$

$SubjectDisSimilarity$ is symmetric, which means $SD_{subj1,subj2} = SD_{subj2,subj1}$

Distance Coefficient. The distance coefficient measures how physically distant a pair of students are with respect to each other. The $DistanceCoefficient_{seat1,seat2}$ is defined as the Euclidean distance between positions of $seat1$ and $seat2$ assuming the seats are arranged in a rectangular grid fashion, with the rows and columns being unit distance apart. It is abbreviated as $DC_{seat1,seat2}$ and is a floating point number. **seat1** and **seat2** are position vectors containing the x and y coordinates of the seat locations in a room.

$$DC_{seat1,seat2} = \sqrt{(seat1_x - seat2_x)^2 + (seat1_y - seat2_y)^2} \tag{2}$$

$$seat = \begin{bmatrix} seat_x \\ seat_y \end{bmatrix} \tag{3}$$

NonVisibility Coefficient. The Visual coefficient is a measure of how visible other examiness are with respect to a particular examinee according to the human field of view. This is important because, examinees find it easiest to engage in malpractice with an examinee directly in front of them, rather than those placed to their side or behind them. It is expressed as a floating point number. Visual acuity refers to the clarity of vision. It depends on factors such as sharpness of retinal focus, interpretative faculty of the brain and angle of view. Visual acuity tends to be more accurate when the target is presented more centrally to retina, and worsens when the target is further in the periphery of the retina. This phenomenon is called eccentricity and was proven by [9].

We have modelled this behaviour with a mathematical function that closely mimics the empirically obtained result graph. The angles having good vision have been widened to account for the fact that we can also rotate our head in the horizontal plane. The $VisualCoefficient_{seat1,seat2}$ is a continuous and differentiable function that is based on the Gaussian Normal distribution varying with parameter θ. θ refers to the visual angle in radians. The coefficient is abbreviated as VC_θ. It has a maximum value of 1 at $\theta = 0rad$. The value progressively becomes smaller towards both the positive and negative direction. It reaches a minimum value of 0.007192 at the points $\theta = -\pi rad$ and $\theta = \pi rad$. The higher the value of VC_θ, the higher the visual acuity and the higher is the chance for malpractice (Figs. 1 and 2).

$$VC_{seat1,seat2} = exp(-\frac{(\theta_{seat1,seat2})^2}{2}) \tag{4}$$

where $\theta_{seat1,seat2}$ is the angle difference between seat2 and the frontal direction with respect to seat1.

$$\theta_{seat1,seat2} = \arccos(\frac{(seat1 - seat2)}{\|seat1 - seat2\|} \cdot \binom{0}{1}) \tag{5}$$

The corresponding $NonVisibilityCoefficient_{seat1,seat2}$ is abbreviated as $NC_{seat1,seat2}$. The higher the value of $NC_{seat1,seat2}$, the lower the visual acuity and the lower is the chance for malpractice. It is defined as:

$$NCseat1, seat2 = 1 - VCseat1, seat2 \tag{6}$$

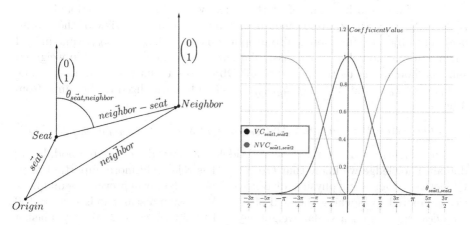

Fig. 1. Vector diagram to explain Eq. 5

Fig. 2. Vertical axis displays $VC_{seat1,seat2}$. Horizontal axis shows $\theta_{seat1,seat2}$ in radians

2.3   Fitness Function

The Fitness of a particular chromosome solution $Fitness_{chromosome}$ is defined as the average Fitness of each seat within the chromosome $Fitness_{seat}$:

$$Fitness_{chromosome} = \frac{\sum_{seat \in chromosome} Fitness_{seat}}{|chromosome|} \tag{7}$$

Where the Fitness of a seat $Fitness_{seat}$ is given by the minimum pairwise Fitness of the seat with each of it's neighboring seats $Fitness_{seat,neighbor}$.

$$Fitness_{seat} = min_{neighbor \in Neighborhood_{seat}}(Fitness_{seat,neighbor}) \tag{8}$$

Objective 1 ensures that examinees with similar subjects do not sit physically close to each other. Therefore the objective function is proportional to the $DC_{seat,neighbor}$ (maximized when distance between seat and neighbor is high). The objective function is also proportional to $SD_{seat,neighbor}$ (maximized when seat and neighbors have dissimilar subjects). Guideline 2 in weighted sum method needs us to normalize all Objectives to have similar range.

$SD_{seat,neighbor}$ already lies in range between 0 to 1. However, $DC_{seat,neighbor}$ ranges between minimum value 1 to maximum value of the room's diagonal length. This value is normalized to lie between 0 to 1 by dividing by room's diagonal length. The room's diagonal length is found by applying Pythagorean theorem to the number of columns and rows in the room.

$$Objective\ 1 \Rightarrow\ maximize\{\frac{DC_{seat,neighbor} \times SD_{seat,neighbor}}{\sqrt{room_{rows}^2 + room_{columns}^2}}\} \qquad (9)$$

Objective 2 prevents examinees with similar subjects from being in the field of vision of one another. Therefore the objective function is proportional to the $NC_{seat,neighbor}$ (maximized when neighbors not in field of view of the examinee). The objective function is also proportional to $SD_{seat,neighbor}$ (maximized when seat and neighbors have dissimilar subjects). The Guideline 2 in weighted sum method needs us to normalize all Objectives to have similar range. The $SD_{seat,neighbor}$ and $NC_{seat,neighbor}$ are already normalized in the range from 0 to 1.

$$Objective\ 2 \Rightarrow maximize\{NC_{seat,neighbor} \times SD_{seat,neighbor}\} \qquad (10)$$

The weights are determined using Guideline 3 in weighted sum method. Using domain knowledge we know that Objective 1 is relatively more important than Objective 2. Increasing physical distance is a bigger factor in preventing malpractice compared to blocking the field of view. We assign a scalar weight $w_1 = 100$ for *Objective* 1 and a scalar weight $w_2 = 10$ for *Objective* 2. We are biasing the Genetic Algorithm to give more priority towards solving *Objective* 1 over solving *Objective* 2.

$$Fitness_{seat,neighbor} = 100(\frac{DC_{seat,neighbor} \times SD_{seat,neighbor}}{\sqrt{room_{rows}^2 + room_{columns}^2}}\})$$
$$+ 10(NC_{seat,neighbor} \times SD_{seat,neighbor}) \qquad (11)$$

2.4   Global Optimum Convergence Proof

We prove the genetic algorithm's ability to always converge to the global optimum given sufficient epochs by basing off the mathematical approach taken by [10]. Let us consider the following Mathematical Model. M is a finite set of all possible solutions(chromosomes). The number of possible solutions is proven to be finite and dependent on the number of seats ($NumSeats$) and is given by Permutation theory.

$$Fitness(x) \rightarrow max$$
$$x \in M \qquad (12)$$

$$|M| =^{NumSeats} P_{NumSeats} = (NumSeats)! \tag{13}$$

In each iteration t of the Genetic Algorithm, multiple possible solutions are considered denoted by population set X_t, containing of p "parent" solutions. Each of the solutions $x_t^i \in M$, where $X_t = \{x_t^1, \cdots, x_t^p\}$. A set of "children" solutions denoted by $\overline{X}_t$ are generated from the parent set X_t. The generation rules involve crossovers and mutations. The solutions $\overline{x}_t^i \in M$, where $\overline{X}_t = \{\overline{x}_t^1, \cdots, \overline{x}_t^p\}$. A neighborhood structure is a mapping N from M. For each solution x it defines a neighborhood $N(x)$ of x and each $y \in N(x)$ is called a neighbor of x.

A generation mechanism is a rule of selecting a solution y from the neighborhood N(x) of a given solution x. In the context of genetic algorithms such a generation rule consists of crossover and mutation rules. The generation mechanism can be described by a transition probability matrix R, where X_t denotes the state of the system at iteration t.

$$R(x,y) = P\{X_{t+1} = y | X_t = x\} \tag{14}$$

By (14), a Markov chain is defined over the set M of feasible solutions. A locally optimal solution is an $x \in M$ such that:

$$\forall y \in N(x), Fitness(x) \leq Fitness(y) \tag{15}$$

While a globally optimal solution is defined by:

$$\forall y \in M, Fitness(x) \leq Fitness(y) \tag{16}$$

In order for the algorithm not to get stuck in a local optimum (which is not globally optimal), it is necessary to also accept deterioration of the objective function with positive probability. In our Genetic Algorithm, a child with lesser fitness than the parents can be generated, and can also be a future parent if it is within the top 25% of overall population. Therefore, our algorithm does not get stuck inside local optimums.

After generating the children population $\overline{X}_t$ from the parent population X_t, the new parent population X_{t+1} for the next iteration has to be selected. In our case the top 20% fittest solutions out of union of the parent and children set $(X_t \bigcup \overline{X}_t)$ is selected as the parents for the next generation (X_{t+1}). The Genetic Algorithm is biased towards selecting more fitter individuals as parents for the next generation.

A state y is said to be "reachable" from state x if there exists a set of solutions $\{z_1, z_2, \cdots, z_m\} \in M$ such that $z_1 \in N(x), z_2 \in N(z_1), \cdots, y \in N(z_m)$.

Now the sequence of populations computed by the Genetic Algorithm can be described by a Markov-chain with the following properties. The state Y_t in iteration t is the combined vector concatenation of all individuals in population X_t. On the other hand $Y_t = y_0$ if one of the elements $\{x_1, \cdots, x_p\}$ of X_t is a globally optimal solution.

$$Y_t = \begin{cases} y_0 \ (if \ \exists x_t^i \in X_t \ where \ x_t^i \ is \ globally \ optimal) \\ x_t^1 \frown x_t^2 \frown \cdots \frown x_t^p \end{cases} \tag{17}$$

The globally optimal solution is the solution with highest fitness value. Once the globally optimal solution is selected, it always remains because the top 20% of the solutions are always selected to be next generation parents. Therefore, the state y_0 is an absorbing state of the Markov-chain. We also make an assumption that the globally optimal solution is reachable from any other solution. In other words, the absorbing state y_0 is reachable from any other state Y_t in the new Markov chain. This is a reasonable assumption given that mutation and crossover rules allow children solutions that are genetically different from the parent solution. Mutation allows for random exploration in the M solution space. Also, we have seen previously that solutions do not get stuck and can escape inflection points such as local minima. From the above observations, we can imply that for every state $Y_t \neq y_0$ is transient(non-absorbing) and that:

$$lim_{t \to \infty}\{Y_t = y_0\} = 1 \tag{18}$$

Thus, we have proved the convergence of fitness value of our Genetic Algorithm to the global optimum given a sufficiently large number of generations.

2.5   Parent Selection and Population

In this stage of the genetic algorithm, we select which chromosome solutions go on to produce future children solutions for the next generation. These parents chromosomes are a subset of the population that crossover with each other and mutate to produce children chromosome solutions. Only the top 20% of chromosomes by fitness value are selected to be parents. Each of these parent solutions are randomly paired up with another parent solution. Genetic Crossover and Mutation on each pair of parents produces 4 pairs of children solutions. Therefore, 20% of the population consists of the fittest solutions of the previous generation(parents), and 80% consists of children generated by those parents. This ratio ensures the chromosome population size remains constant over every generation.

2.6   Genetic Crossover and Mutation

Crossover is an operation that combines information from a pair of parent chromosomes to produce new children chromosome solutions. Since selected parents have high fitness values, crossover attempts to make the child chromosome contain features from both the parents. As a result, the child solution has a high probability of having high fitness levels as well. Our Genetic Algorithm uses the Order 1 Crossover variant proposed by [11]. A pair of parents $Parent_1$, $Parent_2$ produces a pair of children $Child_1$, $Child_2$. First, a random continuous section of chromosome positions is selected. The seats in this section is copied from $Parent_1$ onto the corresponding positions in $Child_1$. Exclude the seats present in the selected section from $Parent_2$. Place the remaining seats of $Parent_2$ in left to right sequence order into the unfilled positions of $Child_1$ from left to right. The same section of chromosome positions is also used to produce $Child_2$. The seats in this section is copied from $Parent_2$ onto the corresponding positions in $Child_2$. Exclude the seats present in the selected section from $Parent_1$. Place the remaining seats of $Parent_1$ in left to right sequence order into the positions of $Child_2$ from left to right. Each section of positions produces a pair of children. We need each pair of parents to produce 4 pairs of children each to maintain constant population size. Thus for each pair of parents, we apply the Ordered Crossover algorithm 4 times, each time with different randomized sections.

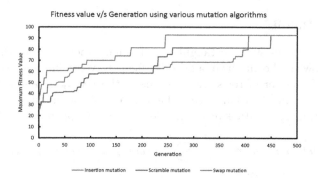

Fig. 3. Speed of fitness convergence comparison between various mutation algorithms.

Mutation is an action performed to bring out about small random changes in the chromosome. Mutation is responsible for the exploration of the search space. It is essential for the convergence of the fitness to the global optimal values. This ensures that the genetic algorithm can escape from local maxima points by preventing the population of chromosomes from becoming too similar to each other. We experimented with various mutation algorithms such as Insertion mutation [12,13], Scramble mutation [14] and Swap mutation [15]. For our Genetic Algorithm, Swap mutation produced the fastest convergence to the globally optimal fitness solution. Figure 3 shows a comparison of speed of fitness convergence between the various mutation types. The swap operation selects 2 seats on the chromosome at random and interchanges the positions. Swap mutation works by performing the swap operation multiple times on the same chromosome solution. It works best when the swap operator is performed with a low probability. So, we allow the swap operation to occur a random integer between 0 and $\frac{|chromosome|}{4}$ number of times.

2.7   Chromosomal Structure

Each chromosome represents a single seating allocation solution, characterized by a set of parameters known as genes. Genes are joined together in an order to form a chromosome. The size of a chromosome is defined by the number of genes present in it. The number of genes is given by the total number of seats present in all the rooms. Each gene represents a single seat and contains the following properties:

- The room in which the seat is present in.
- The row number of the seat.
- The column number of the seat.
- The subject taken by the examinee located on that seat. Seats can also be unoccupied by examinees.

2.8   Room Details

The algorithm works with rectangular and square rooms where the seats are arranged in rows and columns in a grid-like fashion. We define each $room$ to contain details of number of rows and columns in the $room_{rows}$ and $room_{columns}$. There can be multiple rooms, each having a variable number of rows and columns. All the $room$ data is placed inside a set of multiple rooms called $Rooms$.

$$|chromosome| = \sum_{room \in Rooms} room_{rows} \times room_{columns} \qquad (19)$$

The overall set of possible chromosomal solutions considered in each generation is called a Population. The Population size is an input to the genetic algorithm.

3   Results

The final seat allocation of the genetic algorithm is compared with conventional examination seat allocation on multiple test cases. In the conventional I shape seating methodology adopted by the [2], students of the same subject are not allocated to nearest column, but are allocated to the nearest row. At least one column distance is confirmed between two columns having same subject students. A comparative study between the fitness of the conventional algorithm allocation versus the fitness of the genetic algorithm allocation is used to prove the efficacy of our approach.

A brute force method of finding the optimal seating allocation is to generate all possible permutations of seating arrangements. Students who are writing the same subject form identical repeating objects in the student set. Algorithms like [17] can be used to find all possible permutations of a set with repetitions. We also do a comparative study between the number of solutions examined by our genetic algorithm versus the number of solutions examined when using the brute force permutation generation algorithm. This gives insight into the speed improvement our algorithm provides.

We practically cannot allow the Genetic algorithm to run infinitely to ensure an optimal solution. [16] shows that running a Genetic Algorithm for a finite number of generations can guarantee convergence to the global optimum within a certain level of confidence. The more the number of generations run, the higher the probability that the optimal solution lies inside the current population. Thus, the stopping criteria employed is to stop at a fixed practical large number of generations where multiple runs have saturated at the same fitness value. This step further improves the probability that the achieved allotment is the most optimal solution.

The *SubjectSimilarity* coefficient between all the subject pairs is given in Table 2. The subject set used is $\{S1, S2, S3, S4\}$. The subjects which are not related or similar to each other have a *SubjectSimilarity* value of 0.1. The subjects which are related and similar to each other have a *SubjectSimilarity* value of 0.4. *SubjectSimilarity* for a subject with respect to the same subject has the highest value which is 0.9. Subjects $S1$ and $S2$ are similar to each other. Subjects $S3$ and $S4$ are also similar to each other. The remaining subject pairings are unrelated.

Table 1. Genetic algorithm input parameters for Test Case 1 and 2

Input parameter	Test case 1	Test case 2
Maximum generations	2000	10000
Population size	300	300
$S1$ population	10	20
$S2$ population	10	10
$S3$ population	10	20
$S4$ population	10	10
Room 1 dimension	5 rows × 4 columns	5 rows × 4 columns
Room 2 dimension	5 rows × 4 columns	5 rows × 4 columns
Room 3 dimension	—	5 rows × 4 columns

Table 2. *SubjectSimilarity* correlation table where $SubjectSimilarity_{subject_1, subject_2}$ is given by the float value in $subject_1$ row and $subject_2$ column

	$S1$	$S2$	$S3$	$S4$
$S1$	0.9	0.4	0.1	0.1
$S2$	0.4	0.9	0.1	0.1
$S3$	0.1	0.1	0.9	0.4
$S4$	0.1	0.1	0.4	0.9

3.1 Test Case 1

The input parameters used by the genetic algorithm for running Test Case 1 is given in Table 1. The *SubjectSimilarity* coefficients used are in Table 2. The algorithm was run 3 separate times and the graphical plot of the maximum population fitness versus generation number graph is shown by Fig. 4. Since all 3 runs plateau at the same maximum fitness value of 92.93 and do not show signs of increasing further, we can assume with a high probability that the globally optimal solution was found. Table 3 visually contrasts the final seat allocation generated by our genetic seat allocation algorithm and the conventional seat allocation algorithm for Test Case 1. The conventional seat allotment has a fitness value of 10.20. Our genetic algorithm seat allotment has a fitness value of 92.93. Based upon our fitness heuristic measure, our genetic algorithm seat allocation is a 9.11 times improvement upon the conventional seat allocation. Run 3 reached the maximum fitness value of 92.93 the fastest in only 429 generations. This means that it analyzed $429 \times 300 = 128700$ solutions before finding the optimal solution. The brute force permutation generation algorithm would need to analyze $(40!)/(10! \times 10! \times 10! \times 10!) = 4.705 \times 10^{21}$ solutions before finding the optimal solution. Our genetic algorithm is 3.656×10^{16} times computationally faster than the brute force permutation generation algorithm.

Table 3. Test Case 1 genetic algorithm seat allocation versus conventional seat allocation

Genetic algorithm allotment								Conventional allotment							
Room 1				Room 2				Room 1				Room 2			
S1	S3	S1	S3	S4	S2	S4	S2	S1	S2	S3	S4	S1	S2	S3	S4
S4	S2	S4	S2	S1	S3	S1	S3	S1	S2	S3	S4	S1	S2	S3	S4
S1	S3	S1	S3	S4	S2	S4	S2	S1	S2	S3	S4	S1	S2	S3	S4
S4	S2	S4	S2	S1	S3	S1	S3	S1	S2	S3	S4	S1	S2	S3	S4
S1	S3	S1	S3	S4	S2	S4	S2	S1	S2	S3	S4	S1	S2	S3	S4

3.2 Test Case 2

The input parameters used by the genetic algorithm for running Test Case 2 is given in Table 1. The *SubjectSimilarity* coefficients used are in Table 2. The algorithm was run 3 separate times and the graphical plot of the maximum population fitness versus generation number graph is shown by Fig. 5. Since all 3 runs plateau at the same maximum fitness value of 82.02 and do not show signs of increasing further, we can assume with a high probability that the globally optimal solution was found. Table 4 visually contrasts the final seat allocation generated by our genetic seat allocation algorithm and the conventional seat allocation algorithm for Test Case 2. The conventional seat allotment has a fitness value of 12.14. Our genetic algorithm seat allotment has a fitness value of 82.02. Based upon our fitness heuristic measure, the genetic algorithm seat allocation is a 6.76 times improvement upon the conventional seat allocation. Run 1 reached the maximum fitness value of 82.02 the fastest in only 5053 generations. This means that it analyzed $5053 \times 300 = 1515900$ solutions before finding the optimal solution. The brute force permutation generation algorithm would need to analyze $(60!)/(20! \times 10! \times 20! \times 10!) = 1.068 \times 10^{32}$ solutions before finding the optimal solution. Our genetic algorithm is 7.043×10^{25} times computationally faster than the brute force permutation generation algorithm.

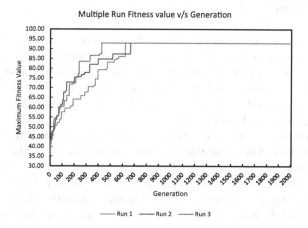

Fig. 4. Test Case 1 graph of maximum population fitness value versus generation number

Table 4. Test Case 2 genetic algorithm seat allocation versus conventional seat allocation

Genetic algorithm allotment												Conventional allotment											
Room 1				Room 2				Room 3				Room 1				Room 2				Room 3			
S1	S3	S1	S3	S1	S3	S1	S3	S3	S1	S3	S1	S1	S2	S3	S4	S1	S2	S3	S4	S1	S2	S1	S2
S4	S2	S4	S2	S4	S2	S4	S2	S2	S4	S2	S4	S1	S2	S3	S4	S1	S2	S3	S4	S1	S2	S1	S2
S1	S3	S1	S3	S1	S3	S1	S3	S3	S1	S3	S1	S1	S2	S3	S4	S1	S2	S3	S4	S1	S2	S1	S2
S4	S2	S1	S1	S4	S2	S4	S2	S2	S4	S3	S3	S1	S2	S3	S4	S1	S2	S3	S4	S1	S2	S1	S2
S1	S3	S1	S3	S1	S3	S1	S3	S3	S1	S3	S1	S1	S2	S3	S4	S1	S2	S3	S4	S1	S2	S1	S2

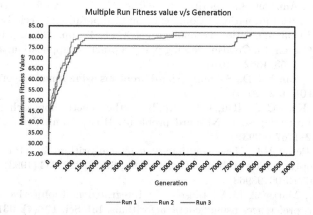

Fig. 5. Test Case 2 graph of maximum population fitness value versus generation number.

4   Conclusion

The results prove that our genetic seating algorithm does a better job in preventing malpractice compared to conventional seating algorithms by a huge margin. The possibility of examinees copying from other examinee's answer scripts is greatly reduced as determined by our fitness heuristic. We also see that our genetic algorithm based method is many orders times faster than brute force permutation generation based methods.

However, there are some limitations to the current algorithm, which further research can reduce. One limitation is that the genetic algorithm is still computationally slow. For example, each run of $TestCase2$ took 197 hours to run on a 3.8 GHz Intel Cascade Lake Scalable Cloud Processor. Creating a parallel implementation [18] of our currently serial genetic algorithm to utilize multiple processors, will likely reduce computation time enormously. Another limitation is that currently only rectangular room geometries where seats are arranged in rows and columns are supported. Alternate room geometries should also be considered. Comparison of results using alternate metaheuristic methods such as particle swarm optimization, simulated annealing and ant colony optimization should also be done.

We hope that our research will arm examination bodies and universities with an additional tool to smartly combat malpractices. With millions of students taking up mega public examinations around the world, untoward cases of cheating are bound to occur no matter the precautions. However, scientific approaches like ours can make all the difference between rampant organized cheating versus rare unfortunate occurrences.

References

1. Moffatt, M.: Undergraduate cheating (1990)
2. Chaki, P.K., Anirban, S.: Algorithm for efficient seating plan for centralized exam system. In: 2016 International Conference on Computational Techniques in Information and Communication Technologies (ICCTICT), pp. 320–325. IEEE (2016)
3. Lewis, R., Carroll, F.: Creating seating plans: a practical application. J. Oper. Res. Soc. **67**(11), 1353–1362 (2016)
4. Panchal, G., Panchal, D.: Solving np hard problems using genetic algorithm. Transportation **106**, 6-2 (2015)
5. Lin, F.T., Kao, C.Y., Hsu, C.C.: Applying the genetic approach to simulated annealing in solving some NP-hard problems. IEEE Trans. Syst. Man Cybern. **23**(6), 1752–1767 (1993)
6. Bac, F.Q., Perov, V.L.: New evolutionary genetic algorithms for NP-complete combinatorial optimization problems. Biol. Cybern. **69**(3), 229–234 (1993). https://doi.org/10.1007/BF00198963
7. Sanchis, J., Martínez, M.A., Blasco, X.: Integrated multiobjective optimization and a priori preferences using genetic algorithms. Inf. Sci. **178**(4), 931–951 (2008)
8. Marler, R.T., Arora, J.S.: The weighted sum method for multi-objective optimization: new insights. Struct. Multidiscip. Optim. **41**(6), 853–862 (2010). https://doi.org/10.1007/s00158-009-0460-7

9. Wertheim, T., Dunsky, I.L.: Peripheral visual acuity. Optom. Vis. Sci. **57**(12), 915–924 (1980)
10. Hartl, R.F., Belew, R.K.: A global convergence proof for a class of genetic algorithms. University of Technology, Vienna (1990)
11. Davis, L.: Applying adaptive algorithms to epistatic domains. In: IJCAI, vol. 85, pp. 162–164 (1985)
12. Fogel, D.B.: An evolutionary approach to the traveling salesman problems. Biol. Cybern. **60**, 139–144 (1988). https://doi.org/10.1007/BF00202901
13. Michalewicz, Z.: Genetic Algorithms + Data Structures = Evolution Programs. Springer, Heidelberg (2013)
14. Syswerda, G.: Schedule optimization using genetic algorithms (1991)
15. Oliver, I.M., Smith, D., Holland, J.R.: Study of permutation crossover operators on the traveling salesman problem. In: Genetic Algorithms and their Applications: Proceedings of the Second International Conference on Genetic Algorithms, 28–31 July at the Massachusetts Institute of Technology, Cambridge, MA, p. 1987. L. Erlhaum Associates, Hillsdale (1987)
16. Greenhalgh, D., Marshall, S.: Convergence criteria for genetic algorithms. SIAM J. Comput. **30**(1), 269–282 (2000)
17. Chase, P.J.: Algorithm 383: permutations of a set with repetitions [G6]. Commun. ACM **13**(6), 368–369 (1970)
18. Cantu-Paz, E.: Efficient and Accurate Parallel Genetic Algorithms, vol. 1. Springer, Heidelberg (2000). https://doi.org/10.1007/978-1-4615-4369-5

Big Data: Does BIG Matter for Your Business?

Wei Zhou[1] and Selwyn Piramuthu[2(✉)]

[1] Information and Operations Management, ESCP Europe, Paris, France
[2] ISOM, University of Florida Gainesville, Gainesville, FL, USA
selwyn@ufl.edu

Abstract. With the emergence of big data and business analytics, many new concepts and business models driven by data have been introduced in recent years. Does "big" really matter? We attempt to explain when and why big does not matter in many business cases. In those occasions where "Big" does matter, we outline the data strategy framework that differentiates the degree of big data requirements. In conclusion, we offer practical advice on strategic usage of big data for best practice management and sound decision-making.

The ease of generation and storage of large volumes of data, specifically in applications that include social media, transaction (e.g., online and brick-and-mortar retail store check-out data), sensor networks, Internet of Things (IoT), among others have resulted in the global phenomenon that is also known as "big data." As such large data volumes are not restricted to specific domains or application areas, it is not uncommon to witness such data in disparate real-world scenarios. With this development of generation and storage of big data invariably come the hype that is associated with such data in terms of its effect on the way business practices operate or on our everyday lives. While the benefits that are associated with huge volumes of relevant data in any application domain that are appropriately processed for actionable intelligence cannot be overstated, there is a concomitant interest on how big is big enough for big data and whether such huge data volumes necessarily generate useful actionable intelligence or heretofore unknown insights.

While big data as a term has existed for a while now, it does not have a generally agreed upon definition. The 'big' in big data is a fuzzy concept that generally represents data sets that are too big to be able to capture, organize, and analyze under commonly encountered resource constraints. Rooted from early 2000, the industry continues to use the so-called '3Vs' to describe big data in terms of Volume, Velocity and Variety. The volume of big data comes from various sources, that include historical transaction-data, unstructured data from social media, and automatically generated sensor network data. Velocity in big data signifies the very high data generation speed/frequency from RFID tags, sensor network and IoT devices. Variety refers to the fact that while data origin spans several sources, the different format types supported include audio,

S. M. Thampi et al. (Eds.): SoMMA 2020, CCIS 1366, pp. 146–156, 2021.
https://doi.org/10.1007/978-981-16-0419-5_12

video, text messages, business transactions, financial markets, and operational physical parameters (temperature, humidity, density, etc.). Nowadays we often add a fourth "V" as Veracity, which stands for uncertainty that may come from both internal and external environments, such as economic factors, weather conditions, etc. The fifth "V" as Value is often considered indispensable for business data strategy making [1].

Clearly, it is a challenging task to process big data with high volume, velocity, variety, and veracity for value creation. Thanks to recent advances in data storage technologies (cloud, non-mechanic flash storage, direct attached storage architecture, etc.), storage cost is no longer a serious constraint for most practical purposes. While it is in general difficult to deal with decision-making situations in real-time, the "high velocity" aspect of big data adds to the complexity when such data are used to make real-time decisions. RFID tags are commonly used in manufacturing, supply chains, retailing, and by customers to facilitate ease of operations and to achieve better operational efficiency and effectiveness. Nevertheless, big data seems to have found its way out to claim its place as a serious contender for strategic purposes in a large number of firms. Overall, similar to other information and communication technologies (ICT), big data delivers on various fronts when appropriately used to generate actionable intelligence for improved decisions.

While no longer new, big data still remains largely mysterious to many business practitioners with regard to the best practices associated with how to appropriately handle big data. It is natural to ask "for big data, is bigger indeed the better?" In this article, we explain why big indeed does not matter in many cases in a wide spectrum of industries. In those occasions where "Big" does matter, we outline the data strategy framework that differentiates the degree of big data requirements. In conclusion, we offer practical advices on strategic usage of big data for best practice management and sound decision-making.

1   Why Big Does Not Matter?

Big Data Analytics Decomposed: In order to explain why "big doesn't matter", it helps to first understand big data analytics, which is the knowledge and pattern discovery process from existing big data. Big data analytics may involve various statistics and pattern recognition methods that help capture and analyze a very large data set from different perspectives. The fundamental assumption in big data analytics is that it needs at least a pre-defined problem with one or several objective functions to solve. Data doesn't create problems by itself; managers create them. Once a problem is specified, the big data set with different variables can be visualized, for example, as a map that displays the mutual relationship between any two variables. Figure 1 illustrates a simple example of room brightness (in lumens) that is generated by four electric lights. In a perfect big data scenario, the room brightness is continuously monitored, including all functionalities of the four lights and the electricity power supply. This generates 6 data input with status (lumen, lights 1 to 4, and electricity) and 8 possible relationships in this case. If the problem is to determine the lumen value in the room, given information that light #4 is broken, all that is necessary in this big data map are the representations in blue. In other words, once the status of lights 1 to 3 are known, there is no need to know the other data on electricity and light 4 and their relationship. This problem only needs data from three nodes (lights 1 to 3) and three relationships. The blue elements in Fig. 1 together comprise the 'Markov blanket' in data mining. Therefore, for big data, big really doesn't matter as long as the extra data input doesn't lie on the Markov blanket because when this small set of (Markov blanket) data is known, the rest of the big data set are irrelevant to the given problem.

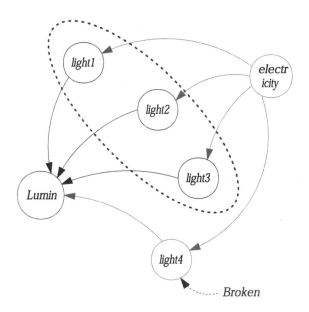

Fig. 1. Big data for a room lighting example (Color figure online)

There's another technical perspective to illustrate that "big doesn't matter": the feature selection problem. Feature selection is considered a pre-processing step that generally helps reduce the complexity of data in data analysis. Feature selection results in the selection of a subset of features that are necessary to learn the target concept [2]. While keeping features that form the core of concept description, feature selection eliminates those features that are deemed to irrelevant. In general, a feature contributes at least in terms of two components: noise and useful information. A useful or relevant feature is one that contributes more useful information than noise and an irrelevant feature introduces more noise than useful information to learn the concept of interest [3]. With irrelevant features in the dataset, the complexity [4] associated with learning the concept of interest increases. Irrelevant features also lowers the quality of learned concepts due to modeling of their inherent noisiness. While feature selection is important while analyzing small data sets, its significance increases multi-fold in big data analysis due to the sheer volume of data that are handled. Feature selection also results in a precipitous drop in the number of dimensions which may indeed transform a big data set to one that is not big. In a sense, big data can be reduced to one that is not through data pre-processing steps.

While feature selection essentially removes columns from a data set, its *dual*, *instance selection* results in the removal of rows from a data set. Instance selection generally operates by eliminating those examples (rows) that are not near the boundary that separate classes that describe concepts. This is simply because the examples that are near the boundary of a given class are more useful to draw the boundary, which is necessary to learn the concept of interest. This property is exploited by support vector machines (SVM) through appropriate data transformations. The idea is that the examples that are farther away from the boundary do not provide significant information to draw the boundary and therefore can be eliminated without any significant degradation on the concept learned.

The overall learning performance can be improved through improvement in the algorithm itself or through reduction in complexity of data used as input to these algorithms. Scalability is an issue with most learning algorithms. Feature selection as well as instance selection effectively improves scalability through reduction in data complexity. In other words, the same "big" data set is essentially transformed into one that is not, thereby rendering it possible to be handled by existing learning algorithm with no significant issues that are related to scalability.

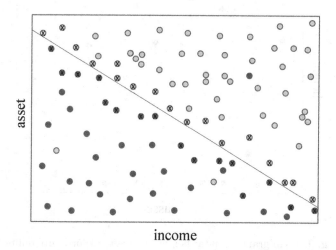

Fig. 2. Loan-granting data: asset vs. income (Color figure online)

For example, a big data set used for loan granting decisions may be 'big' because of irrelevant variables such as the applicant's height (e.g., Figs. 3 and 4). Consider a 'big data' set with a large number of instances and three attributes (asset, income, height). Two-dimensional plots of all possible pairs of these are given in Figs. 2, 3, and 4. In these figures, the green circles represent the 'good' (i.e., loan-grantable) cases and the red circles represent the 'not-good' cases. Clearly, there is a gradation in the 'good'ness and 'not-good'ness among these cases. We ignore those gradations since the decision to grant loan in its simplest form is binary (yes/no) in character, as represented by the line in Fig. 2. This (discriminant) line separates cases that were granted loan from those that were not. Now, assuming that only asset and income are relevant features that are used to decide whether or not to grant loan to a loan applicant, Figs. 2, 3 and 4 show the existence of a pattern in the first and the non-existence of any pattern in the latter two. In other words, the pattern is only visible upon projection of all data points on the asset-income axes. Here, a *feature selection* algorithm would select asset and income as the *relevant* attributes (from asset, income, and height).

Figure 2 has a set of x-inscribed circles (both red and green) that are at the boundary between 'good' and 'not-good' cases. For learning the concept of 'good' or 'not-good,' the only cases or instances that are relevant are those marked with an x since ultimately learning occurs by determining the 'line' or 'curve' that separates the 'good' from 'not-good' cases. Here, an *instance selection* algorithm would select these 'x' cases. The green circles among the red ones and the red circles among the green ones are most likely due to *noise* in the data set.

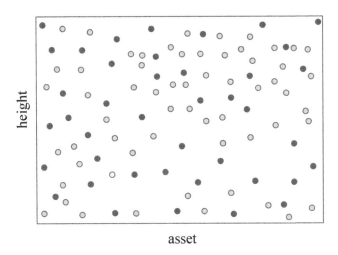

Fig. 3. Loan-granting data: height vs. asset (Color figure online)

At this point, we can safely state that only a small and regular set of data matters to the managers and decision makers with the assumption that big data itself doesn't create problems. The rest of the data do not matter as long as they are outside of the Markov blanket or too remote to be selected.

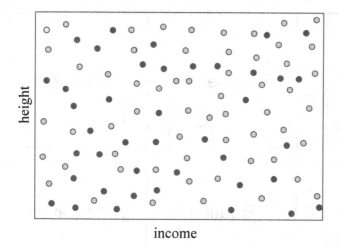

Fig. 4. Loan-granting data: height vs. income (Color figure online)

2   When It Matters, What's the Right Data Strategy?

So far, recent discussions on big data strategy are often referred to the model presented by (Davenport et al. 2012). Its main strategic perspectives include: the access to data and the capabilities of data processing. Driven by data, the existing models focus on data performance. A company's vision and business drive, for example everyday's operational dynamics, is missing in existing data models. We consider it essential to understand supply chain dynamics and aim to integrate this part into the existing data strategy. In this section, we introduce four new big data strategies (routine, integration, strategic, and excellence) by mixing data streaming capability and the data analytical capability as one broad perspective of as "data capability".

In Fig. 5, we consider both operational and supply chain uncertainty (dynamics) and a company's data capability (including both data acquisition and analytical capabilities). The operational dynamics can be classified as low or high depending on how often and how different are the decision-making situations. We use "big data capability" that takes values high or low to represent group data acquisition and analytical capabilities of the organization. To operationalize this, we develop the following strategies that include routine, integration, strategic, and excellence.

Routine: The Routine strategy is chosen in situations in which there is stability in operational activities as well as a general absence of varying dynamics overall. This strategy is also recommended for scenarios where large volumes of data are unavailable or inaccessible in addition to the capability to process data in such high volume. In the real-world context, a significant number of raw material suppliers satisfy these constraints as data request is generally at significantly low levels and data are processed in a routine manner with no obvious signs of

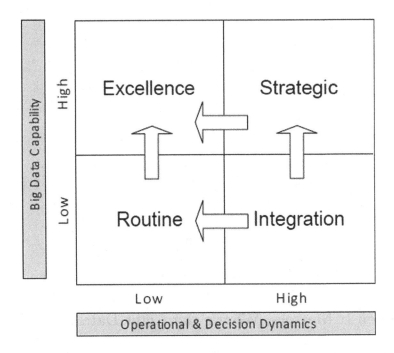

Fig. 5. The right data strategy regarding decision dynamics

deviations. Moreover, the uncertainly in such an environment with routine data processing operational decisions is rather low.

Integration: The data integration strategy is recommended to address data need in situations where the amount of data available or accessible is limited, while the company simultaneously experiences a wide variety of operational dynamics in addition to a large number of decision-making requests. An anecdotal evidence is that of French public hospitals that are generally known for their high number of demands while also presenting with delayed service provision. In addition, these characteristics are exhibited primarily due to a sheer lack of financial resources that are necessary for the implementation of appropriate advanced computer-based or automated systems that help alleviate the difficulty to deal with complex operational circumstances. This strategy recommends the integration of abilities of various suppliers. For example, the data capabilities of entities such as equipment manufacturer, labs, blood bank could all be integrated together to achieve better outcome. Overall, data integration is used to alleviate the stress that develops as a result of mismatch between data need and constrained data capability.

Strategic: The strategic case is witnessed when the firm is able to easily accommodate a high volume of dynamic decision-making situations through use of its ability to easily process big data without much difficulty. An example of this scenario is the fast fashion industry which requires this capability to stay afloat when operating in a highly dynamic environment in which important decisions are made frequently aided by results from analyses of high volumes of data. An example is a company like Zara that strategically utilizes its big data that are generated across its resources to develop quick and responsive marketing campaigns. With the capability to generate, access, process, and interpret big data and related analysis, data analytics plays a significant role in a large number of business processes and associated decision-making situations. For example, an "A/B testing" can be used as a part of a design process to choose among different colors for a product with the goal of selecting the color that invokes the best market response. Similarly, big data analytics can be used to guide the process to design the product form, the best size portfolio, among others. Clearly, big data can be considered a strategic element in this context. Through big data analytics and related accuracy and timeliness, the dynamics in the system can therefore be controlled to a good extent.

Excellence: When the operational and supply chain dynamics are not high, it is possible for the firm to use big data solutions to reach "excellence" in terms of customer satisfaction, quality management, service provision, among others. Moreover, from a strategic transition perspective, the model can readily be used to illustrate the firm's transition over time (Fig. 5). For example, a firm with minimal (i.e., routine) variations in requirements, the ability to utilize big data translates to the possibility to reach excellence through best business and operational practices. On the other hand, when exposed to a situation that simultaneously has high operational dynamics and limited data capability, it is possible to use integration of such capabilities from buyers and suppliers to render it strategic or the operational dynamics can be reduced to render the operations routine. In other words, firms that simultaneously experience a high level of operational uncertainty along with a similar level of data involvement can utilize data capacity to effectively decrease the variations associated with dynamics to achieve excellent operations. An example of this scenario is the minimal involvement of humans in automated systems.

3   Managerial Advice on Using the Right Big Data Strategy

In this section, we provide some managerial advice on how big data can be strategically dealt with in everyday practice: 1. be problem-driven more than data-driven; 2. prioritize and understand your data needs; 3. pay attention to the big data long tail; 4. human expert knowledge is still valuable.

3.1   Be Problem-Driven More Than Data-Driven

With today's technology, we can not solely rely on data-driven strategy and wait for some breakthrough machine learning innovation that enables the data to create business objectives and decision problems by itself. We can certainly set it as a goal for next generation research to create innovative yet relevant and useful decision problems from data but, given currently available technology, practitioners should be more focused on discovering valuable decision problems and business objectives, and by knowing very precisely the problem before attempting to deal with the data.

Paying more attention to the existing problems and possible problem discoveries doesn't mean that managers should give up on their way to big data. To the contrary, a problem-driven manager can gain valuable insights on business practice from examining the big data. Purely data-driven business strategy, however, would be dangerous because data itself in today's technology doesn't have an innovative spirit that could lead to new problem definition, break-through product design, or innovative business operations. Therefore, big data should be used as a powerful tool in the hands of a manager who values solving existing problems and setting new business goals.

3.2   Prioritize and Understand Your Data Needs

Once the business objectives and decision problems are clearly defined, evidences from big data could help form a map based on all available variables and, more importantly, to prioritize and select the most relevant data in a manageable format and volume. When using big data, it helps to categorize the relevancy of data based on its problem-resolving capability into critical data, marginal data, and long tail data. Critical data is a small set of data that is located on the Markov blanket or in the basket of selected features. They are directly related to the pre-defined problems and on availability of complete information of the critical data, the rest of the data becomes conditionally irrelevant. The marginal data are the second tier data set that is aligned to the critical data. When the critical data is incomplete, we can make probabilistic inference from the marginal

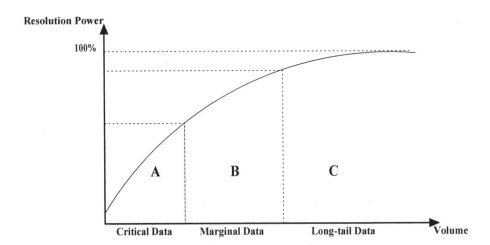

Fig. 6. The long tail model of big data

data towards achieving the optimal solutions. The long tail data represents the extra information that doesn't need to be processed if an optimal solution can be reached by critical and marginal data (Fig. 6).

By understanding and prioritizing our data needs, we can simplify the workflow of data acquisition and, more importantly, keep the managerial decision making procedure resistant to unnecessary information noises that come from big data.

3.3 Pay Attention to the Long-Tail of Big Data

The long tail in the big data may not be immediately important for a specific problem but it may conceal some pleasant surprise that is useful but ignored for a very long time. The long tail in big data refers to the very large set of data that is remotely related (or completely irrelevant) to the core problem. Similar to the long tail phenomena in other business fields, such as in marketing and supply chain management, it applies to the big data domain that this large amount of irrelevant data not directed clustered to the existing major business problems may carry the key to some specific problems that haven't been brought to the managers' direct attention. It may also carry hidden relationship to the critical data. Therefore, big data long tail may bring nice results to the practitioners on discovery of niche business problems or niche business solutions. The long tail of big data may also help the designers, managers, scientist, and engineers to sparkle innovative ideas by examining the data that they don't usually pay attention to.

3.4 Human Expert Knowledge Is Still Valuable

Expert knowledge from managers, marketing personnel, assembly operator, produce/service design team, engineers, and research scientist are extremely valuable even in the era of big data. They have the insights that could integrate marketing response, business process, manufacturing, product design, and engineering all together and discover new and pertinent business problems for further (big) data analytics. They have the practical knowledge from everyday working experience to simplify the data, to link the various data variables, and to recommend proper data analytics methods to accurately analyze the big data towards achieving meaningful and valuable analytical results. Data scientists carry another set of valuable human expert knowledge in big data that could bridge the domain-specific human experts with the existing big data by providing help on problem (model) formation, data prioritization, data analysis, and post-analytics documentation.

3.5 Conclusion

With the emergence of big data and business analytics, many new concepts and business models driven by data have been introduced in recent years. Does "big" really matter? We attempt to explain when and why big does not matter in many business cases. In those occasions where "Big data" matters, a company should choose the right data strategy that is able to differentiate the degree of big data requirements and depth of involvement. In conclusion, we offer practical advice on strategic usage of big data for best practice management and sound decision-making.

Above all, we have only a finite number of business objectives and a few decision problems to make everyday. Infinitely increasing the amount of data would eventually overload our very limited business practice and cost the society if we don't have a right strategy to this ever-increasing data noise and associated storage and processing cost. A sound understanding of big data strategy and when big matters could lead us to reach more valuable business insights than a blind application of big data software. Understanding it helps us to reach the critical data from the much larger data lake. With the continuous expansion of big data, we foresee that the marginal value of each new byte of data will decrease. Eventually a break-even point will be reached when the cost to store, process, and analyze extra data along with other costs equals its marginal benefit for each company. To understand its data need and the break-even points will help today's company to rationally consider its big data investment and align its data strategy with its business goals.

References

1. Arcondara, J., Himmi, K., Guan, P., Zhou, W.: Value oriented big data strategy: analysis & case study. In: Proceedings of the 50th Hawaii International Conference on System Sciences (2017)
2. Kira, K., Rendell, L.A.: A practical approach to feature selection. In: Proceedings of the Ninth International Conference on Machine Learning, pp. 249–256 (1992)
3. Piramuthu, S.: Evaluating feature selection methods for learning in data mining applications. Eur. J. Oper. Res. **156**(2), 483–494 (2004)
4. Rendell, L.A., Seshu, R.M.: Learning hard concepts through constructive induction: framework and rationale. Comput. Intell. **6**(4), 247–270 (1990)

Modelling Energy Consumption of Domestic Households via Supervised and Unsupervised Learning: A Case Study

Shahid Mehraj Shah[✉]

Communication Control and Learning Lab,
Department of Electronics and Communication Engineering,
National Institute of Technology, Srinagar, Jammu and Kashmir, India
shahidshah@nitsri.net
https://sites.google.com/view/shahidshah/

Abstract. Electricity energy billing system is prevalent in most of the places in the world. Also digitization of these electricity bills has also been successfully implemented in various underdeveloped countries as well. The vast amount of data is available regarding the energy consumption of consumers. In this paper we consider a case study of one city, about which we have electricity energy data for several years. We first classify consumers based on their average energy usage via clustering algorithms. We also have survey data of several houses. In that survey, we have building information, family information and also appliance information. We use various regression techniques to disaggregate the energy usage corresponding to various appliances.

Keywords: Energy analytics · Machine learning · LASSO · Regression · AIC · Clustering

1 Introduction

Domestic households are the main source of electric energy consumption. While the energy demand is increasing day by day, at the same time the inefficient utilization of energy, especially electric energy, is also a common phenomenon. There have been several efforts to study the behavior of domestic household consumers and propose appropriate interventions to motivate the consumers to utilize energy properly. While some of the existing techniques either depends upon high resolution and detailed survey or on mounting large number of sensors or IoTs in houses.

The interest in understanding the relationship between energy consumption of buildings has increased in recent times.

© Springer Nature Singapore Pte Ltd. 2021
S. M. Thampi et al. (Eds.): SoMMA 2020, CCIS 1366, pp. 157–171, 2021.
https://doi.org/10.1007/978-981-16-0419-5_13

1.1   Literature Survey

In [1] the authors study various clustering techniques on the residential consumer data to forecast the load of the consumers. The authors use data from various houses in Texas, Austin, USA. Collaborative data analytics based techniques are explored in [2] where the authors explore the possibility of using human feedback based data in addition to the sensors mounted in buildings for collecting energy consumption data in buildings. Gaussian Mixture Model (GMM) based clustering of huge amount of time series data from the case study of United Kingdom was studied in [3], where smart meters were used to capture high granular data sets. Several machine learning algorithms were compared for efficiency of predicting electricity demand of buildings and individuals in [4]. Deep neural network model was used in [5] to predict the effect of heating load and cooling load on the overall forecasting of electricity consumption of building. Recurrent Neural Networks (RNN) based novel technique of Deep Learning called sequence to sequence algorithm was used in [6] for forecasting energy. For state-of-the-art research survey of application of machine learning algorithms in the building life analysis the reader is referred to [7]. A review of various data analytics and mining techniques for estimation and detection of building occupancy is provided in systematic way in [8]. In [9] the case study of residential estate of Milan city is considered, where clustering is done using self-organizing map and k-means algorithm to obtain energy model of residential buildings of the city. A case study regarding the usage of air conditioner in Hong Kong is studied in [10], where occupant behavior is analyzed with respect to the usage of ACs. One more important case study of United States is studied in [11] where American Time Use Survey (ATUS) is used to develop schedule of occupants of domestic households for modeling stochastic appliance schedule. Time Use Survey (TUS) is also used in [12] to develop high resolution occupancy model for domestic buildings. A case study of Chinese city is studied in [13], where authors use survey data alongwith clustering technique to analyze and develop model for building occupancy. One more interesting case study of Chinese study in context of energy consumption of cooling devices is presented in [14], where authors use bottom up physics based model for the analysis.

While these approaches may be applicable in some developed countries or for experimental purposes, these approaches may not be feasible in some countries, e.g., in India for various reasons: 1) Due to social structure of various urban population, people hesitate to reply to detailed survey as one needs for Time of Use data. 2) The common households feel it to be insecure to allow to mount various IoTs or sensors to monitor energy consumption patterns very closely.

Because of these reasons, the existing methodology may not be applicable at the mass level in countries like India, Sri Lanks etc. In this paper we propose a survey based approach, where with minimal survey, and the monthly energy bill, we will try to model the energy consumption pattern of a household. Also IoT based smart meter, which is mounted in very few houses, is used to get detailed consumption pattern of some houses. This will be used to refine the survey based model.

The rest of the paper is organized as follows: In Sect. 2 we introduce the model. In Sect. 3 the clustering algorithm is discussed. In Sect. 4 we study the regression based model for getting factors of households. Finally we conclude the paper in Sect. 5.

2 Monthly Energy Data Set

In this paper we perform the case study of an Indian state Kerala, in particular a city called Aluva. The data is available at two levels, one is the bi-monthly billing data of the whole region, the other is survey data of some houses which contains building and occupancy information. In this section, we will first analyse the bi-monthly survey data. Aluva region of Kerala is divided into seven areas, and each area is designated by area code. The details of these areas is illustrated in Fig. 1.

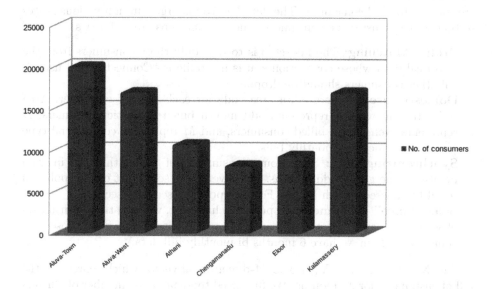

Fig. 1. Population statistics of Aluva region

In Kerala, the Kerala State Board Electricity (KSEB) provides bi-monthly electricity usage bills in contrary to monthly bills (as is common in various regions in India). Further KSEB has divided areas into two categories, one will get bi-monthly bill in even month and others get in odd month. Hence to perform any data analytics operation on the billing data, we need to make it uniform. For this purpose we use following methodology to fill the missing months (Table 1).

Table 1. Acnoryms

Acnorym	Full form
KSEB	Kerala State Board Electricity
LASSO	Least Absolute Shrinkable and Selection Operator
SVM	Support Vector Machine
RBF	Radial Basis Function
AIC	Akaike Information Criterion
BIC	Bayesian Information Criterion
RNN	Recurrent Neural Network

3 Cleaning the Data and Filling Missing Months

The data that is provided to us in excel files has lot of issues. First of all there are some industrial consumers. The data had to undergo through various stages so that we can cluster the consumers. The various steps are as follows

- **Profile Matching:** The first step is to take only those consumers from the historical data whose connection status in profile is "Connected and using". All other consumers should be dropped.
- **Domestic users:** There is an area code for each type of consumer. Area code starting with A represents odd month billed domestic consumers, B represents even month billed consumers, and M represents commercial type consumers which get monthly bills.
- **Synchronizing data:** Since some consumers get bi-monthly bill in even months, some get in odd months. We have to use some sort of interpolation to fill the missed month billing. For interpolation see next section.
- **Select "nice" consumers:** To perform clustering, we need those consumers of which we have atleast one year bill data. So we need to filter those consumers for whom we have 6 months bi monthly bill data.

Let $\mathbf{X}^{(i)} = (X_1^{(i)}, \ldots, X_M^{(i)})$ be a M-dimensional vector which represents the bill of customer i for M months. We first need to identify the number of clusters which will classify the consumers in some meaningful way. To that end, we use a very simple K-means clustering algorithm, which is simple and famous algorithm used for unsupervised learning in Machine learning [15]. We first briefly describe the K-means algorithm. Say we have total of N consumers which we want to cluster into K clusters. Let the partitions be represented as $\mathcal{P} = \{P_1, P_2, \ldots, P_K\}$. The objective is to find

$$\arg\min_{\mathcal{P}} \sum_{i=1}^{K} \sum_{\mathbf{X} \in S_i} \|\mathbf{X} - \mu_i\| \tag{1}$$

We use first elbow method to denote the optimal number of clusters. A total of 40 clusters were identified by the algorithm, which were characterized by the

overall trend for three year cycle (2013–2015), see Fig. 2. The encircles number
is the cluster number (we call it cluster ID) and the number written below the
ID is number of consumers in this cluster. Since we observe that there are some
clusters whose average monthly bill is close to Rs. 5000. In this work our focus
is on those households with nominal average consumption (typically between
200 to 1500 Indian Rupees). Hence we reproduce the cluster analysis of those
households in Fig. 3.

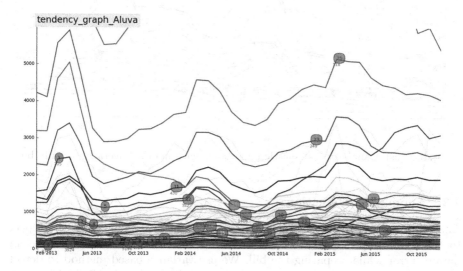

Fig. 2. Clustering of monthly billing data of whole Aluva region

4   Results

4.1   Classification of Consumers

The consumers are classified based on the trend shown by their energy consumption over 36 months, which is taken care by clustering. Also to give more
meaningful insight to a consumer about its behavior, we need to make similar groups within same geographical area also. In our case, the Aluva region is
divided into three major area namely: Aluwa town, Kalamassery, Aluwa west.
We observe from Fig. 2 and Fig. 3 that the consumers are divided into several
groups, each group having a distinct energy usage trend across the year. Some
clusters like cluster No. 25 have a usual trend, where there is more energy usage
in the months of march to may (when AC is used in most of the houses), whereas
during moderate whether the energy usage is less. There are some clusters which
show anomolous behaviour, like cluster No. 17, where the energy usage is continuously increasing throughout the year.

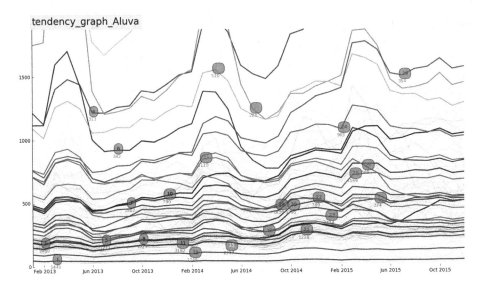

Fig. 3. Cluster analysis of domestic households with nominal average monthly bill

4.2 Anomalous Detection

There are some outliers or consumers with anomalous behavior with respect to their consumption over the three years. This may be due to insufficient data or error while preparing the bill. We use variance based method to detect such anomoly in the consumption pattern over the 36 months. From Fig. 4, Y-axis is normalized monthly bill and X- axis is the consumer number. We take mean+standard deviation as the threshold for anomalous detection. Any consumer with bill more than this threshold or below the lower bound (which is chosen in similar way), we eliminate such consumers from clustering.

5   Regression of Survey Data

Out of 25000 experimental houses, the survey is done in 2000 houses. Now there are 30 clusters, in each cluster we have roughly 800 households and on an average the survey of 60 houses is available. This rough data is available because of logistic constraints. In the survey the following factors are obtained from the houses (Table 2 and Table 3).

The energy consumption of different appliances for different factors was collected from the sources available online. We used the detailed data available about the consumption, e.g., for a single door refrigerator, with 150 L capacity, of age 3–4 years, the average consumption in kW-Hr is 0.4. In this way we obtained the consumption of different appliances like AC, Washing machine, CFL etc. Let the consumption of different devices be denoted by E_i, $i = 1, \ldots, 23$,

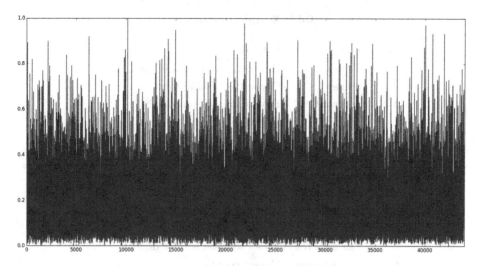

Fig. 4. Anomalous detection using variance approach

Table 2. Family survey

S. No	Factor	Definition
1	num_adult	How many years old is your AC
2	num_child	Capacity of AC in tonnes
3	num_elder	How many AC you have?
4	wkday_10_to_5_AM	Number of family members available during 10PM to 5AM
4	wkday_10_to_5_AM	Number of family members available during 10PM to 5AM
4	wkday_10_to_5_AM	Number of family members available during 10PM to 5AM
4	wkday_10_to_5_AM	Number of family members available during 10PM to 5AM
4	wkday_10_to_5_AM	Number of family members available during 10PM to 5AM
5	ac_temp	Temperature you usually set on AC
6	acool_count	How many air cooler you have
7	acool_type	Type of Air cooler
2	cfl_count	How many cfl you have?

corresponding to different appliances, the total consumption can be written as

$$E_t = \sum_{i=1}^{M} w_i E_i + \sum_{i=1}^{K} w_i^{(t)} F_i^{(t)} \tag{2}$$

where the weights w_i correspond to the appliance usage (which does not depend on time, as survey is done once) and the weights $w_i^{(t)}$ correspond to the weight of factors $F_i^{(t)}$ which vary with time, e.g., temperature, wind speed, precipitation (Fig. 5).

Table 3. Appliance survey

S. No	Factor	Definition
1	ac_age	How many years old is your AC
2	ac_cap	Capacity of AC in tonnes
3	ac_count	How many AC you have?
4	ac_rate	Rating of your AC (out of 5)
5	ac_temp	Temperature you usually set on AC
6	acool_count	How many air cooler you have
7	acool_type	Type of Air cooler
2	cfl_count	How many cfl you have?
3	fan_age	Age of fan
4	fan_count	Count of fan in house
5	fan_service	When was last service done?
6	geyser_count	Geyser count
7	geyser_age	Age of geyser
2	geyser_type	Type of geyser
3	pump_type	Type of pump
4	ups_usage	Usage of pump
5	tbl_cnt	Tube light count
6	led_cnt	LED count
7	incand_cnt	Incandecent lamp count
2	wash_cap	Capacity of washing machine
3	TV_cnt	Count of Television
3	TV_size	Size of TV in inches
3	TV_usg	Usage Television

We use Lasso regression to get the weights.

5.1 Cluster-Wise Regression

In order to get more clear picture about the consumption disaggregation of the consumers, we select few important factors and obtain the weights by regressing against the consumption data per cluster. To get a clear idea about the usage of appliances in different clusters we plot percentage of usage of appliance in all clusters in Fig. 6 (Fig. 7).

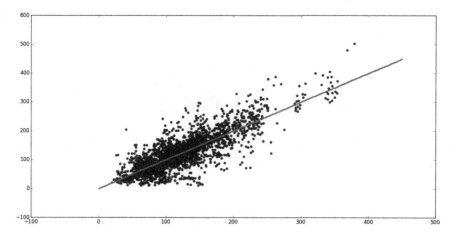

Fig. 5. LASSO regression of particular cluster

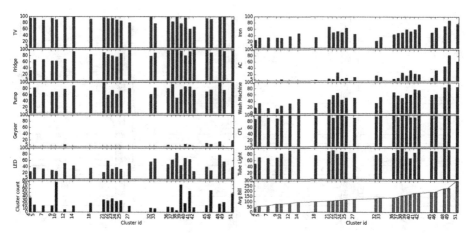

Fig. 6. Appliance usage in different clusters

The monthly billing trend (and hence energy usage trend) of different clusters is presented in Fig. 8.

We also try to estimate the probability density of the monthly bill, we observe that the billing data has exponential flavor as observed in Fig. 9.

Lasso Regression. Since in linear regression without any constraints on the weights, the algorithm can assign unusually high weights to some factors which otherwise does not have impact on the monthly energy consumption, which results in overfitting. Hence we employ LASSO regression, which puts L_1 constraint on the weight, and hence the optimization problem is posed as

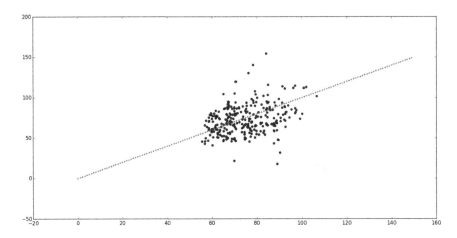

Fig. 7. Linear regression of single cluster

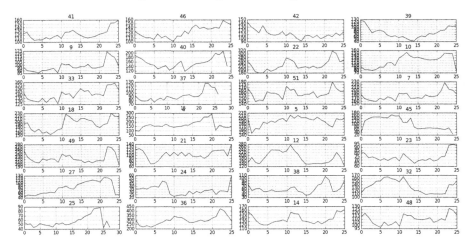

Fig. 8. Linear regression of single cluster

$$\min \sum_{i=1}^{n} \left(y_i - \mathbf{X}_i^T \mathbf{w} \right)^2 + \alpha \left\| \mathbf{w} \right\|_1 \tag{3}$$

where $\left\| \mathbf{w} \right\|_1 = \sum_{i=1}^{n} |w_i|$

Ridge Regression. If instead of L_1 constraint, we impose L_2 constraint on the weights, then we get what is called *Ridge Regression*, which is framed as the following optimization problem:

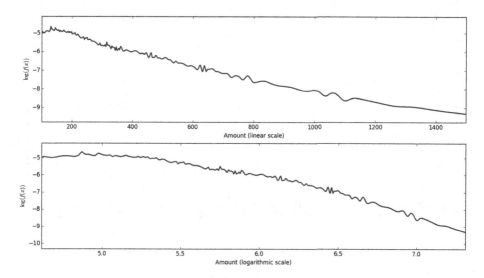

Fig. 9. Probability density of billing data

$$\min \sum_{i=1}^{n} \left(y_i - \mathbf{X}_i^T \mathbf{w} \right)^2 + \alpha \left\| \mathbf{w} \right\|_1^2 \tag{4}$$

where $\left\| \mathbf{w} \right\|_1^2 = \sum_{i=1}^{n} |w_i|^2$

Elastic-Net Regression. In Elastic-net Regression, L_1 and L_2 constraints on the weights are combined, and the optimization problem is posed as:

$$\min \sum_{i=1}^{n} \left(y_i - \mathbf{X}_i^T \mathbf{w} \right)^2 + \alpha\rho \left\| \mathbf{w} \right\|_1 + \frac{1}{2}\alpha(1 - \rho) \left\| \mathbf{w} \right\|_2^2 \tag{5}$$

Support Vector Machine Regression: RBF Kernel Method. We also used SVM based technique to perform the regression of the billing data with the appliance and building survey data.

The error performance of various regression techniques can be observed in Figs. 10 and 11.

We observe one thing that Lasso Regression is the preferred choice of regression, because of two reasons: 1) LASSO automatically assigns zero weights to those factors which do not play major role in monthly bill 2) In comparison to SVM, the weight assigned to a factor is directly related to the energy usage by that factor.

168   S. M. Shah

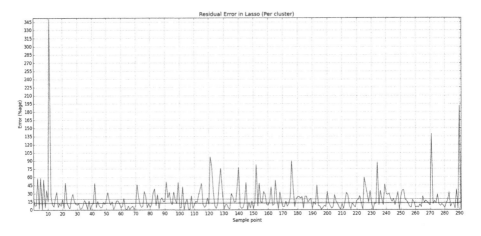

Fig. 10. Error performance of Lasso regression

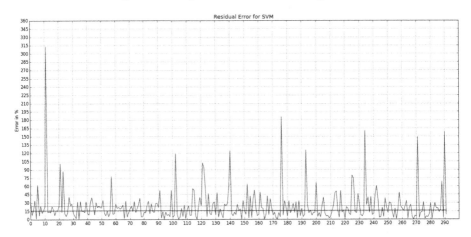

Fig. 11. Error performance of support vector machine

5.2 Disaggregation

The weights obtained via regression corresponding to any appliance can be used to get the disaggregation of the energy usage. Say the factor for a particular appliance if E_i then the fraction of energy consumed by that appliance is proportional to $w_i E_i$. By using this information we can give personalized consumption disaggregation to a particular consumer, see Fig. 12.

To validate the reliability of LASSO regression model, we use Akaike Information Criterion (AIC) [16] and Bayesian Information Criterion (BIC) [17] as shown in Fig. 13.

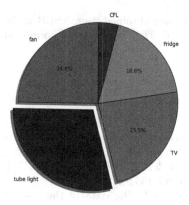

Fig. 12. Disaggregation of energy usage using LASSO

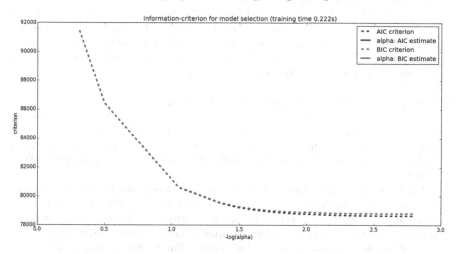

Fig. 13. Information criterion validation of LASSO

6   Conclusions

In this paper we study the case of one city of Kerala, called Aluva. We obtain
monthly billing data of the region and perform clustering using K-means algorithm to divide the consumers into different classes. Then we use the survey
data, obtained from 1000 houses, and use supervised learning techniques like
LASSO, SVM, to disaggregate the total consumption into the usage of different
appliances. We also validate our model using Information Criterions like AIC
and BIC. Although the results were obtained for the data of particular areas
of Kerala, but the methodology proposed in this paper is appliciable in various
underdeveloped countries where billing data is available in raw form.

Acknowledgement. The author would like to thank TEQIP-III for the support for
this project. Part of the work was carried out when the author was project associate

at IISc Bangalore. The data was obtained from KSEB under the joint project of IISc Bangalore and Clytics Pvt. Ltd. Their support and permission to use the data is highly acknowledged.

References

1. Gajowniczek, K., Zabkowski, T.: Simulation study on clustering approaches for short-term electricity forecasting. Complexity **2018** (2018)
2. Lazarova-Molnar, S., Mohamed, N.: Collaborative data analytics for smart buildings: opportunities and models. Cluster Comput. **22**(1), 1065–1077 (2017). https://doi.org/10.1007/s10586-017-1362-x
3. Ushakova, A., Mikhaylov, S.J.: Big data to the rescue? Challenges in analysing granular household electricity consumption in the United Kingdom. Energy Res. Social Sci. **64**, 101428 (2020)
4. Walker, S., Khan, W., Katic, K., Maassen, W., Zeiler, W.: Accuracy of different machine learning algorithms and added-value of predicting aggregated-level energy performance of commercial buildings. Energy Build. **209**, 109705 (2020)
5. Sadeghi, A., Sinaki, R.K., Young, W.A.: An intelligent model to predict energy performances of residential buildings based on deep neural networks. Energies **13**, 571 (2020)
6. Sehovac, L., Nesen, C., Grolinger, K.: Forecasting building energy consumption with deep learning: a sequence to sequence approach. In: IEEE International Congress on Internet of Things (ICIOT), pp. 108–116. IEEE (2019)
7. Hong, T., Wang, Z., Luo, X., Zhang, W.: State-of-the-art on research and applications of machine learning in the building life cycle. Energy Build. **212**, 109831 (2020)
8. Saha, H., Florita, A.R., Henze, G.P., Sarkar, S.: Occupancy sensing in buildings: a review of data analytics approaches. Energy Build. **188**, 278–285 (2019)
9. Causone, F., Carlucci, S., Ferrando, M., Marchenko, A., Erba, S.: A data-driven procedure to model occupancy and occupant-related electric load profiles in residential buildings for energy simulation. Energy Build. **202**, 109342 (2019)
10. Tang, R., Wang, S., Sun, S.: Impacts of technology-guided occupant behavior on air-conditioning system control and building energy use. Build. Simul. **14**, 209–217 (2021). https://doi.org/10.1007/s12273-020-0605-6
11. Mitra, D., Steinmetz, N., Chu, Y., Cetin, K.S.: Typical occupancy profiles and behaviors in residential buildings in the united states. Energy Build. **210**, 109713 (2020)
12. Buttitta, G., Finn, D.P.: A high-temporal resolution residential building occupancy model to generate high-temporal resolution heating load profiles of occupancy-integrated archetypes. Energy Build. **206**, 109577 (2020)
13. Hu, S., Yan, D., An, J., Guo, S., Qian, M.: Investigation and analysis of Chinese residential building occupancy with large-scale questionnaire surveys. Energy Build. **193**, 289–304 (2019)
14. Hu, S., Yan, D., Qian, M.: Using bottom-up model to analyze cooling energy consumption in China's urban residential building. Energy Build. **202**, 109352 (2019)
15. Lloyd, S.: Least squares quantization in PCM. IEEE Trans. Inf. Theory **28**(2), 129–137 (1982)

16. Akaike, H.: Information theory and an extension of the maximum likelihood principle. In: Parzen, E., Tanabe, K., Kitagawa, G. (eds.) Selected Papers of Hirotugu Akaike. Springer Series in Statistics (Perspectives in Statistics), pp. 199–213. Springer, New York (1998). https://doi.org/10.1007/978-1-4612-1694-0_15
17. Schwarz, G., et al.: Estimating the dimension of a model. Ann. Stat. **6**(2), 461–464 (1978)

Machine Learning and Soft Computing Techniques for Combustion System Diagnostics and Monitoring: A Survey

Amir Khan[1]([✉]), Mohd. Zihaib Khan[2], and Mohammad Samar Ansari[3,4]

[1] University Womens' Polytechnic, Aligarh Muslim University, Aligarh, India
amiramu10@gmail.com
[2] University Polytechnic, Aligarh Muslim University, Aligarh, India
zohaib017@gmail.com
[3] Software Research Institute, Athnlone Institute of Technology, Athlone, Ireland
mansari@ait.ie
[4] Department of Electronics Engineering, Aligarh Muslim University, Aligarh, India

Abstract. Combustion systems are ubiquitous in nature and are employed under varied conditions to comply with the specific demands of the applications they are used in. Combustion control and optimization techniques are essential for efficient and reliable monitoring of the combustion process. This paper presents a comprehensive review of combustion monitoring diagnostics and prognostics which have been researched thoroughly using various soft-computing techniques incorporating state-of-the-art Machine Learning (ML) and Deep Learning (DL) techniques. Regarding the combustion systems, there are three primary areas which have been investigated *viz.* (i) combustion state monitoring, (ii) radical emissions and their concentration measurement, and (iii) 3-D flame image reconstruction. This paper reviews these areas along with recent advancements in the flame imaging techniques.

Keywords: Combustion system · Flame imaging · Radicals · Deep learning · Machine learning · Soft computing

1 Introduction

Combustion systems are the key component of many industries. Different combustion systems like gas turbines, combustion engines, fossil fuel fired boilers, biomass fired combustion systems etc. are in practical use, and there are no signs of these being phased out in the near future and replaced by more futuristic counterparts. In order to make the combustion process efficient, different approaches for combustion systems monitoring and diagnostics have been proposed over the time. There are three primary objectives to be achieved regarding the combustion process. Firstly, anomaly detection in combustion state is investigated. Secondly, 3-D image/temperature reconstruction and characterization

S. M. Thampi et al. (Eds.): SoMMA 2020, CCIS 1366, pp. 172–186, 2021.
https://doi.org/10.1007/978-981-16-0419-5_14

of flame will be discussed. Finally, the estimation of the concentration of emitted radicals like OH*, CH*, C2* *etc.* is dealt with. Anomaly detection is one of the main feature of combustion diagnostics, and is one area where conventional machine learning algorithms are quite mature and widely-used. Many existing works have studied flame imaging through image processing techniques and soft-computing [1–17]. In these research papers, first the images are characterized, and then different transformations are performed such as watershed transformation, and thereafter statistical parameters are evaluated to find the combustion state. Second major group of researchers investigated the radical emission in different combustion systems [18–26]. Emitted radicals are dependent on fuel types and fuel-to-air ratio. These studies have been carried out by studying the chemi-lumninscence emissions through the flame. Luminous distribution of the flame has also been studied. Many other research works [27–44] focus on the flame image reconstruction. For this purpose, varied experimental arrangements have been devised which consist of multiple cameras placed at different locations (w.r.t the flame) to create a number of projections for faithful reconstruction of the 3-D flame image. This survey is different from other surveys, as this incorporates three distinct fields related to industrial flames. Furthermore, this survey covers diverse fuel types and most importantly Soft Computing and Machine learning works have been included at one place.

The work embodied is divided into seven sections. Section 2 deals with flame imaging and monitoring the stability of the combustion flame (normal or abnormal state). Section 3 explains the luminous distribution of the flame and radicals emission through chemi-lumniscence. Section 4 investigates the 3-D flame image reconstruction techniques that have been proposed in the technical literature. Recent trends and future prospects in this field are explored in Sect. 5 and 6 respectively; and the conclusions are discussed in the last section.

2   Flame Instability Monitoring

The combustion diagnostics and monitoring has become an area of excessive concern due to the use of poor-quality fuels, fuel mixtures, oxy-fuels and biomass, which often results in the instability of the flame. This generation of fuels not only causes efficiency reduction but also emits more pollutants (e.g. NOx, SO2). Furthermore, combustion stability is predominantly related to the structure of the burner, types of the fuels used, air-to-fuel ratio, fuel's ignitability, and the balance present between velocities of flame.

Efficient monitoring when coupled with diagnostic techniques could determine the quality of flames which helped to measure the performance of the combustion process. It was found that experimental results are in perfect agreement with the theory. A method to evaluate the flame stability centered around time-frequency analysis and higher order statistics has been investigated in [1]. A multi-objective evolutionary algorithm was presented in [2] for the optimization of the combustion process. The main objectives were (i) To curtail down NO_x emissions, and (ii) Decrement in flame pressure pulsations. Authors in [3] presented a generic algorithm based approach to augment the design of a swirler employed in combustion chambers involving non-premixed flames. In [4], a generalized learning vector neural network framework has been devised to capture the textural features of the flame images for observing the combustion state of a rolling burner. To diagnose the state of combustion, a new methodology has been suggested in [5] through direct flame imaging and kernel PCA (Principal Component Analysis). In 2012, the authors formulated a local neighborhood standardization approach employing PCA for multi-mode processes fault identification in the state of the flame [6]. An augmented dynamic neighborhood preserving embedding technique coupled with PCA approach for monitoring the multi-mode combustion state has been reported in [6,7]. For successful pattern construction and stable monitoring of multi-mode combustion process, techniques such as applied kindependent component analysis-principal component analysis (k-ICA-PCA) have been employed [8]. Jiang et al. devised a novel approach for multi-mode observation for the whole plant which involved techniques such as mutual information-based multi-block PCA, joint probability and Bayesian inference method [9]. Authors in [10] suggested a real-time prognostic model to quantify the furnace performance metrics based upon dynamic imaging when coupled with both the Hidden Markov Model and multiway PCA. It has been proposed in [11] and [12] to devise an extreme learning machine (ELM) model which uses flame image features to classify over burning, normal burning or under burning in a rotary kiln.

Research papers exploring several modern imaging techniques are next discussed, with an emphasis on those works incorporating intelligence into the system employing Deep Learning (DL) techniques. In [13,14], images of the flame are first watershed transformed, and then soft-computing has been applied. Watershed transformation has been performed for feature extraction of the image. 14 texture features and 3 color features have been extracted. Figure 1 shows the segregation of flame image regions into *pre-mixing* and *diffusion* regions using watershed transformation which is further processed to generate different features as used by [13,14]. In [13], Principal Component Analysis has been used to reduce the dimensions of the captured flame features, and Kernel Support Vector Machine (KSVM) has been implemented for image classification into two categories: anomalous or normal. In [14], another soft-computing technique referred to as Random Weight Network has been applied preceded by the PCA. It needs to be pointed out that in all these discussed works, the difference is not only in the soft-computing method employed, but also in type of fuel considered in each is different which translates to different flame characteristics and parameters. Oxy-fuels (Fuel/O_2/CO_2) and pulverized fuels have been used in [13] and [14] respectively. In [13], it has been demonstrated that its classification accuracy is better than [14] and also better than existing classifiers such as Nearest Neighbor (NN) and k-NN. In both the cases, statistical parameters such as Hotelling's T-squared (T^2) and Squared Prediction Error (SPE) have been evaluated for predicting the state of the flame. The above-mentioned research employs the supervised learning technique and the image identification has been performed by Deep Learning techniques. A generalized representation of the technical strategy has been shown in Fig. 2 for [13,14].

The DL algorithms may have the potential to surpass all the existing state-of-the-art ML approaches ranging from classification to dimensionality reduction. DL models can easily handle the very large dimensional data and can acquire the hierarchical features of the data. DL techniques have also been applied in flame monitoring and diagnostics. In [15], a deep convolutional selective auto-encoder has been used for correctly predicting the combustion instabilities arising from high-speed flame video, and estimated an instability parameter which credibly measures the distance of the results from the image frames for every transition when compared to the results for a stable flame frame; while in [16] early detection of instability in flame is studied using DL and Symbolic Time Series Analysis (STSA). The works in [15,16] deal with the thermo-acoustic instability in combustion in the aircraft and gas turbines. Auto-encoder structure along with selective mask used in [15] is shown in Fig. 3. In [16], Deep Belief Network (DBN) are implemented and the top layer implemented Symbolic Time Series Analysis (STSA) to acquire sequential nature of images. DBN provides a diverse capability that has made it a key deep learning technique. It can be used for dimensionality reduction, collaborative filtering, solving classification problem, topic modelling, feature learning etc. STSA is fast time-series feature extraction method that qualitatively represents the temporal progression of quasi-stationary time series via symbolization [16].

Another less explored approach is to classify the combustion regime which can provide information similar to flame image characterization. Similar to [13,14,17] used laboratory burner rig for capturing the data, and used a Convolutional Neural Network (CNN) for classification. In [17], researchers proposed an automated approach for determination of combustion regime involving CNN with a regime classification accuracy of 98%. Authors in [45] devised a novel DL algorithm to create a robust diagnostics for combustion flame instability. This study has been performed for hydrogen methane gas (syngas) turbine. Authors proposed a DL technique where sequential flame images are presented as inputs to correctly predict the combustion state for the last frame. A test accuracy of 95.1–98.6% and a very small processing time of 5.2–12.2 ms were achieved. Authors used ResNet [46] as the backbone architecture and added two extra sequential layers namely Early Fusion Layer (EFL) and Late Fusion Layer (LFL) before and after ResNet respectively. EFL takes flame images frames as input and extract the relevant features to be provided to ResNet architecture as inputs. Weights of the EFL are automatically adjusted by the algorithm. But the authors have shown that LFL is useful when the weights are set manually which is a clear drawback of this architecture. Han et al. [47] proposed new monitoring technique using Sparse Stacked Autoencoder (SSAE) based deep neural network. A distinct feature of the method is that proposed SSAE mines the important and relevant features from the flame images in an unsupervised manner. Furthermore, the characterization of combustion stability has been performed using SSAE through classification and regression. The network gave an F1-score of 0.99 and R-squared of 0.98, and was tested on gas combustor and is open to be tested for other types of fuel.

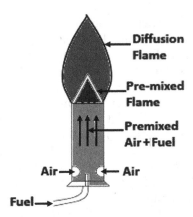

Fig. 1. Sample flame diagram depicting different combustion regions

3   Radical Emission

One of the key factors affecting the combustion stability and efficiency is radical emissions. Carbogen (CH) is a molecule which is usually found in rich flames has a high temperature dependent emission intensity. Moreover, hydroxide (OH) has the maximum emission intensity under stoichiometric conditions. Diatomic carbon (C2) is an intermediate class of molecule often found in rich flames in a combustion reaction [20]. These molecules in excited state form radicals and chemilumniscence is observed at respective wavelengths.

Various methodologies and systems have been proposed to measure the concentration of emitted radicals which exploit the separate spectral signature of an individual radical. Combustion researchers have exploited molecular spectroscopy in various diagnostic techniques, such as Laser Induced Fluorescence (LIF), Laser Induced Incandescence (LII), Coherent anti-Stokes Raman Spectroscopy (CARS) and chemilumniscence. Work embodied in [21] used ultraviolet LEDs for the detection of OH and CH radicals in a methane/air fuel mixture. However, the LEDs used in that work can only detect these two radicals which is a major limitation of this work. Other devices having broader spectrum can be implemented in order to detect other radicals like C_2, CN, etc. The clear advantage of the work is its low cost as the detector ultraviolet LEDs are cost effective. Recently, more focus is on the emission of NO_x because it is the major pollutant in biomass combustion systems. Li et al. published a series of papers looking into the aspect of radical emissions using different soft computing techniques [18,19]. A method that involves flame radical imaging and Support Vector Machines (SVM) for on-line identification of biomass fuels has been investigated in [18]. Characteristic parameters of flame radicals, including OH*, CN*, CH* and C_2*, are extracted and used real-time fuel identification technique for reconstructing the SVM. In another work, they employ radial basis function based neural network techniques to achieve a similar objective [19].

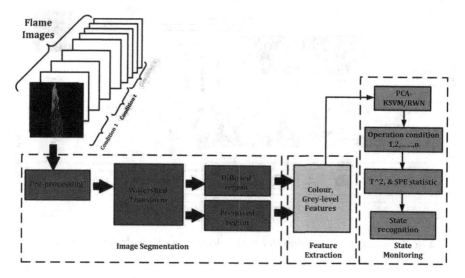

Fig. 2. Diagram illustrating the general technical strategy employed in [13,14] (Adapted from [13])

The work in [22] used a biomass-gas fired test rig, as shown in Fig. 4, to obtain the images of the flame. Flame images emanating radicals are processed by morphological component analysis, and thereafter a DL-based prediction model is employed to predict the NO_x emission. The developed model performs three tasks: feature extraction, feature fusion and emission prediction. Performance of this work has been compared with other machine learning based works [23–25], which employed hand-crafted feature extraction on the basis of Root-Mean-Squared-Error (RMSE). It has been shown that the DL model has surpassed all other works. However, it does not consider the NO_x emission at higher temperature (which is the case in practical industry systems), and also the complex combustion process of industry has not been considered. The proposal in [24] is more diverse with respect to type of fuels it considered. The work in [26] demonstrated a diagnostic set-up for experimental measurements of mole fraction and temperature of OH radical in atmospheric air and methane premixed laminar flat flames. The drawback is that it takes only 1-D simulation of flame images which clearly leads to oversimplification and approximation of original flame. This work also utilized ultraviolet LEDs.

4   Flame Image Reconstruction

The previous section also discussed about the temperature measurement. Rigorous efforts have been done in this direction for faithful reconstruction of the flame image and its temperature variation profile. In recent past, several methods were devised to reconstruct the 3-D flame temperature distribution profile. The various techniques can be categorized as laser-based diagnostic [31,32],

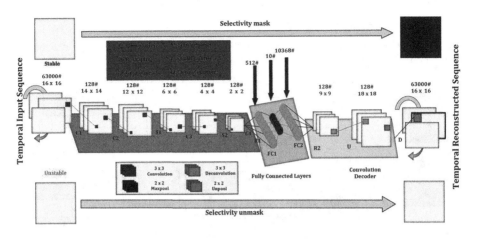

Fig. 3. Structure of autoencoder with selective mask (Adapted from [15])

image-based techniques [27–30, 33–38] and acoustic techniques [39]. Laser-based techniques are efficacious but are mostly implemented in a laboratory owing to their intricate set-up and considerable cost. In various acoustic processes, acoustic transmitters and receivers are employed to sample acoustic signal (acoustic propagation speed). However, in these techniques the spatial resolution is not high owing to multiple transmitters and receivers. For image-based models, usually charge coupled device (CCD) camera or complementary metal-oxide semiconductor (CMOS) camera are engaged. The flame images are first captured using cameras and sampling of flame radiations is then performed. The biggest advantage of the image-based technique is that presence of external signal (laser) is not mandatory. Therefore, they present a straightforward sampling approach when compared to the two previously discussed techniques. Single and multi-camera system have been used depending on the type of flame used. Multiple camera set-up is used in [40, 41] for dealing with unstable and turbulent flames whereas a single camera arrangement [38] is useful for stable and steady flames.

Authors in [27] presented a framework based on neural networks and fuzzy logic which is a vision-guided flame controlling system. The authors claimed that the fuzzy control approach avoided the issue of constructing a burning model for the flame, and the use of neural network made it easier to increase the number of control parameters and inculcate the possibility to adjust the performance of the overall system in an automated manner. The work contained in [28] highlighted an approach to control the combustion flame of a pre-mixed gas burner based upon fuzzy logic. An attentive observation of the colours of the flame to achieve acceptable characteristics for a combustion flame while retaining its size was the desired objective. By employing two stepper driven valves, the flow rates of air and gas can be independently tuned using a fuzzy logic controller. In another related work, authors in [29] classified the fire pixels using an augmented generic colour model based upon fuzzy-logic. To separate the luminance from the chrominance, a YCbCr color space was chosen and proved to be more efficient than

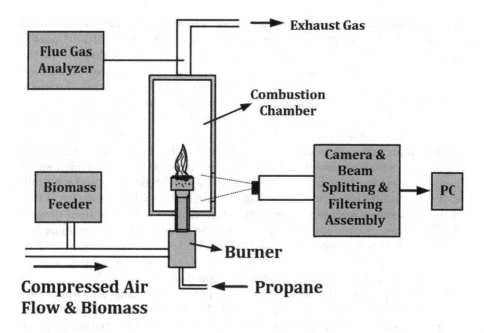

Fig. 4. Experimental setup used in [22] (Adapted from [22])

other color configurations such as RGB. An effective approach to discriminate fire from other fire-like coloured objects is by employing fuzzy logic techniques instead of heuristic models to make the classification process more efficient and reliable. The work in [30] proposed an approach for effective identification of fire regions by using a generic color model and a background difference model. Careful monitoring of flame characteristics such as motion variations, shape and size was achieved using Gaussian membership functions and these generated features were forwarded to fuzzy logic system for real-time fire verification.

Different algorithms have been implemented in order to reconstruct the 3-D temperature distribution profile. The work in [33] used filtered back propagation (FBP) and algebraic reconstruction techniques (ART). Authors in [34] used truncated singular value decomposition (TSVD), and [38] utilized inverse algorithms (like Least Square QR-factorization) *etc.*. Authors in [35] proposed a focused camera based imaging system and a non-negative least square (NNLS) algorithm was implemented for reconstruction of the flame temperature variations. The reconstruction accuracy has been expressed as a function of distance from micro-lens array (MLA) and it has been found that focused camera is better than traditional camera.

Different setups with different number of cameras and their arrangements have been proposed. Although [40] is an old work, it is still quite relevant. The work embodied investigated tomographic reconstruction of burner flames which is based upon optical fiber imaging system. The setup includes two CCD cameras with 8 optical fiber bundles, each containing 30 thousand optical fibers for a higher resolution, connected to each camera. These eight bundles are arranged on a semicircle, burner at the center, having a maximum angle of 180° among them. The setup is really effective as it takes total of eight projections of the flame and successfully reproduces a high resolution reconstructed 3-D image (version) of the flame. The image projections were acquired through the imaging system to faithfully represent the cross and longitudinal sections of a 3-D burner flame. Experimental tests were performed to ascertain the effectiveness of the imaging system as well as the computer algorithm. However, one limitation of such an approach is that the system may suffer from synchronization of different projections obtained and that can also be a bottleneck for high speed monitoring systems. Misalignment of fiber and flame height can also be a problem. A tomographic algorithm combining logical filtered back-propagation (LFB) and simultaneous algebraic reconstruction technique (SART) has been devised [40]. This setup can be updated by keeping the number of cameras same but changing their types. Instead of using RGB CCD cameras, hyper-spectral CCD cameras are employed. Advanced tomographic algorithms can be used for 3-D reconstruction. The set-up used in [40] has been depicted in Fig. 5.

Qi et al. [48] proposed a novel flame imaging technique using multi-plenoptic camera. This multi camera system provides the flame radiative information in two directions along with the accurate reconstruction of distribution of flame temperature. Non Negative Least Square algorithm has been used to rebuild the flame temperature distribution. The proposed system delivered better results in terms of relative error and reconstruction quality when compared with single plenoptic camera arrangement and other traditional multiple camera set-ups.

4.1 Recent Advancements in the Field of Flame Imaging

With the advent of advanced methods, several new techniques have been evolved for flame imaging. A DL approach which can predict Online in-situ evolution of 3-D flames from the previously captured 2-D projections has been reported in [41]. In this work, the experimental technique involved time-resolved volumetric tomography in conjunction with DL algorithms to offer a quick prognostic of 3-D flame progression. The experimental results suggested that progression of both the laminar diffusion flame and a typical non-premixed turbulent swirl-stabilized flame could be measured on a time scale exhibiting accuracy in milliseconds and showed an extra dip with the addition of more GPUs. Furthermore, an unsupervised classification algorithm for flame imaging was also employed.

An unlabelled classification algorithm centered around convolutional auto-encoder (CAE), the hidden Markov model (HMM) and the principal component analysis (PCA) for efficient monitoring of the combustion conditions having uniformly spaced flame images obtained through furnace combustion monitoring system has been reported in [42]. The results obtained from the classification framework provides good classification accuracy (95.25%: training samples and 97.36%: testing samples) and the desired results for identifying the semi-stable state (85.67%: training samples and 77.60%: testing samples) can be obtained.

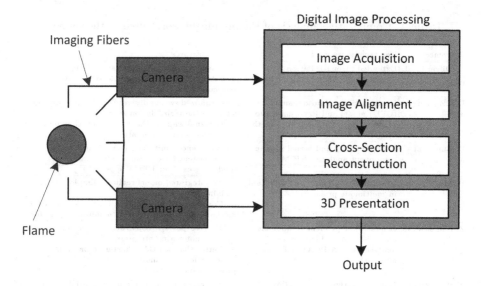

Fig. 5. Camera fibers diagram (Adapted from [40])

Thus, it can be concluded the proposed framework is efficient enough to credibly identify the changes in combustion environment as the combustion process deteriorates with the decreasing coal feed rates.

Another dimension that can be further investigated is a 3-D rapid Flame Chemi-luminescence Tomography (FCT) based upon deep learning algorithm [43]. An illustrative 3D rapid FCT reconstruction technique based on convolution neural networks (CNN) model has been presented for practical combustion measurements. After the completion of the training process, the model had the capability for an efficient reconstruction for a 3-D flame distribution. Initially, three cases of phantoms have been created to mimic the 3-D conical flame using a numerical simulation approach. The next step involved the computation of the loss function and the training time in order to determine and quantitatively certify an optimal CNN architecture.

Lastly, a real FCT system is realized which comprises of 12 CCD cameras that can extract t CH^* and $C2^*$ components using multi-spectral separation algorithm. The proposed CNN model can faithfully reconstruct the 3-D flame structure using real time captured projections with a high degree of similarity and a credible accuracy. The reconstruction, thus obtained, can be authenticated by practical measurements testing. Moreover, when compared with traditional iteration reconstruction approach, the proposed CNN model exhibits an improved performance in terms of reconstruction speed which enabled fast 3-D monitoring of flames (Table 1).

A research work which investigates temperature and concentration distribution profiles for flame images is presented in [44]. A machine learning algorithm for the measurement of species concentrations and temperatures using spectral

Table 1. Comparative analysis of the prominent works used in the survey

Reference	Key techniques used	Salient features
C. Oliver et al. [2]	Extended Strength Pareto Evolutionary Algorithm (E-SPEA)	— Chemiluminescence results: Uniform distribution profile of heat release in the recirculation zone
D.A.Z. Luna et al. [3]	Computational fluid dynamics (CFD) model and Renormalization group (RNG) k-" turbulence method	— Optimized swirler design: Stabilization was sensitive to the recirculation zone — External walls of the combustion chamber: Experiences low temperatures
D. Sun et al. [5]	Flame imaging and kernel principal component analysis (KPCA)	— Confidence limit: 95% (KPCA approach) — Consistent false warning: 0% (Statistical modelling used for KPCA approach)
H. Ma et al. [6]	Novel LNS-PCA for fault detection in multimode processes	— An integrated model realized: Employed scaled training data — Conventional MSPM approach and PCA/PLS methods: Multimode process monitoring possible
Z. Zhu et al. [8]	A new k-independent component analysis–principal component analysis (k-ICA-PCA) modeling approach	— Process pattern construction and multi-mode process monitoring are proposed — Better than k-PCA (Clustering based pattern construction) and multi-PCA (Multi-mode process monitoring)
J. H. Chen et al. [10]	Hidden Markov model (HMM) and multiway principal component analysis (MPCA)	—The cross-correlation among spatial features: Obtained using MPCA technique — Reduced dimensionality space — Temporal behaviour of the sequence of spatial features obtained: HMM approach — State-based segmentation
X. Bai et al. [14]	PCA-RWN (Principal Component Analysis and Random Weight Network)	— Condition recognition success rate: >91% (employed PCA-RWN technique) — Reduced training time. — Detect abnormalities with varied oscillation frequencies: Used T^2 and SPE statistical modelling
X. Li et al. [18]	Combination of flame radical imaging and radical basis function (RBF) neural network (NN) techniques.	— Accurate modelling of RBF NNs: Using performance metrics (Intensity contours and mean intensity) — RBF networks are better than traditional SVM.
N. Li et al. [22]	Flame radical imaging and deep learning (DL) algorithms	— Improved FRI dataset — Enhanced computational efficiency — Algorithms: Morphological component analysis, region of interest (ROI) extraction — Feature fusion and fine-tuning strategies: Enhances accuracy of prediction results.
N. Li et al. [24]	Radial basis function network modelling, SVR modelling, and the LS-SVR modelling	— Soft-computing model for NOx prediction based on flame radical features: Employed LS-SVR model (found better than MSRE and MRE) — NOx emissions: 27.79 ppm for LS-SVR and RMSEV (9) and 7.23 ppm for MRE V (9)
M. M. Hossain et al. [33]	Combined logical filtered back-projection (LFBP) and simultaneous iterative reconstruction and algebraic reconstruction technique (SART)	— Black body source (1000–1200 C): Metrics (Temperature and emissivity measurements) — Max. relative error: 1.04% (temperature) and 8.65% (emissivity) — Max. temperature difference of thermocouple and imaging system ≯±9%
J. Huang et al. [41]	Time-resolved volumetric tomography) with deep learning algorithms	— Enhanced computational efficiency: Simple algorithmic operations (solutions to complex partial differential equations can be omitted)
T. Qui et al. [42]	Unlabelled classification framework based on convolutional auto-encoder (CAE), PCA and HMM	— High classification accuracy (training: 95.25% and testing:97.36%) — Improved performance for semi-stable state (training: 85.67% and testing:77.60%)

infrared emission technique has been investigated. The 2010 high-temperature molecular spectroscopic database (HITEMP) for the gaseous combination of CO_2, H_2O, and CO was employed to obtain the training spectra for the ML algorithm. The technique produced credible results for various line-ofsight temperature and concentration distributions, several gas path lengths and different spectral intervals. The measurement of spectral emission was experimentally validated using a set-up which comprised of a Hencken flat flame burner and a Fourier-transform infrared spectrometer having multiple spectral resolutions. The temperature fields above the burner for combustion with equivalence ratios of $\phi = 1$, $\phi = 0.8$, and $\phi = 1.4$, were determined and were in perfect accordance with temperatures realized through Rayleigh scattering thermometry.

5   Future Prospects

Ever expanding domains of ML/DL are most promising and have already been exploited to some extent. But the real potential of these techniques is yet to be unlocked through the application of fully unsupervised techniques. Different unsupervised techniques like Deep Boltzmann Machines, Deep Belief Network, Non-linear auto-encoder *etc.* can be further investigated and incorporated in this area to make their implementation truly unsupervised. Furthermore, there are several advanced cameras are there which can be used over the whole range of flame spectrum and in turn can identify the emission of all types radicals at any wavelength of spectrum. Lastly, latest tomography algorithms like modified delay-and-sum reconstruction and other relevant approaches may be explored for an improved reconstruction of 3D flame images and variations in temperature.

6   Conclusion

A comprehensive study of the methods and techniques that have been put forward for monitoring of combustion system has been discussed in this paper. This includes flame instability monitoring, radical emission study and concentration measurement, and finally the 3-D image reconstruction of the flame. The work embodied in this paper incorporates advanced machine learning and deep learning classifiers to categorize various combustion states. It has been identified that the development of advanced experimental setups involving improved tomographic techniques presents a promising opportunity for future work.

References

1. Zhang, H., Zhou, M., Lan, X.: A fuzzy synthetic evaluation method of flame stability based on time-frequency analysis and higher-order statistics. Energies **12**(7), 1196 (2019)
2. Paschereit, C.O., Schuermans, B., Buche, D.: Combustion process optimization using evolutionary algorithm. In: Turbo Expo. Sea, and Air, vol. 36851, pp. 281–291 (2003)

3. Zavaleta-Luna, D.A., Vigueras-Zúñiga, M.O., Herrera-May, A.L., Zamora-Castro, S.A., Cueto, M.E.T.: Optimized design of a swirler for a combustion chamber of non-premixed flame using genetic algorithms. Energies **13**(9), 2240 (2020)
4. Wang, J.-S., Ren, X.-D.: GLCM based extraction of flame image texture features and KPCA-GLVQ recognition method for rotary kiln combustion working conditions. Int. J. Autom. Comput. **11**(1), 72–77 (2014)
5. Sun, D., Gang, L., Zhou, H., Yan, Y.: Condition monitoring of combustion processes through flame imaging and kernel principal component analysis. Combust. Sci. Technol. **185**(9), 1400–1413 (2013)
6. Ma, H., Hu, Y., Shi, H.: A novel local neighborhood standardization strategy and its application in fault detection of multimode processes. Chemometr. Intell. Lab. Syst. **118**, 287–300 (2012)
7. Song, B., Ma, Y., Shi, H.: Multimode process monitoring using improved dynamic neighborhood preserving embedding. Chemometr. Intell. Lab. Syst. **135**, 17–30 (2014)
8. Zhu, Z., Song, Z., Palazoglu, A.: Process pattern construction and multi-mode monitoring. J. Process Control **22**(1), 247–262 (2012)
9. Jiang, Q., Yan, X.: Monitoring multi-mode plant-wide processes by using mutual information-based multi-block PCA, joint probability, and bayesian inference. Chemometr. Intell. Lab. Syst. **136**, 121–137 (2014)
10. Chen, J., Hsu, T.-Y., Chen, C.-C., Cheng, Y.-C.: Online predictive monitoring using dynamic imaging of furnaces with the combinational method of multiway principal component analysis and hidden markov model. Ind. Eng. Chem. Res. **50**(5), 2946–2958 (2011)
11. Li, W., Wang, D., Chai, T.: Flame image-based burning state recognition for sintering process of rotary kiln using heterogeneous features and fuzzy integral. IEEE Trans. Industr. Inf. **8**(4), 780–790 (2012)
12. Chen, H., Zhang, J., Hu, H., Zhang, X.: Recognition of sintering state in rotary kiln using a robust extreme learning machine. In: International Joint Conference on Neural Networks (IJCNN), pp. 2564–2570. IEEE (2014)
13. Bai, X., Lu, G., Hossain, M.M., Yan, Y., Liu, S.: Multimode monitoring of oxy-gas combustion through flame imaging, principal component analysis, and kernel support vector machine. Combust. Sci. Technol. **189**(5), 776–792 (2017)
14. Bai, X., et al.: Multi-mode combustion process monitoring on a pulverised fuel combustion test facility based on flame imaging and random weight network techniques. Fuel **202**, 656–664 (2017)
15. Akintayo, A., Lore, K.G., Sarkar, S., Sarkar, S.: Prognostics of combustion instabilities from hi-speed flame video using a deep convolutional selective autoencoder. Int. J. Prognost. Health Manage. **7**(023), 1–14 (2016)
16. Sarkar, S., et al.: Early detection of combustion instability from hi-speed flame images via deep learning and symbolic time series analysis. In: Annual Conference of the Prognostics and Health Management (2015)
17. Abdurakipov, S.S., Gobyzov, O.A., Tokarev, M.P., Dulin, V.M.: Combustion regime monitoring by flame imaging and machine learning. Optoelectron. Instru. Data Process. **54**(5), 513–519 (2018)
18. Li, X.L., Li, N., Lu, G., Yan, Y.: On-line identification of biomass fuels based on flame radical and application of support vector machine techniques (2013)
19. Li, X., Mengjiao, W., Gang, L., Yan, Y., Liu, S.: On-line identification of biomass fuels based on flame radical imaging and application of radical basis function neural network techniques. IET Renew. Power Gener. **9**(4), 323–330 (2014)

20. Stamatoglou, P.: Spectral analysis of flame emission for optimization of combustion devices on marine vessels. Lund Reports on Combustion Physics LRCP-176 (2014)
21. Schorsch, S., Kiefer, J., Leipertz, A., Li, Z., Alden, M.: Detection of flame radicals using light-emitting diodes. Appl. Spectrosc. **64**(12), 1330–1334 (2010)
22. Li, N., Gang, L., Li, X., Yan, Y.: Prediction of nox emissions from a biomass fired combustion process based on flame radical imaging and deep learning techniques. Combust. Sci. Technol. **188**(2), 233–246 (2016)
23. Li, X., Sun, D., Lu, G., Krabicka, J., Yan, Y.: Prediction of nox emissions through flame radical imaging and neural network based soft computing. In: IEEE International Conference on Imaging Systems and Techniques Proceedings, pp. 502–505. IEEE (2012)
24. Li, N., Gang, L., Li, X., Yan, Y.: Prediction of pollutant emissions of biomass flames through digital imaging, contourlet transform, and support vector regression modeling. IEEE Trans. Instrum. Meas. **64**(9), 2409–2416 (2015)
25. Li, N., Lu, G., Li, X., Yan, Y.: Prediction of nox emissions from a biomass fired combustion process through digital imaging, non-negative matrix factorization and fast sparse regression. In: Proceedings of the IEEE International Instrumentation and Measurement Technology Conference (I2MTC), pp. 176–180. IEEE (2015)
26. White, L., Gamba, M.: Underresolved absorption spectroscopy of oh radicals in flames using broadband UV leds. J. Quant. Spectrosc. Radiat. Transf. **209**, 73–90 (2018)
27. Tao, W., Burkhardt, H.: Application of fuzzy logic and neural network to the control of a flame process. In: Second International Conference on Intelligent Systems Engineering, pp. 235–240. IET (1994)
28. Tuntrakoon, A., Kuntanapreeda, S.: Image-based flame control of a premixed gas burner using fuzzy logics. In: Zhong, N., Raś, Z.W., Tsumoto, S., Suzuki, E. (eds.) ISMIS 2003. LNCS (LNAI), vol. 2871, pp. 673–677. Springer, Heidelberg (2003). https://doi.org/10.1007/978-3-540-39592-8_98
29. Celik, T., Ozkaramanlt, H., Demirel, H.: Fire pixel classification using fuzzy logic and statistical color model. In: IEEE International Conference on Acoustics, Speech and Signal Processing-ICASSP 2007, vol. 1, p. I-1205. IEEE (2007)
30. Ko, B.C., Jung, J.-H., Nam, J.-Y.: Fire detection and 3D surface reconstruction based on stereoscopic pictures and probabilistic fuzzy logic. Fire Saf. J. **68**, 61–70 (2014)
31. Yang, H.-N., Yang, B., Cai, X.-S., Hecht, C., Dreier, T., Schulz, C.: Three-dimensional (3-D) temperature measurement in a low pressure flame reactor using multiplexed tunable diode laser absorption spectroscopy (TDLAS). Lasers Eng. (Old City Publishing) **31** (2015)
32. Ma, L., et al.: Tomographic imaging of temperature and chemical species based on hyperspectral absorption spectroscopy. Opt. Express **17**(10), 8602–8613 (2009)
33. Hossain, M.M., Lu, G., Sun, D., Yan, Y.: Three-dimensional reconstruction of flame temperature and emissivity distribution using optical tomographic and two-colour pyrometric techniques. Meas. Sci. Technol. **24**(7), 074010 (2013)
34. Liu, D., Yan, J., Cen, K.: On the treatment of non-optimal regularization parameter influence on temperature distribution reconstruction accuracy in participating medium. Int. J. Heat Mass Transf. **55**(5–6), 1553–1560 (2012)
35. Sun, J., Hossain, M.M., Xu, C., Zhang, B.: Investigation of flame radiation sampling and temperature measurement through light field camera. Int. J. Heat Mass Transf. **121**, 1281–1296 (2018)

36. Sun, J., Hossain, M.M., Xu, C.-L., Zhang, B., Wang, S.-M.: A novel calibration method of focused light field camera for 3-D reconstruction of flame temperature. Opt. Commun. **390**, 7–15 (2017)

37. Chuanlong, X., Zhao, W., Jianghai, H., Zhang, B., Wang, S.: Liquid lens-based optical sectioning tomography for three-dimensional flame temperature measurement. Fuel **196**, 550–563 (2017)

38. Sun, J., et al.: Three-dimensional temperature field measurement of flame using a single light field camera. Opt. Express **24**(2), 1118–1132 (2016)

39. An, L.S., Wang, R., Shen, G.Q., et al.: Overview of furnace three-dimensional temperature field reconstruction algorithms based on acoustic theory. Power Syst. Eng. **30**, 9–12 (2014)

40. Hossain, M.M.M., Gang, L., Yan, Y.: Optical fiber imaging based tomographic reconstruction of burner flames. IEEE Trans. Instrum. Meas. **61**(5), 1417–1425 (2012)

41. Huang, J., Liu, H., Cai, W.: Online in situ prediction of 3-D flame evolution from its history 2-D projections via deep learning. J. Fluid Mech. **875** (2019)

42. Qiu, T., Liu, M., Zhou, G., Wang, L., Gao, K.: An unsupervised classification method for flame image of pulverized coal combustion based on convolutional auto-encoder and hidden markov model. Energies **12**(13), 2585 (2019)

43. Jin, Y., et al.: Three-dimensional rapid flame chemiluminescence tomography via deep learning. Opt. Express **27**(19), 27308–27334 (2019)

44. Ren, T., Modest, M.F., Fateev, A., Sutton, G., Zhao, W., Rusu, F.: Machine learning applied to retrieval of temperature and concentration distributions from infrared emission measurements. Appl. Energy **252**, 113448 (2019)

45. Choi, O., Choi, J., Kim, N., Lee, M.C.: Combustion instability monitoring through deep-learning-based classification of sequential high-speed flame images. Electronics **9**(5), 848 (2020)

46. He, K., Zhang, X., Ren, S., Sun, J.: Deep residual learning for image recognition. In: Proceedings of the IEEE Conference on Computer Vision and Pattern Recognition, pp. 770–778 (2016)

47. Han, Z., et al.: Combustion stability monitoring through flame imaging and stacked sparse autoencoder based deep neural network. Appl. Energy **259**, 114159 (2020)

48. Qi, Q., Hossain, M.M., Zhang, B., Ling, T., Xu, C.: Flame temperature reconstruction through a multi-plenoptic camera technique. Meas. Sci. Technol. **30**(12), 124002 (2019)

Traffic Sign Classification Using ODENet

Yaratapalli Nitheesh Chandra Sainath$^{(\boxtimes)}$, Reethesh Venkataraman,
Abhishek Dinesan, Ashni Manish Bhagvandas, and Padmamala Sriram

Department of Computer Science and Engineering, Amrita Vishwa Vidyapeetham,
Amritapuri, India
nitheesh.my@gmail.com, reetheshv.rv@gmail.com, abhishekdinesh3@gmail.com,
ashnibhagvandas16@gmail.com, padmamala@am.amrita.edu
https://www.amrita.edu

Abstract. In the family of deep neural network models, deeper the model is, the longer it takes to predict and larger the memory space it utilizes. It is very much likely that use-cases have constraints to be respected, especially on embedded devices, i.e, low powered, memory-constrained systems. Finding a suitable model under constraints is repeated trial-and-error to find optimal trade-off. A novel technique known as Neural Ordinary Differential Equation Networks (ODENet) was proposed in NeurIPS2018, where instead of a distinct arrangement of internal hidden layers of a Residual Neural Network (RNN), they used parametrized derivatives of internal states in the neural system. Any differential equation solver can be used to calculate the final output. These models have constant depth and can trade between speed and accuracy. We propose a methodology for Traffic Sign Detection using ODENet and subsequently conclude that ODENets are more robust and perform better in comparison to ResNets. We also conclude that though training time is high in ODENets, they can trade-off between speed and accuracy when it comes to both training and testing.

Keywords: Differential equations · Neural networks · Embedded systems · Traffic sign · Deep learning

1 Introduction

1.1 Traffic Sign Detection(TSD)

An innovation by which a vehicle can discern the road signs that are placed on sides of the road such as, "Speed Limit", "No Parking" or "No U-Turn". It is being innovated by various self-driving automotive manufacturers. It can use various techniques ranging from image processing to Lidar analysis to locate and identify traffic signs. The techniques can be commonly grouped based on the color, shape and the type of learning [5,7].

TSD is a real world task which involves lot of constraints and complications. Even a minor misclassification of the traffic sign could lead to catastrophic outcomes and can even lead to loss of life. This is implemented as a sub system in various ADAS and in autonomous vehicles [13].

© Springer Nature Singapore Pte Ltd. 2021
S. M. Thampi et al. (Eds.): SoMMA 2020, CCIS 1366, pp. 187–197, 2021.
https://doi.org/10.1007/978-981-16-0419-5_15

Typically, a camera facing the forward direction will be present on the dashboard of the vehicle and it captures the real time video feed which is sampled into frames and fed to a series of methods and techniques. One of which is a deep learning model which is deployed inside an automotive embedded board. As the vehicle is driven in various environments, lighting conditions, speeds and geographies it is essential for the deep learning algorithm to be robust and reliable at all times. The camera can catch the traffic sign in different orientations and positions but the algorithm should recognize the correct sign [13].

Detection and classification are the 2 main parts of the algorithm. The detection module takes the image and localizes any traffic signs in them after which the classification module identifies which sign it is. Also, both modules work based on the colour, shape and edges of traffic signs. There are ways to determine both detection and classification in the same technique [18].

1.2   Neural Networks as Differential Equations

All different variants of residual networks (ResNets) create complicated changes to hidden state with each transformations:

$$\mathbf{h}_{t+1} = \mathbf{h}_t + f(\mathbf{h}_t, \Theta_t) \tag{1}$$

where $t \in \{0...T\}$ and $h_t \in \mathbb{R}^D$.

Ordinary differential equation can be used as a substitute for 1:

$$\frac{d\mathbf{h}(t)}{dt} = f(\mathbf{h}(t), t, \theta)) \tag{2}$$

The initial layer $\mathbf{h}(0)$ and designate the output layer $\mathbf{h}(T)$ is the result of this initial value problem at a certain depth T. By utilizing any differential equation solver, referred as black-box solver in [7] that computes the concealed dynamics f. These solvers can consists of tunable parameters which in this case are used for speed-accuracy trade off.

For other advantages of NeuralODEs, refer [7].

2   Related Work

2.1   Traffic Sign Detection (TSD)

Can be broken down to subsets which include tasks like detection, classification and tracking. There has been extensive research effort carried by researchers in this area.

Computer Vision Feature Extraction. Computer vision algorithms and methodologies were few of early approaches before the advent of machine learning. Techniques like Histogram Oriented Gradients (HOG) [12] is initially popularized for the detection of pedestrians. In this method the usage of color gradients in images are computed along with various weighted, normalized histograms.

Scale Invariant Function Transform, popularly know as SIFT [10] was used to classify and the sliding window method was used simultaneously to perform both classification and detection tasks.

Machine Learning. Machine learning algorithms uses many techniques namely Support Vector Machines [14], Linear Discriminant Analysis [17], Ensemble Classifiers, Random Forest, and KD-Trees [23].

Linear Discriminate Analysis (LDA) is based on the maximum posterior estimation of the class membership. Class densities are assumed to have multivariate Gaussian and common co-variance matrix [21].

Random Forest is an ensemble classifier method [20] which is a set of decision trees. Each decision tree is trained using randomly taken training data. Testing data is analyzed by all different decision trees for classification. The classification output is based on majority voting, which takes into account the majority decision trees' decisions.

Support Vector Machines (SVMs) are classification algorithms that use a hyperplane to divide the n-dimensional data [14]. SVM can also isolate data distributed non-linearly by projecting the classification hyperplane into higher dimensions using a non-linear kernel function.

Machine learning approaches [1] were unable to manage images of various aspect ratios, sizes and dimensions and had to be manually produced which is a very time-consuming operation that can produce a lot of errors.

Deep Learning. To overcome the disadvantages of above mentioned conventional methodologies new implementations based on deep learning algorithms which presented a novel approach than previous methods. In recent years with an increase in computing power and availability of standardized data sets and access to a huge amount of data.

LENET Architecture was the first CNN architecture for traffic sign classification. Convolutional neural networks are multi-stage neural network architecture that learns the invariant features automatically [6]. Each stage consists of convolution layer, a RELU layer, and a pooling layer [19]. The pooling layer lowers spatial information and functions as complex cells within the visual cortex. A gradient descent based optimizer is used for training and updating each filter to minimize the loss function. The output of all the layers is fed to the classifier for improving the accuracy of classification.

2.2 Neural Ordinary Differential Equation

There was no practical application of adjoint training approach for continuous-time neural networks, even though it was proposed [8]. The concept of exploiting reversibility and approximate computation came into research after viewing residual networks [4] as an approximate ODE solver [24]. The different sections of the said concepts that came under research were adaptive computation (ODE solvers give generalizable and resource and CPU non-intensive solutions to adjust the computation number) [3], constant memory backpropagation (reversible resnets made of restricted architectures with the same memory work-load as normal approach, except our approach does not have such restricted architectures) [2], approximate differential equations from given data (fluid simulation applications are one such example) [22] and using adjoint sensitivity analysis which uses linear-time number of variables in comparison to forward analysis which is quadratic-time [11].

3   Reverse-Mode Automatic Differentiation of ODE Solutions

A package provided by the authors of Neural Ordinary Differential Equations at https://github.com/rtqichen/torchdiffeq.git [3] is being used with Scikit-learn [15].

In training continuous-depth networks, the key technological challenge is to execute backpropagation via the ODE solver. In forward pass operations, differentiating is easy, but it involves a high processing cost and introduces unnecessary computational error.

By using a BlackBox ODE solver, gradients are calculated using *the adjoint sensitivity technique* [16]. This method measures gradients in time, solving an increased ODE backwards. This solving is valid to all ODE solvers. This method also has low memory expenses, scales and problem size are linearly proportional and manages computational error directly.

$$\mathbf{L}(\mathbf{z}(t_1)) = \mathbf{L}\left(\mathbf{z}(t_0) + \int_{t_0}^{t_1} f(\mathbf{z}(t), t, \theta) dt\right) \tag{3}$$

$$= \mathbf{L}\left(ODESolve(\mathbf{z}(t_0), f, t_0, t_1, \theta)\right) \tag{4}$$

where $\mathbf{L}()$ is ascalar-valued loss function and input is the result of an ODE solver:

Gradients corresponding to θ are required to optimize L. In the first step, the dependency between the hidden state $\mathbf{z}(t)$ and the gradient of loss is determined. Also known as the Adjoint $a(t) = \frac{\partial L}{\partial \mathbf{z}(t)}$. Another Ordinary Differential Equation gives the dynamics:

$$\frac{d\mathbf{a}(t))}{dt} = -\mathbf{a}(t)^T \frac{\partial f(\mathbf{z}(t), t, \theta)}{\partial \mathbf{z}} \tag{5}$$

Common ODE solvers can output the state $\mathbf{z}(t)$ at any point. The reverse-mode derivative is seperated inot multiple solutions each bearing the middle of 2 consequtive output times as the loss depends on the in between states. At each iteration, the Adj (Adjoint) matrix will be updated in the direction of the respective partial derivative $\frac{\partial L}{\partial t_i}$. Full derivation can be found in [7].

3.1   ODE-Nets: Error Control

Tolerance of the true solution can be ensured by setting parameters for ODE solvers. Tolerance has direct effect on the behavior of the network. Also the number of feature evaluations is proportional to the amount of time.

Adjusting the tolerance value allows trade-off between accuracy and computational costs. Training for sensitive changes can be done with high precision and test the same system with test will lower tolerance as a trade-off for speed and vice-versa.

3.2 Network Depth

As of now, number of internal evaluations (depends on the initial state) for hidden state dynamics can be used as depth for an ODE solution, but the term is still unclear.

4 Experimental Setup

4.1 Dataset

The GTSRB dataset (German Traffic Sign Recognition Benchmark) [20] is a multi-class classification dataset accumulated as part of IJCNN 2012. It has over 50000 images and 43 different classes. The annotations are given in CSV files with details such as: height and width of the image, bounding box co-ordinates, filename and class label of the traffic sign. A more in-depth review of the dataset was worked upon in Wen Lihua et al. 2017 [9].

4.2 Augmentation and Preprocessing Techniques

Resizing all images to the most prominent width, height and depth of the dataset i.e, $(33 \times 34 \times 3)$. Also, the dataset is unbalanced which could be handled by using some augmenting techniques with rules like

- Allowed rotation: $\pm 25°$ more than this could cause changes to certain samples
- Horizontal shift: $\pm 20\%$
- Vertical shift: $\pm 20\%$, most of the image has to be retained
- Horizontal flip: *False*
- Vertical flip: *False*, As flipping could change the sign
- Color space transformation: ± 0.1, as signs are subject to lighting under different seasons
- Scale in: 0.5
- Scale out: 2.0, to make predictions size invariant
- crop: Allowed with a min height or width as at least 40%
- Noise Injection: Gaussian or Salt and Pepper, adding noise to prevent adversarial attacks

4.3   Additional Augmentation Techniques

In the real-world, data can exist in a variety of unpredictable circumstances which can not be accounted for by the simple methods described above. Conditional GANs have the power to generate images with variations in the wild with input images.

The above method is robust but computationally intensive. Anything called neural design transfer would be a cheaper option. This takes one image's texture/ambience/appearance (aka, the "style") and combines this with another's material.

The only downside to this approach is that rather than practical, the performance appears to look more artistic. However, there are other advancements that have amazing effects, such as Deep Picture Style Transfer, shown below.

4.4   Brief on Interpolation

In general, the original image size has to be maintained after performing the above transformations. Our picture has no knowledge about what's outside its borders. In general, the space outside the boundary of the image is zeros. Therefore you get a black area when you do these transformations where the image is not specified.

But the images do not have a black colour group of pixels which may not be what is desired. There are various algorithms both in image processing and Machine Learning algorithms to fill the missing padding or empty space:

- **Constant** A simplest gap filler would be to fill the empty part with a fixed value.
  This works monochromatic images but not for images but does work for.
- **Reflect** Image values will be reflected along the missing values from the boundary of the image.
  Useful for natural or continuous contexts.
- **Edge** The image's edge values are extended beyond the boundary.
  For mild translations, this method can work
- **Symmetric** Similar to reflecting, despite the fact that a copy of the edge pixels is rendered at the boundary of reflection.
  Noticeable when dealing with very small scale patterns or images.
- **Wrap** The picture is only replicated as if it were tiled outside its limits.
  This does not make sense for a lot of scenarios, not as popularly used.

Custom methods can be used for handling missing values. For most classification problems, these methods will typically do well.

4.5   Deep Learning Techniques

Choosing an impainting approach is both temporally consistent and maintains a clear object boundary.

4.6   Network Architecture

The architecture used for the TSD consists of 2 convolutional layers as with 64 and 128 filters respectively. Followed by an ODE Block with two convolutions with a flatten and a dense layer for output. Above mentioned each convolution is a group of Convolution, Batch Normalization, MaxPooling.

Input Layer. Input Layer is used to instantiate a tensor. This layer takes the images as input thus the size will be ($33 \times 34 \times 3$) to take RGB image as input.

Convolutional Layer. The 2D convolution layer is the most common form of convolution used and is typically abbreviated as conv2D. In a conv2D layer, a filter or kernel has a height and a width. It is usually smaller than the image input and so it is transferred over the entire image. The region in which the filter appears on the image is called the receptive field.

Every filter in this layer is initialized randomly into some distribution (Normal, Gaussian, etc.). Each filter is trained slightly differently by having different initialisation criteria. Eventually, they learn how to detect various features in the image. Unless they both were equally configured, then the odds of two filters learning similar features are significantly rising. Random initialization helps each filter to learn to recognise different characteristics.

Since each conv2D filter learns a separate feature, many of them are used to identify different features within a single layer. The best part is that every filter is learnt automatically. Here a kernel size of 3×3 is used along with 64, 128 filters in conv_1 and conv_2.

Pooling Layer. Its purpose is to gradually bring down the spatial size which in turn allows to decrease trainable parameters, thereby decreasing network computation. Pooling layer functions independently on every function diagram.

Max and average pooling are the most common methods employed in pooling.

Batch Normalization Layer. By modifying and scaling the activations, the input of a layer is normalized. This allows all layers to work independently.

It eliminates overfitting, since it has a small effect of regularization. Hence, less dropout is used along with batch normalization, which is a good thing since the loss of details is minimised. Nonetheless, for regularization, batch normalization cannot be solely relied on; its better to be used along with dropout.

Dropout Layer. On a neural network, Dropout is implemented per row. Almost all layers can be used with a dropout layer. Dropout parameter specifies probability of an output retaining for next layer. Generally a probability of 0.5 is used.

ODEBlock Layer. A chain of residual blocks in a neural network is basically a solution of the ODE with the Euler method as

$$y_{n+1} = y_n + f(t_n, y_n) \tag{6}$$

in this case, the the system's initial condition is "time" 0, which indicates the very first layer of the neural network, and as x(0) will serve the normal input, which can be time series, image, whatever you want! The final condition at "time" t will be the desired output of the neural network: a scalar value, a vector representing classes or anything else.

These residual connections are discrete time steps of the Euler method, which means that the depth of the neural network can be regulated just by choosing the discretizing scheme, hence, making the solution (aka neural network) more or less accurate, even making it a pseudo-infinite-layer.

Flatten Layer. The spatial dimensions of the input collapse into the channel dimension by a flattening layer.

Dense Layer. Every node in this layer is connected to every other node in the previous layer. Also know as fully connected layer. In this case, a dense layer with 43 nodes is used for output.

5   Results

The model is compared with ResNet, a similar network. The model is evaluated using the testing data set of 12,630 testing images (Table 1).

$$Accuracy = \frac{\Sigma Correctly Identified}{Total images} \tag{7}$$

Table 1. Comparison of results

Model	Loss (training)	Accuracy (training)	Loss (testing)	Accuracy (testing)	Best epochs
ResNet	0.1066	0.9689	0.7283	0.8046	15
ODENet*	0.0100	0.9968	0.1990	0.9561	17

*Our approach

Training was done using 128 batch size, and categorical cross entropy was used as the loss function. Adam optimizer was been used.

Based on the loss and accuracy metrics of the best epoch, it is concluded that ODENets perform better in comparison to ResNets. It is observed that the number of epochs (iterations) for ODENets is higher, proving that ODENets take longer to converge.

6   Conclusion

Traffic sign detection is a challenging task as they are implemented on a embedded device, thus having a constraint on processing power. By using Neural Ordinary Differential Equation techniques, a trade-off between speed and accuracy of the system can be facilitated to correctly perform image classification and recognition tasks faster, even on blurred, rotated and distorted images. Also as concluded in the previous section, even though training time is longer than in other similar methods, ODENets provide a flexible and faster way of getting results.

7   Future Work

7.1   Minibatching

Usage of mini-batches do not currently have standardization as a regular neural networks. Evaluations are batched together through the differential solver by joining states of batches together to create a combined ODE with a dimension of value **DxK**. For a case of different errors for each batch, a combined error is required, which is K times more system intensive to solve individually. But, no substantial change was noticed in number of evaluations during the practical usage of mini-batches.

7.2   Setting Tolerances

The usage of adaptive solver for ODEs has a trade off between precision vs speed, but this requires the manual setting of tolerances for both forward and backward passes in training. The tolerance was brought down to $1e-3$ and $1e-5$ for atol and rtol respectively without any changes in performance.

7.3   Functions Neural ODEs Cannot Represent

Classes of functions are introduced in arbitrary dimension d which NODEs cannot represent. Let $0 < r1 < r2 < r3$ and let $g : \mathbb{R} \to \mathbb{R}$ be a function such that

$$\begin{cases} g(\mathbf{x}) = -1 & if \, \|x\| \leq r_1 \\ g(\mathbf{x}) = 1 & if r_2 \leq \|x\| \leq r_3 \end{cases} \tag{8}$$

References

1. Andreas Mogelmose, M.M.T., Moeslund, T.B.: Vision-based traffic sign detection and analysis for intelligent driver assistance systems: perspectives and survey. IEEE Trans. Intell. Transp. Syst. **13**(4), 1484–1497 (2012)

2. Chang, B., Meng, L., Haber, E., Ruthotto, L., Begert, D., Holtham, E.: Reversible architectures for arbitrarily deep residual neural networks. In: Thirty-Second AAAI Conference on Artificial Intelligence (2018)
3. Chen, T., Rubanova, Y., Bettencourt, J., Duvenaud, D.: Neural ordinary differential equations. In: Advances in Neural Information Processing Systems, vol. 31, pp. 6571–6583. Curran Associates, Inc. (2018). http://papers.nips.cc/paper/7892-neural-ordinary-differential-equations.pdf
4. He, R., Lin, C., Wang, J., McAuley, J.: Sherlock: sparse hierarchical embeddings for visually-aware one-class collaborative filtering (2016)
5. Hecht, J.: Lidar for self-driving cars. Opt. Photon. News **29**(1), 26–33 (2018)
6. Stallkamp, J., Schlipsing, M., Salmen, J., Igel, C.: Man vs. computer: benchmarking machine learning algorithms for traffic sign recognition. Neural Netw. **32**, 323–332 (2012)
7. Lim, K., Hong, Y., Choi, Y., Byun, H.: Real-time traffic sign recognition based on a general-purpose GPU and deep-learning. PLOS One **12**(3), 1–22 (2017). https://doi.org/10.1371/journal.pone.0173317
8. LeCun, Y.A., Bottou, L., Orr, G.B., Müller, K.-R.: Efficient backpropagation. In: Montavon, G., Orr, G.B., Müller, K.-R. (eds.) Neural Networks: Tricks of the Trade. LNCS, vol. 7700, pp. 9–48. Springer, Heidelberg (2012). https://doi.org/10.1007/978-3-642-35289-8_3
9. Lihua, W., Jo, K.H.: Traffic sign recognition and classification with modified residual networks. In: 2017 IEEE/SICE International Symposium on System Integration (SII), pp. 835–840, December 2017
10. Lowe, D.G.: Object recognition from local scale-invariant features. In: International Conference on Computer Vision, vol. 2, p. 1150. Computer Society, Washington (1999)
11. Melicher, W., Uet al.: Fast, lean, and accurate: modeling password guessability using neural networks. In: 25th USENIX Security Symposium (USENIX Security 16), pp. 175–191. USENIX Association, Austin, August 2016. https://www.usenix.org/conference/usenixsecurity16/technical-sessions/presentation/melicher
12. Dalal, N., Triggs, B.: Histograms of oriented gradients for human detection. In: 2005 IEEE Computer Society Conference on Computer Vision and Pattern Recognition, vol. 1, pp. 886–893, June 2005
13. Deepika, N., Variyar, V.: Obstacle classification and detection for vision-based navigation for autonomous driving. In: International Conference on Advances in Computing, Communications, and informatics (ICACCI)(2017), pp. 2092–2097 (2017). https://www.semanticscholar.org/paper/Obstacle-classification-and-detection-for-vision-Deepika-Variyar/1100b4de94fc4ca6307c09d57901d52a01e18b74
14. Park, J.G., Kim, K.J.: Design of a visual perception model with edge-adaptive gabor filter and support vector machine for traffic sign detection. Expert Syst. Appl. **40**(9), 3679–3687 (2013)
15. Pedregosa, F., et al.: Scikit-learn: machine learning in Python. J. Mach. Learn. Res. **12**, 2825–2830 (2011)
16. Pontryagin, L., Lohwater, A.: Ordinary differential equations (1962). https://cds.cern.ch/record/113444
17. Rabia Malik, J.K., Ahmad, S.N.: Road sign detection and recognition using color segmentation, shape analysis, and template matching. In: International Conference on Machine Learning and Cybernetics, vol. 6, pp. 3556–3560. IEEE (2007)
18. Rani, N.S., Rao, P., Clinton, P.: Visual recognition and classification of videos using deep convolutional neural networks. Int. J. Eng. Technol. (UAE) **7**, 85–88 (2018)

19. Sermanet, P., LeCun, Y.: Traffic sign recognition with multi-scale convolutional networks. In: IJCNN, pp. 2809–2813. IEEE (2011)
20. Stallkamp, J., Schlipsing, M., Salmen, J., Igel, C.: The German traffic sign recognition benchmark: a multi-class classification competition. In: The 2011 International Joint Conference on Neural Networks (IJCNN), pp. 1453–1460. IEEE (2011)
21. Wu, Y., Liu, Y., Li, J., Liu, H., Hu, X.: Traffic sign detection based on convolutional neural networks. In: The 2013 International Joint Conference on Neural Networks (IJCNN), pp. 1–7 (2013)
22. Xie, X., Zhang, G., Webster, C.: Data-driven reduced order modeling of fluid dynamics using linear multistep network (2018)
23. Zaklouta, F., Stanciulescu, B.: Real-time traffic sign recognition in three stages. Robot. Auton. Syst. **62**(1), 16–24 (2014)
24. Zhang, Z., et al.: Modeling of a CO_2-piperazine-membrane absorption system. Chem. Eng. Res. Des. **131**, 375–384 (2018)

Analysis of UNSW-NB15 Dataset Using Machine Learning Classifiers

Anne Dickson[1,2(✉)] and Ciza Thomas[1,2]

[1] College of Engineering, Trivandrum, Thiruvananthapuram, Kerala, India
`annedickson@cet.ac.in`, `cizathomas@gmail.com`
[2] Directorate of Technical Education,
Thiruvananthapuram, Kerala, India

Abstract. Benchmark datasets are the inevitable tool required to scrutinize vulnerabilities and tools in network security. Current datasets lack correlation between normal and the real-time network traffic. Behind every evaluation and establishment of attack detection, such datasets are the cornerstone deployed by research community. Creating our own dataset is a herculean task. Hence analyzing the subsisting datasets aids to provide a thorough clarity on the effectiveness when deployed in real time environments. This paper work focus on analysis and comparison of UNSW-NB15 with NSL-KDD dataset based on performance analysis and accuracy using machine learning classifiers. Feasibility, reliability and dependability of the dataset is reviewed and discussed by considering various performance measures such as precision, recall, F-score, specificity using various machine learning classifiers Naïve Bayes, Logistic Regression, SMO, J48 and Random Forest. Experimental results give out its noticeable classification accuracy of 0.99 with the random forest classifier having 0.998 recall and specificity 0.999 respectively. Research studies reveal the fact that threat diagnosis using conventional dataset and sophisticated technologies cover only 25% of threat taxonomy and hence the poor performance of existing intrusion detection systems. Thorough analysis and exploration of the dataset will pave the way for the outstanding performance of the intelligent Intrusion Detection System.

Keywords: Statistical traffic properties · Traffic classification · Segmentation · Deep packet inspection · Intrusion detection system

1 Introduction

Social engineering is the ultimate data source of real-time cyber threats. Recently available benchmark datasets will not exhibit real-time properties. A quality or trustworthy dataset is supposed to have real network traffic, and it should be sharable, adaptable and labelled. Available benchmark datasets include the DARPA, KDD'99, NSL-KDD, DEFCON, CAIDA, LBNL, CDX, Kyoto, ISCX 2012, UNS ISCX and UNSW-NB15. We use these datasets mainly for evaluating intrusion detection systems (IDS). Old benchmark datasets use simulated

© Springer Nature Singapore Pte Ltd. 2021
S. M. Thampi et al. (Eds.): SoMMA 2020, CCIS 1366, pp. 198–207, 2021.
https://doi.org/10.1007/978-981-16-0419-5_16

datasets. The enormous growth in internet applications leads to the challenging growth in cyber security. Countering this challenge, the research community introduced UNSW-NB15 dataset to evaluate network anomaly intrusion detection systems [1]. Exponential growth of network threats in adversely affected the confidentiality, integrity and availability which are the basic principles of information security. Firewall, IDS which are considered as the wall of defence failed to detect modern attack scenario. Deep network packet inspection and network behaviour analysis is not done appropriately by current IDS. Hence, analysing and monitoring the network systems to detect anomalies and network threats are supposed to perform using variant approaches such as machine learning, deep learning and other hybrid methods.

When coming to network trouble shooting for threat detection, we need network visibility. As intrusions increased with technology expansion, exploration of flow data traffic structure turn into an irreplaceable procedure. It is mandatory to identify the source and destination of packet flows and its configurations. Packet format should be identified precisely regardless of on-demand or full packet dissection. When the world bloom with technology exploration using computers and automation, the core challenge faced in current decade is in modelling secure network applications. IDS also faces different challenges in the areas of network topology, hardware involvement and in other functionality. The performance and availability differs with highly accessible and limited resources with different protocols. Remaining part of the paper is organized as follows. Sect. 2 depicts the related works on analysis of various datasets used in network intrusion detection. Sect. 3 deals with methodology used for analysing this dataset and its insight using distinct machine learning classifiers using various evaluation metrics along with the results. Sect. 4 gives the comparison between the datasets UNSW-NB15 and NSL-KDD. Finally, the paper is concluded with future directions and discussions.

2 Related Works

This section reviews related works on analysing various available intrusion detection datasets. Here we consider the review based on anomaly based intrusion detection dataset among network and host based systems. The UCI repository, Kaggle, Hogzilla, Netresec data, Digital Corpora, ICS cyberattack data set, UMass trace are some of the common repositories of intrusion detection dataset. Intrusion detection models are evaluated usually using both train and test datasets [1]. If the dataset is huge with numerous features, feature reduction is deployed to reduce its computational complexity. Markus et al. [2] claims that irrespective of the type of data, labelled data sets are required for judging anomaly based intrusion detection. Anomaly based detection draws more attention than signature based due to its effectiveness in disclosing novel attacks [3]. Preliminary effort was put forward by DARPA for creating a dataset in 1999 [4] and that was the only trusted one which got international acceptance. The research community deployed this for evaluating IDS models and later several critics arised due to its incapability to cope up with real world network traffic diversity [5]. Based upon the services provided by each network, the type of intrusion and its active duration will differ. Dataset and its attributes adequate for one scenario is not going to work well for other scenario. An intrusion detection dataset should be adaptable, reproducible and labelled, it has to reflect real network traffic according to Viegas et al. [7]. In today's world, networks will always change and analysts have to finger on the pulse of what is happening and identify any unfamiliar activities before it turns into something bad. The motivation behind this paper is the realization that in no way the present IDS can meet the high detection rate, with real time increasing network traffic and complexity of recent cyberspace attacks.

3   Experimental Setup

3.1   Research Methodology

The methodology for the analysis of UNSW-NB15 dataset is summarized as follows. Sklearn library is an open source machine learning tool widely used in python, with various tools for building statistical and machine learning models, including classification, clustering and dimensionality reduction. Initially performance evaluators and model required for analysis are imported followed by the path of the input data set. The dataset is then partitioned into train set and test set for further processing. The required model is fitted using train data. Finally, the response for test data is predicted by calculating accuracy, error matrix, AUC and ROC plot.

3.2   Performance Metrics

For the detailed study regarding the capability of the dataset, various performance evaluators from machine learning classifiers such as Naïve Bayes, Logistic Regression, Support Vector Machine, Decision Tree and Random Forest were taken. Parameters for accessing classifiers such as True Positive, False positive, True negative, False negative are observed. To evaluate effectiveness of the model, accuracy, misclassification, precision, F-measure, sensitivity and specificity are being considered. Performance of a classifier model can be interpreted in a tabular form called confusion matrix or error matrix where each row represents predicted class and column represents actual class. Classification measures can be extended to multiple classes too. As depicted in Table 1, performance measures can be easily calculated from this matrix.

TP: when positively predicts the real occurrence
FP: when negatively predicts the real occurrence
TN: when positively predicts the non-occurrence
FN: when negatively predicts the non-occurrence

Table 1. Confusion matrix

	Actual occurance (true/false)	
Predicted Occurrence (Positive/Negative)	True Positive (TP)	False Positive (FP) Type I Error
	False Negative (FN) Type II Error	True Negative (TN)

Classification Rate or Accuracy is calculated by taking all correct events with total observations. It allows to visualize the performance of algorithm and simple identification of confusion between classes. False positive is the rejection of a true null hypothesis whereas false negative is the non-rejection of a false null hypothesis.

$$Accuracy = (TP + TN)/(TP + TN + FP + FN) \tag{1}$$

$$Classification Error = 1 - Classification Rate \tag{2}$$

Misclassification can be measured by considering all incorrect events with total observations.

$$Misclassification = (FP + FN)/(TP + TN + FP + FN) \tag{3}$$

Precision is taken by considering how much total positives go among predicted positives.

$$Precision = TP/(TP + FP) \tag{4}$$

Sensitivity or recall is the fraction of correctly labelled positive instances from both true positive and false negative. It gives actual positive cases whereas specificity gives actual negative cases.

$$Sensitivity aka Recall = TP/(TP + FN) \tag{5}$$

$$Specificity = TN/(TN + FP) \tag{6}$$

ROC plot is the graph showing the trade-off between sensitivity and specificity for every possible cut-off. A Graph representing false positive rate verses true positive rate. Two dimensional area under the entire ROC is termed as the 'Area Under Curve' (AUC) and it ranges from zero to one. Deploying AUC is an effective way for differentiating IDS performance. An ideal IDS has an area of one and 0.5 for a random IDS. AUC score can be easily calculated using trapezoidal rule.

3.3 Exploring UNSW-NB15 Dataset

The raw network packets of UNSW-NB15 dataset was fabricated in the Cyber Range Lab of the Australian Centre for Cyber Security (ACCS) using IXIA Perfect Storm tool [8,9]. These raw network packets are combination of modern and contemporary network attack characteristics. Argus and BroIDS were the tools used as web based interface remote network monitoring application and for analysing the network traffic to detect behavioural anomalies. TCP dump tool was used for capturing and filtering the packets. This dataset consists of forty-seven features along nine types of attacks such as fuzzers, analysis, backdoors, DoS, Exploits, Generic, Reconnaissance, Shell code and worms. This dataset contains simulated attack types.

3.3.1   Insight of UNSW-NB15 Dataset

The number of records in the training set is 1,75,341 records and the testing set is 82,332 records from different types, attack and normal. Actual number of records consists of 2,540,044 are stored in four CSV files. But for this experimental purpose, 70% of the whole dataset is taken. Numeric, time stamp and categorical are the three data types used to distinguish between various normal and attack instances [10]. This dataset contains a large number of protocols and services with modern security events and malware scenarios. Table 2 mentioned below shows the compartmentalisation of forty seven features other than labelled features from this UNSW-NB15 dataset [31,32].

Table 2. Categorization of UNSW-NB15 attributes

Categories	Attributes
Flow Feature (1–5)	Source IP, Destination IP, Source Port, Destination Port, Protocol Number
Basic Features (6–18)	State, Duration, source and destination bytes, source and destination time to live, source and destination packet loss, service, source to destination packet count and bits per second
Content Features (19–26)	Source and destination window, source and destination TCP base sequence number, packet size mean of source and destination, transaction depth, the data size from server
Time Features (27–35)	Source and destination jitter, start and last time, source and destinaiton inter-packet arrival time, TCP round trip time, TCP connection setup time of SYN and ACK packet
General Purpose Features (36–40)	Is_sm_ips_ports, ct_state_ttl, ct_flw_http_mthd, is_ftp_login, ct_ftp_cmd
Connection Features (41–47)	ct_srv_src, ct_srv_dst, ct_src_ltm, ct_dst_ltm, ct_src_sport_ltm, ct_dst_sport_ltm, ct_dst_src_ltem
Labels (48–49)	Attack or normal

Table 3. Performance Metrics for five classifiers

Machine learning classifier	TP	FP	TN	FN	ROC	Precision	Recall	F-score	Specificity
Naive bayes	4881	2548	7138	1900	0.826	0.657	0.719	0.686	0.736
Logistic regression	6469	889	5912	3197	0.884	0.997	0.999	0.997	0.869
SVM	5622	1708	5242	3895	0.902	0.766	0.590	0.666	0.754
J48	7400	19	9044	4	0.999	0.879	0.669	0.759	0.997
Random forest	7424	5	9030	8	1.000	0.999	0.998	0.009	0.999

The primary goal of analysing the dataset using machine learning classifier is to diagnose performance measures [11]. For this purpose, seventy percentage of the whole dataset is taken for classification and it is classified using Random Forest, J48, Logistic Regression, SVM and Naïve Bayes. Total 16,467 samples were taken. 13174 and 3293 were the training and test samples deployed for analysis. Table 3 shows the details about various performance metrics such as true positive, false positive, true negative, false negative along with accuracy and the ROC area for 16,467 samples.

4   Comparison with NSL-KDD Dataset

Dataset plays a vital role in evaluating the prototype of any problem domain. Existing network traffic datasets which are readily available are either outdated or unreliable. For last decade, NSL-KDD dataset [33] is considered as the most trust worthy and internationally well accepted one even though many criticisms were existing. A fascinating dataset must come with metadata with more decisive properties. When comparing with this NSL-KDD, there are many noticing variations which makes the UNSW more interesting such as methods used in traffic generation, time considered for capturing the network packet, data format, tools used for attribute selection and the rest. UNSW-NB15 dataset [34,35] includes modern attacks and network traffic with six more new features since this is not a simulated one. It is not mandatory that a dataset must include all type of attacks while judging the performance of an intrusion detection system. Research community should find the appropriate data set suitable for their ranking [12].

In UNSW-NB15, three subnets with forty-five distinct internet protocol addresses are used for its experimentation. Here malware is classified into nine different types, whereas in NSL-KDD there are two subnets with eleven internet protocol addresses and classified into four types of attacks. The NSL-KDD data set is expanded version of KDD'99. Benchmark datasets are the inevitable tools utilized to scrutinize, envisage, differentiate and explore data along various dimensions. If we take the record of prior decade, almost all the network threat sensing used the NSL-KDD dataset and hence attacks detected belongs to the usual ones than the advanced one. And the algorithms used for detection are ANN, SVM and K-means [13].

Table 4. Comparison of results for NSL-KDD and UNSW-NB15

Machine learning classifier	NSL-KDD dataset		UNSW-NB15 dataset		
	Accuracy %	FAR %	Accuracy %	FAR %	Classification Error
Naive bayes	70.1	0.101	0.73	15.47	0.271
Logistic regression	76.2	0.54	0.84	5.3	0.247
SVM	84.1	0.23	0.65	10.37	0.341
J48	98.4	0.005	0.98	0.23	0.012
Random forest	98.9	0.004	0.99	0.12	0.002

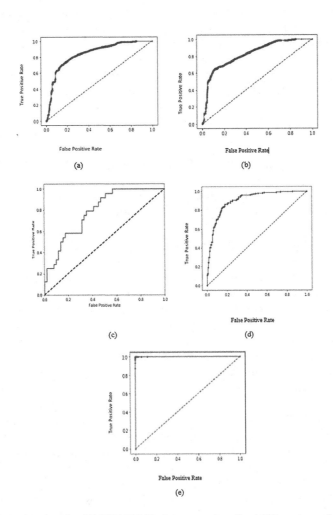

Fig. 1. ROC plot for the UNSW-NB15 dataset using five different machine learning classifiers (a) Naïve Bayes (b) Logistic Regression (c) SMO (d) J48 (e) Random Forest

These datasets are unable to adapt to the persistent changes in the today's networks. Pre-processing of dataset is unavoidable before applying to any machine learning algorithm. Currently, application layer attacks and denial of service attacks are enormously increasing steadily. To improve the performance of IDS, real time datasets has to be incorporated [17]. Figure 1 shows the performance of five different machine learning classifiers such as Naïve Bayes, Logistic Regression, SMO, J48 and Random Forest [18]. Maximum accuracy of 98.9 and 0.99 is attained using the classifier Random Forest with 0.002 minimum classification error as shown in Table 4. Subsisting datasets imparts an immense sample of network threats implanted in normal traffic. Hence, many attack scenarios are managed in the normal traffic data. This is considered as the major cause for the poor performance of IDS and reduced detection rate [21] even now.

5   Conclusion

This manuscript aims at providing an analysis of UNSW-NB15 using machine learning classifiers and calculating performance metrics used for their evaluation criteria for various classification problems. Network threat analysis is possible only with trustworthy datasets. Lack of association between the datasets and the real network traffic is the root cause for the poor performance of intrusion detection. Appreciable results reveal the credibility of UNSW-NB15 dataset and its reliability in the field of network threat analysis. From the performed statistical analysis, credibility of the dataset is proved using performance modelling tool ROC starting from the base classifier Naïve Bayes to the best performer machine learning classifier random forest with a minimum of 0.12% of false alarm rate. Simulating this dataset using various ensemble methods will help the research community to explore more challenges in the field of threat analysis and network security.

References

1. Frank, H., et al.: Optimal design of centralized computer networks. Networks **1**(1), 43–57 (1971)
2. Karnaugh, M.: A new class of algorithms for multipoint network optimization. IEEE Trans. Commun. **24**(5), 500–505 (1976)
3. Newman, M.E.J.: Modularity and community structure in networks. Proc. Natl. Acad. Sci. **103**(23), 8577–8582 (2006)
4. Silander, T., Myllymaki, P.: A simple approach for finding the globally optimal Bayesian network structure. arXiv preprint arXiv: 1206.6875 (2012)
5. Kassabalidis, I., El-Sharkawi, M.A., Marks II, R.J., Arabshahi, P., Gray, A.A.: Gambardella, swarm intelligence for routing in communication networks. Department of Electrical Engineering, Box 352500 (2003)
6. Sharma, P., Khurana, N.: Study of optimal path finding techniques. Int. J. Adv. Technol. **4**(2), 124–130 (2013)
7. Viegas, E., Santin, A., Bessani, A., Neves, N.: BigFlow: real-time and reliable anomaly-based intrusion detection for high-speed networks. Future Gener. Comput. Syst. **93**, 473–485 (2019)

8. Sooda, K., Nair, T.R.: A comparative analysis for determining the optimal path using PSO and GA. arXiv preprint arXiv:1407.5327 (2014)
9. Li, B., et al.: Grid-based path planner using multivariant optimization algorithm, pp. 89-96. Airtilibrary Publication (2015)
10. Attarzadeh, I., Rezaee, A.: A new method for finding the shortest path in network and reducing the time of routing, using gray wolf optimizer (GWO) and chaotic system. Thesis, Slamic Azad University Tehran Science and Research Branch (2016)
11. Singh, V., Bandyopadhyay, M., Singh, M.P.: Geospatial network analysis using particle swarm optimization. Int. J. Comput. Electr. Autom. Control Inf. Eng. (2014)
12. Jin, D., Gabrys, B., Dang, J.: Combined node and link partitions method for finding overlapping communities in complex networks. Sci. Rep. **5**, 8600 (2015)
13. Zhang, L.: Virtual clock: a new traffic control algorithm for packet switching networks. ACM SIGCOMM Comput. Commun. Rev. **20**(4) (1990)
14. Moore, A.W., Zuev, D.: Internet traffic classification using Bayesian analysis techniques. ACM SIGMETRICS Perform. Eval. Rev. **33**(1) (2005)
15. WAN and application solution guide. https://www.cisco.com
16. Huang, S., et al.: A statistical-feature-based approach to internet traffic classification using machine learning. In: 2009 International Conference on Ultra Modern Telecommunications & Workshops. IEEE (2009)
17. Zhen, L., Qiong, L.: A new feature selection method for internet traffic classification using ML. Phys. Proc. **33**, 1338–1345 (2012)
18. Bujlow, T., Riaz, T., Pedersen, J.M.: A method for classification of network traffic based on C5. 0 machine learning algorithm. In: 2012 International Conference on Computing, Networking and Communications (ICNC). IEEE (2012)
19. Bujlow, T., Carela-Espanol, V.: Comparison of deep packet inspection (DPI) tools for traffic classification (2013)
20. Bujlow, T., Pedersen, J.M.: A practical method for multilevel classification and accounting of traffic in computer networks. Technical report, Section for Networking and Security, Department of Electronic Systems, Aalborg University (2014)
21. Singh, K., Agrawal, S.: Comparative analysis of five machine learning algorithms for IP traffic classification (2011)
22. Bakhshi, T., Ghita, B.: On internet traffic classification: a two-phased machine learning approach. J. Comput. Netw. Commun. **2016** (2016)
23. Zhao, S., Zhang, Y., Chang, P.: Network traffic classification using tri-training based on statistical flow characteristics. In: 2017 IEEE Trustcom/BigDataSE/ICESS (2017)
24. Ameur, C.B., Mory, E., Cousin, B.: Combining traffic-shaping methods with congestion control variants for HTTP adaptive streaming. Multimed. Syst. **24**(1), 1–18 (2018)
25. Nguyen, T.T.T., Armitage, G.J.: A survey of techniques for internet traffic classification using machine learning. IEEE Commun. Surv. Tutor. **10**(1–4), 56–76 (2008)
26. Kim, H., et al.: Internet traffic classification demystified: myths, caveats, and the best practices. In: Proceedings of the 2008 ACM CoNEXT Conference. ACM (2008)
27. Nascimento, Z., Sadok, D.: MODC: a pareto-optimal optimization approach for network traffic classification based on the divide and conquer strategy. Information **9**(9), 233 (2018)
28. Ertam, F., Avci, E.: Classification with intelligent systems for internet traffic in enterprise networks. Int. J. Comput. Commun. Instr. Eng. (IJCCIE) **3** (2016)

29. Li, Y., et al.: Survivability optimization and analysis of network topology based on average distance. In: IEEE Asia Communications and Photonics Conference and Exhibition ACP (2009)

30. Hindy, H., et al.: A taxonomy and survey of Intrusion detection system design techniques, network threats and datasets. Article Number 1, vol. 1, pp. 1–35 (2018)

31. Moustafa, N., Slay, J.: UNSW-NB15: a comprehensive dataset for network Intrusion detection systems (UNSW-NB15 network dataset). In: Proceedings of the 2015 Military Communications and Information Systems Conference (MilCIS), Canberra, Australia, pp. 1–6 (2015)

32. UNB. NSL-KDD Dataset (2019). https://www.unb.ca/cic/datasets/nsl.html

33. Dhanabal, L., Shantharajah, S.: A study on NSL-KDD dataset for intrusion detection system based on classification algorithms. Int. J. Adv. Res. Comput. Commun. 4, 446–452 (2015)

34. ACCS. UNSW-NB15 Dataset (2019). https://www.unsw.adfa.edu.au/unsw-canberracybercybersecurityADFA-NB15-Datasets

35. Moustafa, N., Slay, J.: The evaluation of network anomaly detection systems: statistical analysis of the UNSW-NB15 data set and the comparison with the KDD99 data set. Inf. Secur. J.: Glob. Perspect. 25, 18–31 (2016)

Concept Drift Detection in Phishing Using Autoencoders

Aditya Gopal Menon[1]([⊠]) and Gilad Gressel[2]

[1] Amrita Vishwa Vidyapeetham, Kollam, Kerala, India
`adityamenon@am.students.amrita.edu`
[2] Georgia Institute of Technology, Atlanta, GA, USA
`ggressel3@gatech.edu`

Abstract. When machine learning models are built with non-stationary data their performance will naturally decrease over time due to concept drift, shifts in the underlying distribution of the data. A common solution is to retrain the machine learning model which can be expensive, both in obtaining new labeled data and in compute time. Traditionally many approaches to concept drift detection operate upon streaming data. However drift is also prevalent in semi-stationary data such as web data, social media, and any data set which is generated from human behaviors. Changing web technology causes concept drift in the website data that is used by phishing detection models. In this work, we create "Autoencoder Drift Detection" (ADD) an unsupervised approach for a drift detection mechanism that is suitable for semi-stationary data. We use the reconstruction error of the autoencoder as a proxy to detect concept drift. We use ADD to detect drift in a phishing detection data set which contains drift as it was collected over one year. We also show that ADD is competitive within ±24% with popular streaming drift detection algorithms on benchmark drift datasets. The average accuracy on the phishing data set is .473 without drift detection and using ADD is increased to .648.

Keywords: Concept drift · Phishing · Autoencoders · Machine learning

1 Introduction

The most important requirement for any machine learning model to function efficiently is the presence of high quality statistical data. Many machine learning models are designed to make predictions on human created products. Consider for example, prediction of the price of a home, whether or not a piece of software is malware, or the genre of music a song belongs to. All these tasks share the common trait that the subject of the task (homes, software, and music) are created and built by people. Contrast this with physical properties of the world such as the laws of gravity or thermodynamics. In science we can build models which will always predict how long an ice-cube will take to melt in a given set

© Springer Nature Singapore Pte Ltd. 2021
S. M. Thampi et al. (Eds.): SoMMA 2020, CCIS 1366, pp. 208–220, 2021.
https://doi.org/10.1007/978-981-16-0419-5_17

of circumstances, these models once created will never fail. However when we build models to predict if software is malicious or not, given long enough time the models will fail due to changing nature of software.

As new technology is created or as new coding standards emerge, so changes the actual software. Machine learning models are built by extracting features (statistical representations) of the data. We can view the software as a distribution which is generating the features. As software changes with time, the distribution function which generates our features also changes. Simply put, a model trained on malware in 2005 will fail to perform well in 2015 because the underlying software is no longer the same, the underlying distribution of the data has shifted. In machine learning this is termed as concept drift and this causes the performance of the model to degrade significantly.

There has been much work done in concept drift detection, however most approaches have focused on streaming data. Streaming data is continuously generated at such a rapid rate that it is not stored in memory. Many algorithms have been created and studied to detect concept drift in streaming data sets [1,11,22]. Additionally, most concept drift algorithms are supervised [2,7,13]. However most machine learning problems are susceptible to concept drift but are not built on streaming data. These common problems (image detection, text classification, malware detection, etc.) use data sets which are not streaming, yet not stationary. We define these types of data sets as 'semi-stationary' data. For example, a malware data set likely remain useful for a number of years, with diminishing returns depending on the technology landscape.

Perhaps the most vulnerable area is machine learning for security applications. For example, consider phishing detection. The data provided to phishing detection models are features extracted from a website, based on which the model decides whether the corresponding website is malicious or benign. The technology for creating websites has changed a lot over the past 20 years. These changes are concept drift and present a major obstacle to phishing detection models. In this work we take phishing detection as a use-case for semi-stationary data sets.

Autoencoders work on the principles of deconstruction and reconstruction of the input data. This is also known as encoding and decoding the input data. Autoencoders reduce the dimensions of the data in its encoding network layers and restores these reduced dimensions in the decoding neural network layers. We leverage autoencoders' ability to generalize to unseen data. Autoencoders are able to compress and expand similar data with high levels of performance. If the reconstruction error is high, this indicates that the samples are more dissimilar to the training samples. This property of autoencoders proves to be very useful in anomaly detection. For this reason autoencoders are commonly used in credit card fraud detection [24] and intrusion detection systems [14].

For this reason, we create and implement "Autoencoder Drift Detection" (ADD) an unsupervised approach for drift detection that is suitable for semi-stationary data because neural networks excel at handling batch mode data inputs. We leverage the fact that a high reconstruction error indicates the input data is dissimilar to the training data set. We consider a high reconstruction error to indicate a concept drift from the original data. An added benefit is that autoencoders are an unsupervised approach, thus ADD does not require labels to detect drift. An unsupervised approach is superior in that it avoids the high costs of both obtaining labeled data.

We run a series of experiments comparing ADD to Discriminative Drift Detector (D3) [8], Kolmogorov-Smirnov (KS) [23], and Incremental KS Test (IKS) [6], three very popular streaming detection algorithms on the following data sets: ELEC, Weather, Poker hand, Rialto, movingRBF [3,9,13]. We test the drift detection mechanisms in a batch processing manner. Our results show that ADD yields an average batch accuracy of 0.778 for ELEC, 0.243 for Rialto, 0.703 for Weather, 0.577 for Poker, 0.267 for moving RBF, which is competitive with the other algorithms. It is important to note that the autoencoder used in this work contains a very simple architecture, therefore we believe the potential of ADD has not been met yet. With the work done on the phishing data set, ADD was able to achieve an average accuracy of 0.649.

We see the following as our contributions:

- Create "Autoencoder Drift Detection" (ADD) a novel unsupervised concept drift detection algorithm.
- Robust comparison of ADD to similar unsupervised approaches for concept drift detection such as: D3 [8], KS [23] and IKS [6].
- Using ADD to detect the presence of drift in phishing detection data sets.

2   Related Work

Concept drift has solutions that are both supervised and unsupervised. Most concept drift detection algorithms require two separate machine learning models, one model is to detect drift and the other is performing the actual classification task. The solutions in papers like "Early drift detection method" [2], "Learning with drift detection" [7] and "KNN classifier with self adjusting memory for heterogeneous concept drift" [13] are considered supervised approaches because the detection models require labels. The need for labeled data can prove to be expensive. For this reason ADD is an unsupervised approach.

In order to avoid the requirement of labels, researchers have developed unsupervised drift detection mechanisms. In the work by Zhixong Wang and Wei Wang [23], they use Kolmogorov-Smirnov Test (KS) [12] to detect drift in data sets, this does not require labels. KS test is used to determine whether two sample data points belong to the same distribution. When the KS test returns positive for two different sample points, drift is said to have occurred.

Because the KS test performs comparisons between two sample points, it is time consuming for larger data sets. Incremental KS Test (IKS) [6] uses window based logic to enable the KS tests for continuously growing samples from data streams. However this approach cannot be used for multivariate data sets and the authors perform dimensionality reduction before being used with the IKS algorithm. The authors detect drift per feature, rather on the entire data set.

ADD is able to detect drift on the entire input, using neural nets to extract all relevant features which may contribute to drift.

The most similar work to ours is D3 which describes an unsupervised app-roach which uses a discriminative classifier [8]. The discriminative classifier is trained to separate new and old data. It evaluates predictions on a test set after training. The test set is comprised of new (possibly drifted) data. The more accurately the classifier is able to separate the data, the more drift has occurred in the data set. This is an unsupervised approach as the labelling required for the classifier is automatic, it is simply "new" or "old" data. D3 is specifically designed for streaming as the simple classifier is retrained regularly. ADD uti-lizes an autoencoder which encodes the data into a latent space which extracts more information from the data. However ADD is not suitable for streaming data, while D3 is.

It is important to note that all these papers are working in streaming data. Streaming data is continuously generated and normally too large to store in memory. In streaming data the requirement is to detect drift continuously as the classifier may suddenly lose performance. However we are investigating 'semi' stationary data with the a phishing data set. Phishing data changes much more slowly with time, and the evaluation and detection of drift will be done in batches, for example week to week or month to month.

3   Background

3.1   Autoencoders

Autoencoders are neural networks for the purpose of representational learning. They have two phases; encoding and decoding. These layers are separated by a bottleneck which contains the latent space. The network layers on the encoding phase reduce the dimensions of the input data, while the decoding phase expands the dimensions of this compressed latent data back into its original dimensions. The number of layers in the encoding and decoding are typically symmetrical, but not always. Autoencoders are trained by minimizing a loss function. The latent space is the most important quality of the autoencoder, without it the network will simply memorize the input layer. The bottleneck forces the autoen-coder to learn a compression of the input information. An ideal autoencoder would be sensitive enough to accurately decode a latent space, but not overfit to the input data itself. Autoencoders have been used in projects containing data compression [18,20,21] and anomaly detection [14,24] (Fig. 1).

3.2   Drift Speed

Gradual Drift. Gradual drift occurs when the shift in the properties of data occur over a long period of time. Figure 2 shows a plot of accuracy for a general classifier whose data displays a gradual drift. As the time units increases from 0 to 9, the accuracy of the model slowly decreases.

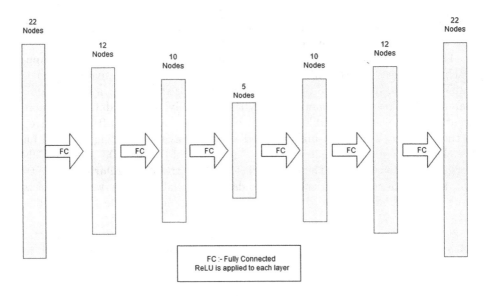

Fig. 1. Autoencoder for concept drift detection in phishing datasets

Sudden Drift. Sudden drift is when the shift in the properties of data occur abruptly causing a sudden drop in accuracy of a general classifier. This is represented by Fig. 3, where there is significant drop in the accuracy of the classifier between the time units 4 and 5.

ADD detects both sudden and gradual drift. If the difference in reconstruction error between two consecutive batches grows suddenly, this is indicative of sudden drift. If the reconstruction error between any given batch and the initial reconstruction error of the trained autoencoder is large this is indicative of a gradual drift. In order to detect both kinds of drifts, ADD implements two different threshold parameters which can be tuned to detect both sudden and gradual drift.

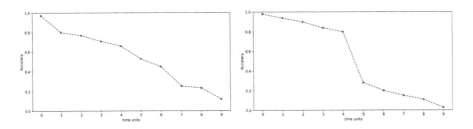

Fig. 2. Gradual drift   **Fig. 3.** Sudden drift

4   Methodology

4.1   Data Collection

We use two kinds of data, streaming and semi-stationary. Streaming data is the data that is generated at a continuous rate. Streaming data needs to be processed incrementally, without guaranteed access to all of the data simultaneously. Semi stationary data is produced in batches. This means that a set of data points are generated together. The next set of data points are produced after an interval. Since, the data remains stationary for an interval of time before a new batch is generated, this type of data can be called semi-stationary.

Streaming Data Collection. In order to compare ADD to other detection algorithms, we used five streaming data sets. One synthetic; Moving RBF [13] and four real world data sets; ELEC, Poker hand, Rialto, Weather [3,9]. These data sets have a varying number of features and number of samples as shown in Table 1.

Table 1. Streaming dataset properties

	Name	#Samples	#Features
Real world	ELEC	45312	6
	Poker Hand	829201	10
	Rialto	82250	27
	Weather	18160	8
Synthetic	Moving RBF	200001	9

Phishing Based Data Collection. We use a phishing data set which contains legitimate and phishing sites from majestic million [10] and phishtank [17] respectively. These websites were crawled using a Selenium based web crawler. This data is semi-stationary in nature as the input data to our models is generated in batches by the web crawler on a day to day basis. Further as discussed earlier phishing data changes slowly with time. The phishing data set has 82553 legitimate websites and 72529 phishing websites.

The phishing data set has 22 features all of which are HTML based features. This includes content based features like the number of forms, redirects, number of iframes, etc. These features are numerical or binary in nature and are widely used in the literature [4,5,15,16,19]. They are mentioned in the Table 2 along with their data types.

4.2   Base Classifier

In concept drift detection, the base classifier is the machine learning model in which would we like to maintain a high level of performance. This can be any sort of classifier that has the ability to train and test on the data. In our experiment we use a Hoeffding tree. The Hoeffding tree supports incremental updates and this makes it an ideal choice for our experiments as it provides a fair comparison to the other drift detection algorithms that use streaming data.

Table 2. Feature set from phishing data set

Feature name	Data type	Feature name	Data type
meta	Count(integer)	redirects	Count(integer)
hidden_text	Count(integer)	rightclick_disable	Binary
images	Count(integer)	submit_to_mail	Binary
iframes	Count(integer)	title	Binary
javascript	Count(integer)	anchor	Count(integer)
href	Count(integer)	SFH	Binary
popup	Binary	insecureforms	Binary
userprompt	Count(integer)	relativeforms	Binary
forms	Count(integer)	abnormalforms	Binary
passwdfield	Count(integer)	text_in_body	Length(integer)
suspicious_word	Count(integer)	onmouseover	Binary

4.3   Autoencoder Architecture

We construct a simple autoencoder in order run our experiments. We use two encoding layers, one latent layer, and two decoding layers. We use the Rectified Linear Unit (ReLU) as the activation function for each layer of the autoencoder. We use mean squared error (MSE) as the loss function to measure reconstruction error of the autoencoder. To perform backpropagation we used the ADAM optimizer. Our autoencoder was implemented with Pytorch. It is important to note that our autoencoder is very simple, perhaps the most simple version possible. We make this choice in order to prototype ADD, and the results indicate that increasing the complexity of the autoencoder may yield much higher performance.

4.4   Autoencoder Drift Detection (ADD)

We now explain how to perform ADD. A key concept of ADD is its ability to detect two kinds of drift, both sudden and gradual. This is done by comparing the reconstruction error between two consecutive batches and the reconstruction

---

Algorithm 1. threshold_compare

Input: $R_i, R_{(i-1)}, R_t, T_g, T_s$
Output: boolean value

1: **if** $R_i - R_t > T_g$ **then**
2:     **return** True
3: **end if**
4: **if** $R_i - R_{i-1} > T_s$ **then**
5:     **return** True
6: **end if**
7: **return** False

---

error between the current batch and the initial batch. This comparison is outlined in Algorithm 1.

We have as inputs to Algorithm 1 the following: R_i (current batch error), R_{i-1} (previous batch error), R_t (error on training batch), T_g (gradual drift threshold), T_s (sudden drift threshold). The output will be a True or False, whether or not drift is detected. If the difference between reconstruction errors $R_i - R_t$ (the current batch and the training batch) is larger than the gradual threshold T_g, then gradual drift has occurred. Otherwise, if the difference between errors $R_i - R_{i-1}$ (the current batch and the previous batch) is larger than the sudden threshold T_s, then sudden drift has occurred. When either of the thresholds are crossed, we return a boolean True value. Otherwise False is returned.

Algorithm 2. Autoencoder Drift Detection

    Input: $Data, bC, aE, Tg, Ts, n$

1: $R \leftarrow [n]$ ▷ array of length n
2: $B \leftarrow [n]$ ▷ array of length n
3: $bC.train(Data_0)$
4: $aE.train(Data_0)$
5: $R_t \leftarrow aE.get\_rec\_loss(Data_0)$ ▷ Training Rec. Error
6: **for** $i \leftarrow index \in make\_batches(Data)$ **do**
7:     $B_i \leftarrow bC.get\_batch\_acc(Data_i)$ ▷ Batch. Accuracy for $Data_i$
8:     $R_i \leftarrow aE.get\_rec\_loss(Data_i)$ ▷ Rec. Error for $Data_i$
9:     **if** threshold_compare$(R_i, R_{i-1}, R_t, T_g, T_s)$ **then**
10:         $Drift \leftarrow True$
11:         $bC.train(Data_i)$
12:         $R_i \leftarrow aE.train(Data_i)$
13:         $R_t \leftarrow R_i$
14:     **else**
15:         $Drift \leftarrow False$
16:     **end if**
17: **end for**

We now describe ADD as presented in Algorithm 2. As inputs we have *Data* (the data), *bC* (base classifier), *aE* (the autoencoder), T_g (threshold for gradual drift), T_s (threshold for sudden drift), and n (number of batches). Two arrays are created R and B, to store the reconstruction error and accuracy respectively. Both *bC* and *aE* are trained on $Data_0$, the first batch. R_t stores the initial reconstruction error on the first batch of data. R_t always symbolizes the reconstruction error on the current trained autoencoder. We then iterate on every batch of the dataset. For each batch i we calculate the batch accuracy and assign it to the variable (B_i) and calculate the reconstruction error and assign to the variable (R_i). At this point we need to compare the reconstruction errors R_i, R_{i-1}, R_t and determine if they are larger than either T_g or T_s the gradual and sudden drift thresholds. This is done using Algorithm 1. If drift detected, then we retrain *bC* (the base classifier) with the current batch of data, this effectively updates it. We also retrain *aE* (the autoencoder) on the current batch. If there is no drift, we simply continue the loop.

There are a number of parameters to tune when using ADD. The most important ones are the two threshold parameters T_g and T_s, each dataset or problem that ADD is used for will have different thresholds that are acceptable. It is also equally important to select batch sizes with enough samples in order to avoid underfitting the autoencoder.

5   Experiments and Results

5.1   Batch Experiments with Streaming Data Sets

We use ADD to detect drift points and calculate batch accuracy in the synthetic data set and four real world data sets Sect. 4.1. Since ADD is designed to detect drift in semi-stationary data, we will be using the batch based ADD algorithm for our experiments. The streaming data sets are divided into training and testing batches.

The objective of the experiment is to compare ADD to KS, IKS, and D3. We use PCA to perform dimensionality reduction in order to use KS and IKS on the entire data set, as KS and IKS only support univariate feature drift detection. We also perform the experiment with no drift detection algorithm at all (no-update) in order to have a baseline model to compare against.

The plots shown in Fig. 4 shows the batch accuracy for the five data sets experimented on. We used T_g of 0.008 and T_s of 0.005, these values were chosen from experimentation. We chose to use the same values across all data sets because we wanted to see how ADD can perform in a general setting. However it would certainly be possible to optimize the thresholds per data set.

We calculated the average batch accuracy of the drift detection models used for each of the data sets which is represented in Table 3. ADD seems to perform well over a period of time as the number of points it has processed increases. It performs the best in ELEC and Poker hand. The highest accuracies of each of the sample data set is marked by bold in Table 3.

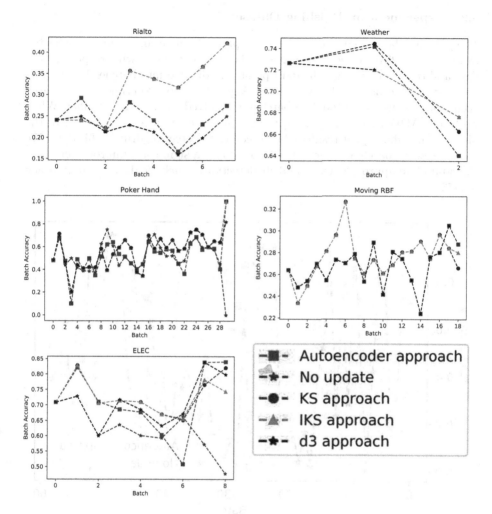

Fig. 4. Accuracy for batch based drift detection

Table 3. Average batch accuracies for the drift detection models

	ADD	KS	IKS	D3	No update
Weather	0.7028	**0.7112**	0.7076	0.7076	0.7076
Rialto	0.2428	**0.3129**	**0.3129**	0.2191	0.2191
ELEC	**0.7784**	0.7303	0.7241	0.7088	0.6197
Poker	**0.5767**	0.5689	0.5689	0.5689	0.513
movingRBF	0.2674	0.2753	**0.2761**	0.2674	0.2674

5.2 Experiment on Phishing Dataset

The phishing dataset contains 155082 samples, 22 dimensions, and was collected from January 2019 to December 2019. The data is ordered with respect to the date and time of crawling. The data points are divided into batches for training and testing. We use batch based ADD Algorithm 2 for experiment. The batch accuracies for the sequential data batches are plotted for the base classifier. When we tested ADD on phishing data, we got mixed results. As seen in Fig. 5, the plot does not show great results when it comes to detecting drift in this data. We got an average batch accuracy of 0.6485. This is a significant improvement over the no-update approach (with no drift detection) which yields a batch accuracy of .473.

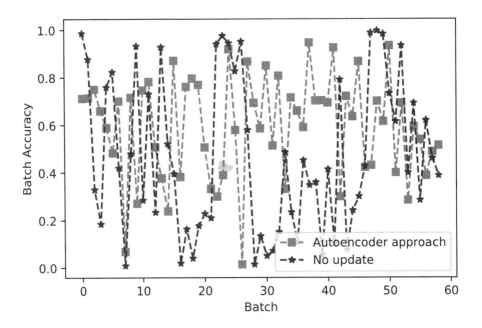

Fig. 5. Batch accuracy for the phishing data

6 Conclusion

Drift detection is a challenge for maintaining a high performing machine learning model over time. There have been many attempts and algorithms introduced to detect drift in streaming data sets. In this work we have introduced ADD an unsupervised approach designed for semi-stationary data. Our results indicate that ADD is competitive with other state of the art unsupervised drift detection algorithms. Additionally ADD is able to detect two kinds of drift, both sudden and gradual. Finally we demonstrate that ADD is able to improve the average batch accuracy by 20% of a semi-stationary phishing data set collected over one year. In the future we plan to experiment with better and more robust parameter tuning of the drift thresholds and also to implement larger and more complex autoencoder architectures. We believe the results in this paper clearly demonstrate the effectiveness of autoencoders to detect drift in semi-stationary datasets and we also believe this performance will only increase with a high model capacity for the autoencoder.

References

1. Anderson, R., Koh, Y.S., Dobbie, G.: Predicting concept drift in data streams using metadata clustering. In: 2018 International Joint Conference on Neural Networks (IJCNN), pp. 1–8. IEEE (2018)
2. Baena-Garcıa, M., del Campo-Ávila, J., Fidalgo, R., Bifet, A., Gavalda, R., Morales-Bueno, R.: Early drift detection method. In: Fourth International Workshop on Knowledge Discovery from Data Streams, vol. 6, pp. 77–86 (2006)
3. Bifet, A., Pfahringer, B., Read, J., Holmes, G.: Efficient data stream classification via probabilistic adaptive windows. In: Proceedings of the 28th Annual ACM Symposium on Applied Computing, pp. 801–806 (2013)
4. Dalvi, S., Gressel, G., Achuthan, K.: Tuning the false positive rate/false negative rate with phishing detection models. Int. J. Eng. Adv. Technol. **9**, 7–13 (2019)
5. Darling, M., Heileman, G., Gressel, G., Ashok, A., Poornachandran, P.: A lexical approach for classifying malicious URLs. In: 2015 International Conference on High Performance Computing & Simulation (HPCS), pp. 195–202. IEEE (2015)
6. dos Reis, D.M., Flach, P., Matwin, S., Batista, G.: Fast unsupervised online drift detection using incremental Kolmogorov-Smirnov test. In: Proceedings of the 22nd ACM SIGKDD International Conference on Knowledge Discovery and Data Mining, pp. 1545–1554 (2016)
7. Gama, J., Medas, P., Castillo, G., Rodrigues, P.: Learning with drift detection. In: Bazzan, A.L.C., Labidi, S. (eds.) SBIA 2004. LNCS (LNAI), vol. 3171, pp. 286–295. Springer, Heidelberg (2004). https://doi.org/10.1007/978-3-540-28645-5_29
8. Gözüaçık, Ö., Büyükçakır, A., Bonab, H., Can, F.: Unsupervised concept drift detection with a discriminative classifier. In: Proceedings of the 28th ACM International Conference on Information and Knowledge Management, pp. 2365–2368 (2019)
9. Harries, M., Wales, N.S.: Splice-2 comparative evaluation: electricity pricing (1999)
10. Jones, D.: Majestic million CSV now free for all, daily (2012)
11. Li, P., Hu, X., Wu, X.: Mining concept-drifting data streams with multiple semi-random decision trees. In: Tang, C., Ling, C.X., Zhou, X., Cercone, N.J., Li, X. (eds.) ADMA 2008. LNCS (LNAI), vol. 5139, pp. 733–740. Springer, Heidelberg (2008). https://doi.org/10.1007/978-3-540-88192-6_78
12. Lopes, R.H.C.: Kolmogorov-Smirnov test. Int. Encycl. Stat. Sci. **30**, 718–720 (2011)
13. Losing, V., Hammer, B., Wersing, H.: KNN classifier with self adjusting memory for heterogeneous concept drift. In: 2016 IEEE 16th International Conference on Data Mining (ICDM), pp. 291–300. IEEE (2016)
14. Madani, P., Vlajic, N.: Robustness of deep autoencoder in intrusion detection under adversarial contamination. In: Proceedings of the 5th Annual Symposium and Bootcamp on Hot Topics in the Science of Security, pp. 1–8 (2018)

15. Mohammad, R.M., Thabtah, F., McCluskey, L.: An assessment of features related to phishing websites using an automated technique. In: 2012 International Conference for Internet Technology and Secured Transactions, pp. 492–497. IEEE (2012)

16. Mohammad, R.M., Thabtah, F., McCluskey, L.: Phishing websites features. School of Computing and Engineering, University of Huddersfield (2015)

17. LLC OpenDNS: Phishtank: an anti-phishing site (2016). https://www.phishtank.com

18. Praveena, R., Kumar, M.A., Soman, K.P.: Chunking based Malayalam paraphrase identification using unfolding recursive autoencoders. In: 2017 International Conference on Advances in Computing, Communications and Informatics (ICACCI), pp. 922–928 (2017)

19. Ramesh, G., Krishnamurthi, I., Kumar, K.S.S.: An efficacious method for detecting phishing webpages through target domain identification. Decis. Support Syst. **61**, 12–22 (2014)

20. Romero, J., Olson, J.P., Aspuru-Guzik, A.: Quantum autoencoders for efficient compression of quantum data. Quantum Sci. Technol. **2**(4), 045001 (2017)

21. Theis, L., Shi, W., Cunningham, A., Huszár, F.: Lossy image compression with compressive autoencoders. arXiv preprint arXiv:1703.00395 (2017)

22. Wang, H., Fan, W., Yu, P.S., Han, J.: Mining concept-drifting data streams using ensemble classifiers. In: Proceedings of the Ninth ACM SIGKDD International Conference on Knowledge Discovery and Data Mining, pp. 226–235 (2003)

23. Wang, Z., Wang, W.: Concept drift detection based on Kolmogorov–Smirnov test. In: Liang, Q., Wang, W., Mu, J., Liu, X., Na, Z., Chen, B. (eds.) Artificial Intelligence in China. LNEE, vol. 572, pp. 273–280. Springer, Singapore (2020). https://doi.org/10.1007/978-981-15-0187-6_31

24. Zamini, M., Montazer, G.: Credit card fraud detection using autoencoder based clustering. In: 2018 9th International Symposium on Telecommunications (IST), pp. 486–491. IEEE (2018)

Detection of Obfuscated Mobile Malware with Machine Learning and Deep Learning Models

K. A. Dhanya[1](✉) [iD], O. K. Dheesha[2] [iD], T. Gireesh Kumar[1] [iD], and P. Vinod[2] [iD]

[1] TIFAC CORE in Cyber Security, Amrita School of Engineering,
Amrita University, Coimbatore, India
`dhannyashibu@gmail.com`, `t_gireeshkumar@cb.amrita.edu`
[2] SCMS School of Engineering and Technology, Cochin, India
`dheeshaprakash@gmail.com`, `vinodp@scmsgroup.org`

Abstract. Obfuscation techniques are used by malware authors to conceal malicious code and surpass the antivirus scanning. Machine Learning techniques especially deep learning techniques are strong enough to identify obfuscated malware samples. Performance of deep learning model on obfuscated malware detection is compared with conventional machine learning models like Random Forest (RF), Classification and Regression Trees (CART) and K Nearest Neighbour (KNN). Both Static (hardware and permission) and dynamic features (system calls) are considered for evaluating the performance. The models are evaluated using metrics which are precision, recall, F1-score and accuracy. Obfuscation transformation attribution is also addressed in this work using association rule mining. Random forest produced best outcome with F1-Score of 0.99 with benign samples, 0.95 with malware and 0.94 with obfuscated malware with system calls as features. Deep learning network with feed forward architecture is capable of identifying benign, malware, obfuscated malware samples with F1-Score of 0.99, 0.96 and 0.97 respectively.

Keywords: Obfuscated malware detection · Machine learning · Deep learning · Random forest · Classification and regression trees · K nearest neighbor

1 Introduction

The significance of mobile phone is countless as it offers a variety of incredible features and opportunities. The tremendous progress in the field of mobile technology together with availability and access to the internet has resulted in an innovative experience in mobile computing. This has been made possible by developing mobile applications. Many factors contributed to the massive growth of mobile applications. Mobile applications are increasingly playing a vital role in the commercial world. A large number of business applications have sprung up with the smart phone industry boom. Some of the most popular types of business

© Springer Nature Singapore Pte Ltd. 2021
S. M. Thampi et al. (Eds.): SoMMA 2020, CCIS 1366, pp. 221–231, 2021.
https://doi.org/10.1007/978-981-16-0419-5_18

applications are banking apps, online shopping apps, mobile payment apps and communication apps. Cyber terrorism is growing exponentially in a sophisticated manner, such that it is mandatory to employ a strong anti-malware strategies to protect the information and digital assets. As per the IT threat evolution Q3 statistics 2018, Kaspersky Lab solutions clogged around 947,027,517 attacks initiated from online assets [1]. McAfee Global Threat Intelligence examined further 1,800,000 URLs, 800,000 files, and 200,000 files in a sandbox each day [2]. Security is becoming more extortionate and hard to manage. The organizations around the world have started spending whopping amounts of money to protect their software from these attacks. Worldwide cyber security spending is said to have reached 96 billion dollars in 2018 [3].

Malware authors have resorted to techniques like obfuscation to evade detection by anti-malware system. Obfuscation has numerous genuine uses, including making software secure and preventing tamper. It also plays an important role in aiding malware to evade different detection mechanisms. Obfuscation is a technique that models programs difficult to interpret. It converts the code to a new version. Originally, this technology was aimed at protecting the intellectual property of software developers. Software developers may also employ obfuscation techniques to conceal flaws and vulnerabilities of the code. Code obfuscation in malicious context has two goals: the malware must elude detection and outlive long enough to accomplish its tasks. Conventional antivirus use signature based or pattern based malware detection. Malware writers can easily defeat the antivirus by changing the syntax without changing the malicious semantics using obfuscation techniques [5]. So it is very crucial to identify obfuscated malware.

Deep learning models are significant in android malware detection since it improves the classification performance. Semantics hidden in the sequence of features can be easily identified by this models [27]. Obfuscated malicious behaviour can be easily revealed with deep learning layers. This work make the following contribution in the area of obfuscated mobile malware detection: Performance of Deep learning models are better than conventional machine learning models for identifying obfuscated malware. Performance of dynamic feature (system calls) is better than static feature (hardware and permission) for conventional machine learning models. Obfuscation transformation attribution requires sophisticated pattern mining methods other than association rule mining with apriori algorithm. Rest of the paper is organised as follows. Section 2 covers literature survey on existing obfuscated malware detection techniques. Section 3 describes architecture and theoretical background of machine learning and deep learning models. Experimental results are demonstrated and analysed in Sect. 4. Section 5 concludes the work.

2   Related Work

Signature-based detection in an anti-malware approach can be easily evaded using simple obfuscation techniques [4]. Static analyses alone are not capable enough to identify malware that incorporates evasion mechanisms. The anti-malware tools that correctly identifies malware failed to detect them after the transformation mechanisms were applied to it. The techniques adopted by malware writers are becoming increasingly sophisticated. This proposes the need for re-designing the malware detection methods so as to effectively protect the smart devices. Numerous experimentation and analysis has been carried out to assess the performance of antivirus tools against obfuscated android mobile malware application. It is observed that many anti-viruses failed to detect obfuscated applications. A detailed literature survey for identifying obfuscated mobile malware given in Table 1.

Table 1. Related work

Author	Methodology and inferences
M. Ikram et al. 2019 [7]	Features from weighted directed graph of API calls. Machine learning models: SVM, KNN, Random Forest. 96% of malware samples were correctly classified
O. Mirzaei et al. 2018 [5]	Features: Dalvik bytecode, control flow graph. Classification models: KNN, SVM, Decision Trees, Random Forest. Accuracy of 92.2% for identifier renaming, 81.41% for string encryption, 68.32% for control flow obfuscation and overall accuracy of 80.66% for the combination of more than one obfuscation technique
G. Suarez-Tangil et al. 2017 [8]	Extra trees are used for malware detection and family identification. Features (API calls, permission, code structure, invoked components, native components, obfuscation artifacts, invariant features underobfuscation). Malware detection accuracy - 99.82% and family identification accuracy - 99.26%
Y. Wang et al. 2017 [9]	Support vector machine for provenance analysis. Features are extracted from data section of DEX files. Obfuscator dentification accuracy - 97%, Configuration recognition accuracy - 90%
J. Garcia et al. 2016 [10]	API based features are used. SVM is used for malware detection and CART is used for family identification. Malicious app detection accuracy - 98% and family identification accuracy - 95%

Most of the works in obfuscated malware analysis concentrates on evaluating the strength of antimalware software on obfuscation techniques and evaluating existing malware detection methods on obfuscation transformation. Obfuscation detection in mobile applcation using batch learning not able to compete in terms of accuracy but save computational resources and time. Androdet [5] claims efficient obfuscated malware detection system. But the authors of Androdet failed to account for the fact that their dataset is biased [6]. As a result machine learning models fail to learn a generalist model for string encryption and might instead learn to classify samples based on characteristic of each malware family. When Androdet is reevaluated with samples never appeared in both the training and testing data, accuracy dropped to around 50%.

3 Methodology

A novel architecture is proposed for identifying obfuscated malicious android application. The model is evaluated with two static features and a dynamic feature. The static features considered here are permission and hardware and dynamic is system call. Figure 1 illustrates the architecture of the proposed model for obfuscated android malware detection.

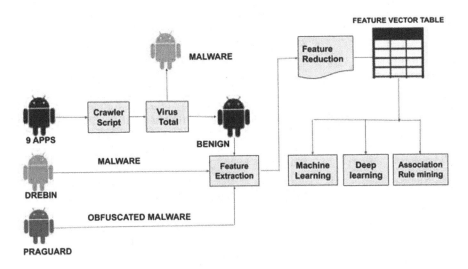

Fig. 1. Proposed system architecture

3.1 Problem Formulation

Let dataset (B, M, O) consist of Benign (B), Malware (M), and Obfuscated Malware (O) samples. Obfuscated Malware samples (O) are generated by applying different obfuscation strategies (Δ) on Malware (M).

$$O = \Delta(M) \tag{1}$$

Each samples are represented as n + 1 tuples such that

$$X_{ij} = (x_{i1}, x_{i2}, x_{i3}.........x_{im}, C_i) \tag{2}$$

where x_{ij} represent the value of jth feature of ith sample and C_i is the class label of sample X_i, $C_i \in$ (B, M, O). Problem is to build a three class classification model capable of mapping the class label of Y($y_1, y_2, ...y_n$) to B, M, O.

3.2 Dataset

The dataset for the proposed system consists of three types of samples-benign, malware and obfuscated malware. A total of 5750 benign samples are collected from the Google Playstore [11] and their genuineness is verified using Virus Total [12]. 5000 malware samples are collected from Drebin [13] and 5000 obfuscated samples are collected from PRAgard dataset [14].

3.3 Feature Extraction

- Static features: Two static features are considered: Permission and hardware features. They are extracted using the Android Asset Packaging Tool [15].
- Dynamic Feature: The dynamic feature considered here is system call. It is extracted using the Android Dumb Bridge [16] and the stress test is performed using the Monkey-runner [17].

3.4 Feature Reduction

Let S be the set of features. Recursive Feature Elimination [18] will generate all combination of features and find $X \in S$ which produce best accuracy with logistic regression. For finding X this approach considers all the subsets of S. For each subset S_j classification model M_{S_j} is generated by Logistic Regression (LR) [19],

$$M_{S_j} = LR(S_j)$$

and its performance is measured. Feature set for which the model produces the maximum performance is selected as X.

$$X = Max(Performance(M_{S_j})|S_j \in (subset(S))) \tag{3}$$

3.5 Feature Vector Table Construction

Classification Model M is generated from the feature vector table F. Feature vector table is a $m \times n$ matrix where m represents the number of samples and n represents the count of the attributes. Feature occurrence matrix is generated for permission and hardware features, whereas frequency matrix for system call features.

Three classification models are generated for identifying obfuscated malware. They are Random Forest [20], Classification and Regression Trees [21] and K-Nearest Neighbour [22].

3.6 Deep Neural Network

Deep learning networks are strong enough to execute feature engineering and thereby can identify relevant features that correlate and then combine features to promote efficient malware detection. In this work a feed forward architecture is proposed with 3 layers with Rectified Linear Unit (ReLU) as activation function in hidden layer and sigmoidal activation function in the output layer. Feed forward network is trained to predict output for all the three features. In order to fit the given data on the feed forward network, the weights of the neural network are updated at the end of every iteration. The hyper-parameters [23,24], used for training deep neural network are epoch, dropout, batch and iteration. They are tuned to get optimised deep network that can identify malware and obfuscated malware efficiently by avoid over fitting of the data and eliminating vanishing gradient problem of deep network.

3.7   Evaluation Metrics

Metrics for evaluating proposed architecture is given in Table 2 [25].
Recall: Sensitivity of classification model is evaluated by recall and it measures the capability of the model to identify the real positive cases.
Precision: Confidence of the model is evaluated by precision. It denotes the true positive accuracy.
F1-Score: F1-Score is the harmonic mean of recall and precision.

Table 2. Evaluation parameters

Precision	$\frac{TP}{TP+FP}$
Recall	$\frac{TP}{TP+FN}$
F1 score	$\frac{2*Precision*Recall}{Precision+Recall}$

3.8   Association Rule Mining

Obfuscation transformation attribution can be performed using association rule mining [26], which is strong enough to find features that are correlated and occur together. In this attribution model, apriori algorithm is used to perform association rule mining for reflection obfuscation with permission, hardware and system call features. Metrics for evaluating quality of mined rules are support, confidence and lift.

Support: Support of a feature P is measured as the proportion of mobile Apps (α) instances in which the feature appears.

$$Support(P) = \frac{\#\{P \in \alpha\}}{\#\alpha} \tag{4}$$

Confidence: Confidence says how likely a feature Q will exist together with feature P. It is expressed as $P \rightarrow Q$.

$$Confidence(P \rightarrow Q) = \frac{Support(P,Q)}{Support(P)} \tag{5}$$

Lift: Lift says how likely a feature P occurs when a feature Q is present.

$$Lift(P) = \frac{Support(P, Q)}{Support(P) * Support(Q)} \qquad (6)$$

4 Results and Discussions

The experiment was conducted on Ubuntu 14.04 platform with the support of Intel core I7 and 8 GB RAM.

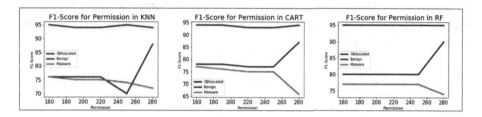

Fig. 2. Performance of classification algorithms with f1-score for permission

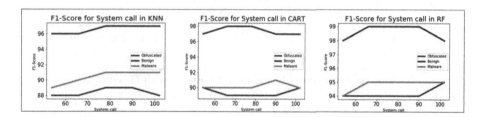

Fig. 3. Performance of classification algorithms with f1-score for system call

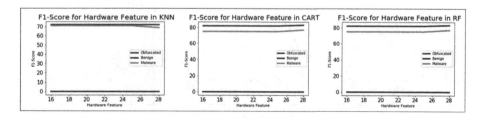

Fig. 4. Performance of classification algorithms with f1-score for hardware feature

4.1   Evaluation of Machine Learning Models

Classification models (CART, RF, kNN) with permission, hardware features and system calls are evaluated using three metrics which are recall, precision and F-Score and results are shown in Fig. 2, Fig. 3 and Fig. 4. Models are generated for different feature length: Permission (160, 190, 220, 250, 280), System Calls (54, 66, 78, 90, 102) and hardware features (16, 19, 22, 25, 28). Experimental results shows that Random forest outperforms other two classifiers with all the three features for malware and obfuscated malware detection due to its ensemble nature. Performance of the hardware features are not appreciable when compared with other two, as its fails to produce much variance among classes due to its limited size. Performance of the system calls are affected much by feature length. As feature length increases, F1-score improves and after a certain limit performance tends to decreases.

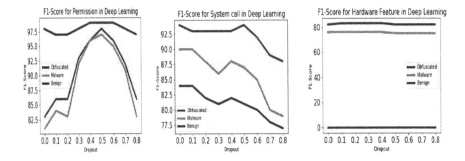

Fig. 5. Evaluation of deep neural network with f1-score

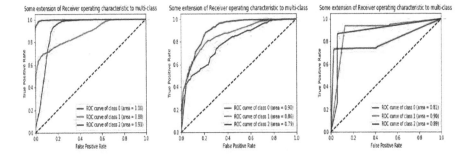

Fig. 6. ROC for permission, system call and hardware feature

4.2 Evaluation of Deep Neural Network (DNN) Models

The DNN is evaluated using recall and F1-score for permission, system calls and hardware features and results are shown in Fig. 5 and Fig. 6. F1-Score for malware and obfuscated malware in permission shows similar trends. F1-Score increases with increase in dropout rate till 0.5 with a value of 97.5 and then shows a gradual decrease. Benign samples show comparatively constant F1-Score values with no steep rises and falls. F1-Score decreases gradually for all the three classes in system calls with increasing dropout values. F1-Score for hardware feature for three classes are not correlated. Permission feature produces best Area under curve (AUC) for benign class and results shows permission and system call features performs much better than hardware feature. Permission features have produced 99% accuracy on deep learning model with dropout 0.5, which is comparatively greater than the existing DaDiDroid [7] model.

Table 3. Association rules

Feature	Rule	Supp.	Conf.	Lift
Permission	android.permission.EXPAND_STATUS_BAR and android.permission.SET_WALLPAPER_HINTS	0.02	1	34.7
System calls	getuid32 and fcntl64 and clock_gettime	0.10	1	4.72
Hardware	gps and network	0.35	0.88	2.5

4.3 Evaluation of Association Rule Mining

Performance of permission, hardware and system call features are evaluated in detecting reflection obfuscation using association rule mining is given in Table 3. Even though the support of permission based feature is poor, confidence factor is maximum for around 20 permissions which indicates the permissions are good for identifying reflection. Moreover highest lift value for around 20 permission is 34.785 which indicates these permissions are strongly bounded to reflection. Support value of system calls are better than permissions. Performance in terms of confidence score is same for all the three features considered. Lift value produced by system calls to identify reflection is less with maximum of 4.72 which depicts the poor associative nature of the system calls with reflection. Further performance of hardware features is less compared with permission and system calls with maximum lift value of 2.52.

5   Conclusion

Machine learning and deep learning models are evaluated for identifying obfuscated malware with features like permissions, hardware features and system calls. Random forest produced best results with permission and system call as it is a strong ensemble decision tree based classifier. Deep learning generates improved results with permission compared to conventional machine learning models. Scope of Association Rule Mining for obfuscation transformation attribution addressed in this work by generating rules for sophisticated reflection obfuscation. In future, various deep learning models can be applied and evaluated for obfuscation detection in malicious mobile application. Obfuscation transformations can be easily identified with resilient features that can be extracted using visualization techniques of malware source code which form the future scope to enrich this research work.

References

1. Kaspersky Lab. https://securelist.com/it-threat-evolution-q3-2018-statistics/88689/. Accessed 4 May 2019
2. McAfee Labs Threats Report. https://www.mcafee.com/enterprise/en-us/assets/reports/rp-quarterly-threats-sep-2018.pdf. Accessed 20 May 2020
3. Gartner Report. https://www.gartner.com/en/newsroom/press-releases. Accessed 15 Apr 2019
4. Scott, J.: Signature Based Malware Detection is Dead. Institute for Critical Infrastructure Technology, Illinois (2017)
5. Mirzaei, O., de Fuentes, J.M., Tapiador, J., Gonzalez-Manzano, L.: AndrODet: an adaptive Android obfuscation detector. Future Gener. Comput. Syst. **90**, 240–261 (2019)
6. Mohammadinodooshan, A., Ulf, K., Nahid, S.: Comment on "AndrODet: an adaptive Android obfuscation detector". arXiv preprint arXiv:1910.06192 (2019)
7. Ikram, M., Beaume, P., Kâafar, M.A.: DaDiDroid: an obfuscation resilient tool for detecting android malware via weighted directed call graph modelling. arXiv preprint arXiv:1905.09136 (2019)
8. Suarez-Tangil, G., Dash, S.K., Ahmadi, M., Kinder, J., Giacinto, G., Cavallaro, L.: DroidSieve: fast and accurate classification of obfuscated Android malware. In: Proceedings of the Seventh ACM on Conference on Data and Application Security and Privacy, pp. 309–320 (2017)
9. Wang, Y., Atanas, R.: Who changed you? Obfuscator identification for Android. In: 2017 IEEE/ACM 4th International Conference on Mobile Software Engineering and Systems (MOBILESoft), pp. 154–164. IEEE (2017)
10. Garcia, J., Hammad, M., Malek, S.: Lightweight, obfuscation-resilient detection and family identification of Android malware. ACM Trans. Softw. Eng. Methodol. (TOSEM) **26**(3), 1–29 (2018)
11. Google Play Store. https://play.google.com/store?hl=en. Accessed 25 Feb 2019
12. Virustotal. https://developers.virustotal.com. Accessed 25 Feb 2019
13. Arp, D., Spreitzenbarth, M., Hubner, M., Gascon, H., Rieck, K., Siemens, C.E.R.T.: Drebin: effective and explainable detection of android malware in your pocket. In: NDSS, vol. 14, pp. 23–26 (2014)

14. PRAGard Dataset. http://pralab.diee.unica.it/en/AndroidPRAGuardDataset. Accessed 5 Mar 2019
15. Android Asset Packaging Tool. https://developer.android.com/studio/command-line/aapt2. Accessed 15 Mar 2019
16. Android Debug Bridge. https://developer.android.com/studio/command-line/adb. Accessed 15 Mar 2019
17. Android Monkey Runner. https://developer.android.com/studio/test/monkey. Accessed 15 Mar 2019
18. Gościk, J., Łukaszuk, T.: Application of the recursive feature elimination and the relaxed linear separability feature selection algorithms to gene expression data analysis. Adv. Comput. Sci. Res. **10**, 39–52 (2013)
19. Zakharov, R., Dupont, P.: Ensemble logistic regression for feature selection. In: Loog, M., Wessels, L., Reinders, M.J.T., de Ridder, D. (eds.) PRIB 2011. LNCS, vol. 7036, pp. 133–144. Springer, Heidelberg (2011). https://doi.org/10.1007/978-3-642-24855-9_12
20. Biau, G.: Analysis of a random forests model. J. Mach. Learn. Res. **13**(1), 1063–1095 (2012)
21. Loh, W.-Y.: Classification and regression trees. Wiley Interdiscip. Rev.: Data Min. Knowl. Discov. **1**(1), 14–23 (2011)
22. Cunningham, P., Delany, S.: K-nearest neighbour classifiers. Technical report. UCD School of Computer Science and Informatics (2007)
23. Srivastava, N., Hinton, G., Krizhevsky, A., Sutskever, I., Salakhutdinov, R.: Dropout: a simple way to prevent neural networks from overfitting. J. Mach. Learn. Res. **15**(1), 1929–1958 (2014)
24. Nwankpa, C., Ijomah, W., Gachagan, A., Marshall, S.: Activation functions: comparison of trends in practice and research for deep learning. arXiv preprint arXiv:1811.03378 (2018)
25. Hossin, M., Sulaiman, M.N.: A review on evaluation metrics for data classification evaluations. Int. J. Data Min. Knowl. Manag. Process **5**(2), 1 (2015)
26. Agarwal, R., Srikant, R.: Fast algorithms for mining association rules. In: Proceedings of the 20th VLDB Conference, pp. 487–499 (1994)
27. Alzaylaee, M.K., Yerima, S.Y., Sezer, S.: DL-Droid: deep learning based Android malware detection using real devices. Comput. Secur. **89**, 101663 (2020)

CybSecMLC: A Comparative Analysis on Cyber Security Intrusion Detection Using Machine Learning Classifiers

Sriramulu Bojjagani[1]([envelope])[ORCID], B. Ramachandra Reddy[1], Mulagala Sandhya[2], and Dinesh Reddy Vemula[1]

[1] Computer Science and Engineering, SRM University-AP,
Amaravati 522502, Andhra Pradesh, India
`sriramulubojjagani@gmail.com`, `brreddy@iiitdmj.ac.in`, `dineshvemula@gmail.com`
[2] Computer Science and Engineering, National Institute of Technology, Warangal,
Warangal 506004, Telangana, India
`msandhya@nitw.ac.in`

Abstract. With the rapid growth of the Internet and smartphone and wireless communication-based applications, new threats, vulnerabilities, and attacks also increased. The attackers always use communication channels to violate security features. The fast-growing of security attacks and malicious activities create a lot of damage to society. The network administrators and intrusion detection systems (IDS) were also unable to identify the possibility of network attacks. However, many security mechanisms and tools are evolved to detect the vulnerabilities and risks involved in wireless communication. Apart from that machine learning classifiers (MLCs) also practical approaches to detect intrusion attacks. These MLCs differentiated the network traffic data as two parts one is abnormal and other regular. Many existing systems work on the in-depth analysis of specific attacks in network intrusion detection systems. This paper presents a comprehensive and detailed inspection of some existing MLCs for identifying the intrusions in the wireless network traffic. Notably, we analyze the MLCs in terms of various dimensions like feature selection and ensemble techniques to identify intrusion detection. Finally, we evaluated MLCs using the "NSL-KDD" dataset and summarize their effectiveness using a detailed experimental evolution.

Keywords: Intrusion detection systems · Machine learning classifiers · Security attacks · NSL-KDD dataset · Feature selection

1 Introduction

An intrusion detection system (IDS) is a system which always monitors the wireless/wired traffic for any malicious activity, or a suspicious action performed. Once any threat happened in the network, it issues alert messages and sends to the intended users. In other words, an IDS is a software application that examines the Internet for malicious activity or policy breaching. In case any violation

© Springer Nature Singapore Pte Ltd. 2021
S. M. Thampi et al. (Eds.): SoMMA 2020, CCIS 1366, pp. 232–245, 2021.
https://doi.org/10.1007/978-981-16-0419-5_19

of security features occurred in the network and reported to the network administrator or collected centrally using security information and event management (SIEM). The SIEM collects data from multiple sources and uses various alert techniques for differentiating the unethical activities over the false alerts. Based on the data analysis IDS classified as two types such as network intrusion detection system (NIDS) and host intrusion detection system (HIDS). The following is the explanation of two IDS:

1. Network Intrusion Detection System (NIDS): It acts as a network monitor and analyzes the traffic from all devices. It identifies the malicious packets flow on the entire subnet and matches the traffic that is passed on the internet by the collection of known vulnerabilities. If any weakness or any abnormal behaviour in the network observed, the alert message directly sent to the network administrator [1,16,17].
2. Host Intrusion Detection System (HIDS): The objective of HIDS monitors the incoming and outgoing packets from the device itself only. If any malicious traffic happened in the network, it alerts the network administrator because these may run on independent devices or hosts on the web [1,16].

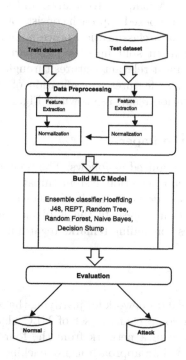

Fig. 1. Organization of a typical MLC model flow

1.1   Machine Learning Classifiers (MLCs)

To detect and to mitigate various unknown (hidden) vulnerabilities existing in the network and to analyze the wired/wireless traffic, several machine learning classifiers developed. Most of these MLCs are detecting vulnerabilities by looking for deviations from a basic (normal) regular traffic model. The models used in the MLCs are trained with the specific attack free and traffic data, i.e. collected from an extended period [11]. There are many works on vulnerability detection using MLCs categorized as three types such as: "supervised learning, unsupervised learning and semi-supervised learning methods".

The primary objective of this paper is we will focus only on the supervised learning classifiers because the supervised learning mechanism provides the trained data which contains no duplicate values and desired outputs. The advantage of a supervised learning mechanism is to provide the predictions on the training data and bring to end only when an acceptable level of performance is achieved so that it allows for the desired target level. The most familiar supervised learning algorithms are "Naive-Bayes (NB), support vector machine (SVM), decision trees (DT), K-nearest neighbours (KNN), logistic regression (LR), artificial neural network (ANN), random forests (RF)", etc.

In this paper, we present a comparative analysis of the various machine learning classifiers (MLCs), the proposed approach consists of two phases: One is data pre-processing and other data classification process. During the pre-processing data stage, the collected input split into the two parts, such as test sets and train datasets. Select the most relevant features through the extraction process. Then normalization of these features, classification of these features, and the evaluation of the classification result as shown in Fig. 1.

1.2   Organization of the Paper

The rest of the paper is organized as follows: The related studies are described in Sect. 2, and the intrusion detection system threat model detailed in Sect. 3. Section 4 provides dataset description. Performance evaluation metrics are described in Sect. 5. Section 6 presents the implementation and experimental results. Section 7 provides concluding remarks regarding this research.

2   Related Work

Nguyen et al. [14] developed framework for justifying the severity of attacks based on the performance of a comprehensive set of MLC algorithms using KDD'99 dataset to identify attacks in a network from the four attack classes. Meera-Gandhi et al. [12] developed an approach using machine learning techniques for prediction of attacks using DARPA-Lincoln dataset. In his proposed method, they were using four ML classifiers for the detection of four types of attacks: U2R, Probe, R2L, and DoS. For results in their approach show that the only J48 ML classifier performs better prediction accuracy for detection of attacks, among others such as NB, MLP, and IBK. Jalil et al. [10] proposed a method for the detection of various attacks using comparing various MLCs. These algorithms were tested based on detection rate, accuracy and false alarm rate using four different classes of attacks. But out of the three classifiers, Decision classifier performs better than other two such as a "neural network (NN) and support vector machines (SVM)".

Dhanabal et al. [7] used NSL-KDD dataset for identifying the intrusion detection in networks system with the study on the effectiveness of various MLCs. In their experimental results shows that they used 20% of NSL-KDD dataset used to compare the accuracy of three MLCs. Decision Tree (J48) classifier produces more accuracy for detection of intrusion in networks than the SVM and NB. Belavagi et al. [2] developed a framework for evaluation of supervised MLCs for detection of various attacks in the network with the NSL-KDD dataset. The algorithms used in her proposed work is "Logistic Regression, Gaussian Naive Bayes, Support Vector Machine, and Random forest method". In their work, the results show that the random forest classifier performs 99% accuracy for detection of attacks in the network. Mahfouz et al. [11] shown a comprehensive analysis of well-known machine learning classifiers for identifying intrusions in the network. Especially, their work considered on various parameters, namely sensitivity to hyperparameter selection, and class imbalance problems that are inherent to intrusion detection.

3   Threat Model

In this section, we develop a threat model for a network intrusion detection system, as shown in Fig. 2. This threat model helps in understanding how an adversary can exploit various attacks in real-time traffic. The main objective of the adversary is to violate the security properties such as confidentiality, authentication, authorization, Non-repudiation and availability [4] in the network. In this paper, the proposed threat model involves an attacker for implements a "Man-in-the-Middle (MitM)". We are not simulating an attacker but for testing and validating the security properties in the network [3,5]. The attacker is actively present in the network and monitors the traffic between end-user and server. The attacker always tries to establish the HTTP traffic instead of HTTPs between the Wi-Fi access point, user, and server. On the other hand, the attacker has a self-signed certificate which is a fake certificate or out-dated certificate [5]. In the diagram first step is the end-user wants to establish the connection with the respective server, but the request is going to the MitM attacker. In step 2, the MitM attacker intends to establish a secure connection (HTTPs) with the desired web server. Now the webserver responds with a real-certificate which is genuine. Meanwhile, the attacker sends a fake-certificate to the mobile application. In this way, the adversary exploits the MitM attack. This scenario is possible only when the mobile app receives a fake certificate and lack of certification pinning [13].

Once the adversary implements MitM attack, other possible associated attacks also exploit over the wired/wireless traffic such as DoS, U2R, R2L, Smurf etc. In this paper, we collect the dataset from NSL-KDD and identify the above all mentioned attacks with maximum and minimum false-positive rates.

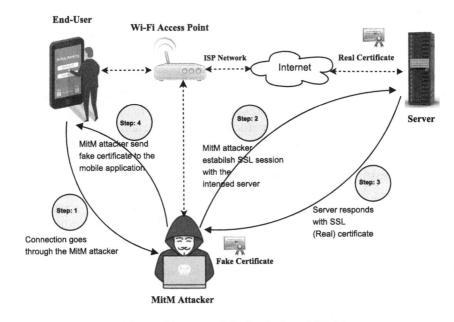

Fig. 2. Threat model: simulation of MitM

4   Dataset Description

The objective of the research is to develop a useful and accurate abnormal (anomalous) behaviour in the network system with a minimum false positive rate based on an ensemble.

To addresses, the various attacks for intrusion detection methods, the security testers, researchers, application developers and bankers have introduced different network traffic datasets. These datasets may be available in public, private, or network simulation datasets—however, these datasets generated by various network monitoring tools that help for capturing the packets for implementing attacks.

4.1   NSL-KDD

In our MLCs, we prefer the well-known dataset, i.e. NSL-KDD [15], which is an improved version of KDDcup99 dataset. Most of data engineering experts, researchers are using the datasets for detecting and analyzing the IDSs in various domains such as cloud computing, Internet of Things, and wired/wireless communication [9]. The file contains all essential records of the full KDD dataset, as shown in Table 1.

Table 1. Description of "NSL-KDD_dataset" files

Sl. no	File name	Description
1	KDDTrain+.TXT	The file consisting of full "NSL-KDD" train set information with vulnerability-type labels and difficulty level in CSV format
2	KDDTrain+.ARFF	The file consisting of full "NSL-KDD" train set data with binary labels in (.ARFF) format
3	KDDTrain+_20Percent.TXT	The file is consisting of 20% subset of the "KDDTrain+.txt" file
4	KDDTrain+_20Percent.ARFF	The file is consisting of 20% subset of the "KDDTrain+.arff" file
5	KDDTest+.ARFF	The file is consisting of full "NSL-KDD" test set data with binary labels in (.ARFF) format
6	KDDTest+.TXT	The file is consisting of full "NSL-KDD" test set data including vulnerability-type labels and difficulty level in (.CSV) format
7	KDDTest-21.TXT	The file is consisting of a subset of the "KDDTest+.TXT". The data does not contain records with difficulty level of 21 out of 21
8	KDDTest-21.ARFF	The file is consisting of a subset of the "KDDTest+.ARFF". The data does not contain records with difficulty level of 21 out of 21

4.2   Feature Selection

The main goal of the feature selection process is selecting a subset of the features from raw data. We ignore the redundant data, so that feature space is optimally reduced to the evaluation criterion. The selection of records in KDD data set are as follows:

1. Duplicate records and unnecessary data are eliminated from the dataset to enable the MLCs to produce unbiased results.
2. The training dataset and test datasets were consisting of a sufficient number of records, which helps to produce results beneficial and accurate in detecting the abnormal behaviour in the network system.
3. The number of records containing in the original KDD data set is inversely proportional to the selected number of records from each difficulty group.

We classify the records into two datasets, one with two classes and another with 24 levels. The former again further classified into two categories one is N stands for Normal, and another one is A for Anomalous. The other classification is 24 classes such as "buffer_overflow, ftp_write, guess_passwd, imap, ipsweep, land, loadmodule, multihop, Neptune, nmap, perl, php, pod, portssweep, rootkit, satan, smurf, spy, teardrop, warezclient, warezmaster, normal, and unknown".

4.3   Ensemble Classifier

In this paper, we have used machine learning ensembled approach [6]. The main idea behind this approach is to construct an accurate intrusion detection system with a low positive rate. In this study, we have used different MLCs for ensemble classifier, such as: "J48, DecisionStump (Decision Tree), IBK (k-nearest neighbour), SVO (SVM), multilayer perceptron (MLP) is a class of feedforward artificial neural network (ANN)". In this model, the seven MLCs executed in parallel and each classifier constructs a dissimilar model of the data. After completed data, it produces output for the seven classifiers are by majority voting method.

5   Performance Evaluation Metrics

Many performance evolution metrics have been proposed in the existing works. In this section, some dimensions used as metrics which are popularly used in evaluating the MLCs for intrusion detection systems.

5.1   Confusion Matrix

To determine the efficiency of various machine learning classifiers, we have used some metrics called sensitivity and specificity. The confusion matrix has three main components. The sensitivity is referred to as true positive rate (TPR), specificity in terms of true negative rate (TNR) and accuracy. These components, defined as follows:

$$Sensitivity = \frac{\mathcal{TPR}}{(\mathcal{TPR} + \mathcal{FNR})} \tag{1}$$

$$Specificity = \frac{\mathcal{TNR}}{(\mathcal{TNR} + \mathcal{FPR})} \tag{2}$$

$$Accuracy = \frac{\mathcal{TPR} + \mathcal{TNR}}{(\mathcal{TNR} + \mathcal{FPR} + \mathcal{TPR} + \mathcal{FNR})} \tag{3}$$

5.2   F-Measure, Recall and Precision

Precision means the percentage of retrieved results which are relevant. On the other hand, recall refers to the portion of relevant total results correctly classified by the algorithm. On the other hand, F-measure is the precision and recall harmonic mean.

$$F - measure = \frac{2 + Precision * Recall}{(Precision + Recall)} \tag{4}$$

$$Recall = \frac{\mathcal{TP}}{(\mathcal{TP} + \mathcal{FN})} \tag{5}$$

$$Precision = \frac{\mathcal{TP}}{(\mathcal{TP} + \mathcal{FP})} \tag{6}$$

To visualize the relation between TPR and FPR rates, generally used receiver operating characteristic (ROC) curve.

5.3   K-Fold Cross-Validation

The term cross-validation is a technique for the re-sampling procedure used to evaluate MLCs on a limited data sample. The method works as first separating the given data sample K spilt into an equal number of groups or folds (instances). As such, the process generally termed as "k-fold cross-validation". When a specific value for k is chosen, then k − 1 folds used to train the system, and the last one is used to place of k about the model, such as k = 10 becoming 10-fold cross-validation. The K folds number depends primarily on the size of the data set. The most used numbers are 3, 5, 7, and 10 [11]. The primary objective of cross-validation in MLCs is to provide a balance between the representation of data and the size of the train and test sets. Apart from that, it estimates the skill of MLCs over unseen data.

6   Implementation and Results

In this section, we discuss the details of the experimental setup and the results of seven MLCs. The parameter metrics used for evaluating the MLCs are correctly classified instances, incorrectly classified instances, percentages of accuracy, inaccuracy, TPR, FPR, precision, recall, f-measure, ROC and PRC area. We identified and chosen seven MLCs to applied for the NSL-KDD data set for intrusion detection. The selected MLCs are J48, DecisionStump, Hoeffding, Random tree, REPT Tree, Random Forest, and Naive Bayes.

The proposed framework has been developed using WEKA [8], which is a data mining tool. It is running a LAPTOP with Intel i7-3770K CPU, 3.50 GHz, 16 GB RAM installed and running a 64-bit OS with Windows 10, x64-based processor.

6.1   Statistical Summary of NSL-KDD

Initially, the dataset is classified and pre-processed and normalized to a range binary to numeric. The action is necessary for individual classifiers to produce better accuracy rate on the normalized dataset. The features of dataset classified as three types: first nomial second binary and third numeric. The more details of the dataset, which is used to identify the intrusion systems are given in [7].

Based on the dataset, the attack types are commonly combined into four groups, and these attacks mapped to the list of vulnerabilities as attack classes shown in the Table 2. The number of sampled data collected for the training set, testing set and occurrences in percentage-wise for normal class and attack classes is shown in Table 3.

6.2   Experimental Results

Our proposed approach is mainly used in the two phases. In the first phase, we compared the performance of various machine learning classifiers without

Table 2. Attack, vulnerabilities types and classes for NSL-KDD

Name of the attack	Name of the vulnerabilities	Description of sampling features	Example
Denial of service (DoS)	Smurf, Teardrop, Neptune, Worm, Land, Back, Mailbomb, UDPstrom, Processtable, Pod	The attacker attempting number of packets to the destination - source bytes	Syn flooding
User to root (U2R)	SQL-injection, Buffer_overflow, Xterm, Perl, Rootkit, HttpTuneel, LoadModule, Ps	The attacker pretends as legitimate user and attempts number of failed login	Password guessing
Probing	Nmap, IPsweep, Portsweep Satan, Saint, Mscan	The attacker uses the collaborative infrastructure to learn the destination location and defensive capabilities	Port scanning
Remote to user (R2L)	SnmpGuess, WarezClient, Phf, Xsnoop, Xlock, Guess_Password, Named, Imap, Ftp_Write, WarezMaster, Sendmail, Worm, Spy, MultiHop, SnmpGuess, SnmpGetAttack	An R2L attack which exploits a bug. - The number of file creations	Buffer overflow

Table 3. Sample data collected for normal and attack classes

Class name	Training data	Occurrences %	Testing data	Occurrences %
Normal (N)	67343	54.62	10123	43.15
Denial of service	45837	38.01	8324	35.48
Probe	8057	6.53	2321	9.90
Remote to user	995	0.80	2635	11.23
User to root	52	0.04	56	0.24
Total	123279	100.0	23459	100.0

data pre-processing using default settings. In the second phase, the data is pre-processed and normalized to provide by selecting the most relevant features.

For the first phase, the values directly submitted to the tool without any preprocessing dataset. But for trained MLCs on the training dataset provided by "NSL-KDD using Stratified Cross-validation of 10-folds" and used the trained models with the testing dataset. For comparing performance for testing datasets also supplied by the NSL-KDD. The results of the first phase of both trained and test datasets, as shown in Table 4 and Table 5, respectively.

For the second phase, the dataset is pre-processed and normalized to reduce its parameter by selecting the most appropriate features. During pre-processing, we choose a subset of input variables by eliminating the features with little or no predictive information. We applied the "InfoGainAttributeEval algorithm with Ranker [11]". The algorithm specifies the ranked the attributes by their evaluation and results in it reduces to 23 selected features out of total 41 features. We also applied the ensemble classified model technique for the seven MLCs executed in parallel, and each classifier constructs a dissimilar model of the data. After completed data, it produces output for the seven classifiers are by majority

Table 4. Results of MLCs with trained class datasets for phase1

Type of tree/classifiers	Accuracy %	Inaccuracy %	TPR	FPR	Precision	Recall	F-measure	ROC area	PRC area
J48	99.7761	0.2239	0.998	0.002	0.998	0.998	0.998	0.999	0.998
DecisionStump	92.215	7.785	0.922	0.079	0.922	0.922	0.922	0.92	0.898
Hoeffding	98.967	1.033	0.99	0.011	0.99	0.99	0.99	0.993	0.99
Random tree	99.8091	0.1929	0.998	0.002	0.998	0.998	0.998	0.998	0.997
REPT tree	99.7952	0.2048	0.998	0.002	0.998	0.998	0.998	0.999	0.999
Random forest	99.9127	0.0873	0.999	0.001	0.999	0.999	0.999	1.000	1.000
Naive Bayes	89.9125	10.0875	0.899	0.107	0.901	0.899	0.899	0.964	0.955

Table 5. Results of MLCs with test class datasets for phase1

Type of tree/classifiers	Accuracy %	Inaccuracy %	TPR	FPR	Precision	Recall	F-measure	ROC area	PRC area
J48	85.42	14.58	0.926	0.392	0.712	0.963	0.759	0.865	0.985
DecisionStump	76.32	23.68	0.912	0.356	0.723	0.923	0.762	0.836	0.965
Hoeffding	78.56	21.44	0.927	0.323	0.721	0.941	0.812	0.841	0.852
Random tree	82.32	17.68	0.916	0.341	0.745	0.956	0.763	0.896	0.932
REPT tree	83.62	16.38	0.926	0.318	0.765	0.932	0.782	0.875	0.963
Random forest	79.23	20.77	0.926	0.393	0.713	0.985	0.754	0.892	0.982
Naive Bayes	71.23	28.77	0.812	0.337	0.789	0.972	0.742	0.841	0.954

voting method. Finally, we compare the performance analysis of phase1 and phase2, and it summarized in Table 6 and Table 7, respectively. The comparative results of phase1 and phase 2 in terms of training and test accuracy are shown in Fig. 3 and Fig. 4 respectively.

Table 6. Results of MLCs with trained class datasets for phase2

Type of tree/classifiers	Accuracy %	Inaccuracy %	TPR	FPR	Precision	Recall	F-measure	ROC area	PRC area
J48	99.7444	0.2556	0.997	0.002	0.997	0.997	0.997	0.999	0.997
DecisionStump	83.198	16.802	0.832	0.116	0.726	0.832	0.772	0.89	0.723
Hoeffding	97.2661	2.7339	0.973	0.005	0.984	0.973	0.977	0.993	0.984
Random	99.6364	0.3636	0.996	0.002	0.996	0.996	0.996	0.998	0.994
REPT tree	99.5309	0.4691	0.995	0.002	0.995	0.995	0.995	0.999	0.996
Random forest	99.869	0.131	0.999	0.001	0.999	0.999	0.999	1.000	1.000
Naive Bayes	45.2375	54.7625	0.452	0.006	0.906	0.452	0.498	0.985	0.923

6.3 Discussion

In this study of experimental results shows that the random tree classifier outperforms other classifiers with the highest accuracy 99.8091% and least accuracy

Table 7. Results of MLCs with test class datasets for phase2

Type of tree/classifiers	Accuracy %	Inaccuracy %	TPR	FPR	Precision	Recall	F-measure	ROC area	PRC area
J48	85.42	14.58	0.782	0.089	0.982	0.782	0.758	0.859	0.985
DecisionStump	75.26	24.74	0.845	0.075	0.852	0.756	0.863	0.859	0.854
Hoeffding	81.64	18.36	0.786	0.086	0.818	0.741	0.861	0.889	0.986
Random	89.56	10.44	0.824	0.082	0.861	0.795	0.952	0.845	0.932
REPT tree	91.23	8.77	0.872	0.075	0.814	0.763	0.954	0.823	0.915
Random forest	92.12	7.88	0.784	0.063	0.851	0.752	0.851	0.856	0.972
Naive Bayes	42.23	57.77	0.792	0.072	0.854	0.763	0.874	0.872	0.932

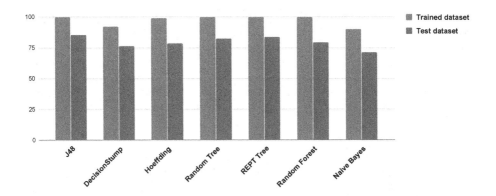

Fig. 3. The comparative results of phase1 of training and test accuracy

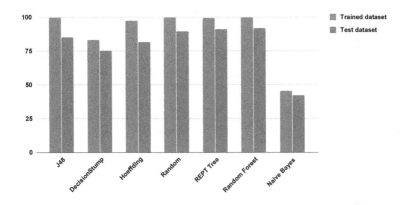

Fig. 4. The comparative results of phase2 of training and test accuracy

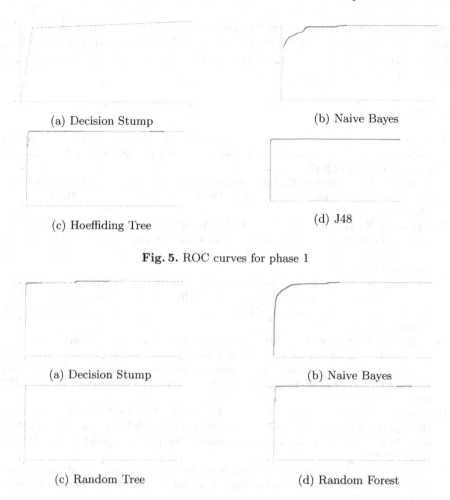

(a) Decision Stump

(b) Naive Bayes

(c) Hoeffiding Tree

(d) J48

Fig. 5. ROC curves for phase 1

(a) Decision Stump

(b) Naive Bayes

(c) Random Tree

(d) Random Forest

Fig. 6. ROC curves for phase 2

of 89.9125% for Naive Bayes. Similarly, for phase 2, the results of Random Forest accuracy 99.869% and least Naive Bayes 45.2375%. The ROC curves of various MLCs for phase 1 and phase 2 is shown in Fig. 5 and Fig. 6 respectively.

7 Conclusion

In this paper, we presented a comparative analysis of anomaly detection using various machine learning classifiers in WEKA using the NSL-KDD data set. The results obtained are beneficial in detecting the abnormal behaviour in the network system with a maximum of 99.84% accuracy and a minimum of 45.23%. Though it is a not satisfiable one we believe as of now this could be the best data set that can be implemented in any network or gateways to detect the attacks and prevent them in best possible way. From this study, we observed that the SMO, Logistic, PART, Random forest REPT Tree, Random, Hoeffding, DecisionStump and J48 produced best results in minimum time which helps in effective intrusion detection.

References

1. Alkasassbeh, M.: An empirical evaluation for the intrusion detection features based on machine learning and feature selection methods. arXiv preprint arXiv:1712.09623 (2017)
2. Belavagi, M.C., Muniyal, B.: Performance evaluation of supervised machine learning algorithms for intrusion detection. Procedia Comput. Sci. **89**(2016), 117–123 (2016)
3. Bojjagani, S., Brabin, D.D., Rao, P.V.: PhishPreventer: a secure authentication protocol for prevention of phishing attacks in mobile environment with formal verification. Procedia Comput. Sci. **171**, 1110–1119 (2020). https://doi.org/10.1016/j.procs.2020.04.119
4. Bojjagani, S., Sastry, V.N.: STAMBA: security testing for Android mobile banking apps. Advances in Signal Processing and Intelligent Recognition Systems. AISC, vol. 425, pp. 671–683. Springer, Cham (2016). https://doi.org/10.1007/978-3-319-28658-7_57
5. Bojjagani, S., Sastry, V.: VAPTAi: a threat model for vulnerability assessment and penetration testing of Android and iOS mobile banking apps. In: IEEE 3rd International Conference on Collaboration and Internet Computing (CIC), October 15–17, San Jose, pp. 77–86, California (2017). https://doi.org/10.1109/CIC.2017.00022
6. Das, S., Mahfouz, A.M., Venugopal, D., Shiva, S.: DDoS intrusion detection through machine learning ensemble. In: 2019 IEEE 19th International Conference on Software Quality, Reliability and Security Companion (QRS-C), pp. 471–477. IEEE (2019)
7. Dhanabal, L., Shantharajah, S.: A study on NSL-KDD dataset for intrusion detection system based on classification algorithms. Int. J. Adv. Res. Comput. Commun. Eng. **4**(6), 446–452 (2015)
8. Eibe, F., Hall, M.A., Witten, I.H.: The WEKA workbench. Online appendix for data mining: practical machine learning tools and techniques. In: Morgan Kaufmann (2016)
9. Ingre, B., Yadav, A.: Performance analysis of NSL-KDD dataset using ANN. In: 2015 International Conference on Signal Processing and Communication Engineering Systems, pp. 92–96. IEEE (2015)
10. Jalil, K.A., Kamarudin, M.H., Masrek, M.N.: Comparison of machine learning algorithms performance in detecting network intrusion. In: 2010 International Conference on Networking and Information Technology, pp. 221–226. IEEE (2010)
11. Mahfouz, A.M., Venugopal, D., Shiva, S.G.: Comparative analysis of ML classifiers for network intrusion detection. In: Yang, X.-S., Sherratt, S., Dey, N., Joshi, A. (eds.) Fourth International Congress on Information and Communication Technology. AISC, vol. 1027, pp. 193–207. Springer, Singapore (2020). https://doi.org/10.1007/978-981-32-9343-4_16
12. MeeraGandhi, G.: Machine learning approach for attack prediction and classification using supervised learning algorithms. Int. J. Comput. Sci. Commun. **1**(2), 11465–11484 (2010)

13. Moonsamy, V., Batten, L.: Mitigating man-in-the-middle attacks on smartphones-a discussion of SSL pinning and DNSSec. In: Proceedings of the 12th Australian Information Security Management Conference, pp. 5–13. Edith Cowan University (2014)

14. Nguyen, H.A., Choi, D.: Application of data mining to network intrusion detection: classifier selection model. In: Ma, Y., Choi, D., Ata, S. (eds.) APNOMS 2008. LNCS, vol. 5297, pp. 399–408. Springer, Heidelberg (2008). https://doi.org/10.1007/978-3-540-88623-5_41

15. NSL-KDD Dataset. https://www.unb.ca/cic/datasets/vpn.html. Accessed 20 Dec 2019

16. Potluri, S., Diedrich, C.: High performance intrusion detection and prevention systems: a survey. In: ECCWS2016-Proceedings of the 15th European Conference on Cyber Warfare and Security, p. 260. Academic Conferences and Publishing Limited (2016)

17. Shashidhara, R., Bojjagani, S., Maurya, A.K., Kumari, S., Xiong, H.: A robust user authentication protocol with privacy-preserving for roaming service in mobility environments. Peer-to-Peer Netw. Appl. **13**, 1–24 (2020). https://doi.org/10.1007/s12083-020-00929-y

Author Index

Printed in the United States
By Bookmasters